THE TECHNIQUE
OF
ORCHESTRATION

Kent Wheeler Kennan

Professor of Music
The University of Texas at Austin

THE TECHNIQUE

OF

ORCHESTRATION

Second Edition

PRENTICE-HALL, INC., Englewood Cliffs, New Jersey

PRENTICE-HALL INTERNATIONAL, INC., London
PRENTICE-HALL OF AUSTRALIA, PTY. LTD., Sydney
PRENTICE-HALL OF CANADA, LTD., Toronto
PRENTICE-HALL OF INDIA PRIVATE LTD., New Delhi
PRENTICE-HALL OF JAPAN, INC., Tokyo

PREFACE

This second edition, which appears some eighteen years after the first, is prompted partly by the need to bring information on instruments and orchestral practice up to date, partly by the desire to make certain changes and additions calculated to give the book greater clarity and completeness. Portions of it have been reorganized; a chapter on special devices has been added; the chapter on infrequently used instruments has been made more comprehensive; and considerable material (including examples) on twentieth-century developments in orchestration has been inserted, especially in the chapter on scoring for full orchestra.

As in the first edition, the emphasis is on the practical fundamentals of orchestration. No attempt has been made to give a detailed account of the construction of instruments, and historical background has been included only where it seemed essential to an understanding of the modern instruments or of scores of an earlier period.

Since most orchestration classes include students who are majoring in music education and who will be working with high school orchestras, certain problems involved in scoring for such groups are mentioned from time to time, and a short chapter is devoted to that subject.

It seems self-evident that a knowledge of various styles of scoring must be gained principally through a direct study of scores themselves. Consequently, this aspect of orchestration has been left largely in the hands of the individual teacher, to be undertaken as scores of different periods are taken up in class. Some thoughts concerning this phase of the work are included in the "Suggestions for the Use of This Book" that follow.

Over the years, the author has consulted virtually every teacher of an orchestral instrument on the staff of the University of Texas at Austin about questions that arose during the writing of this book. His profound thanks go to all these colleagues, past and present, whose number is now such that individual acknowledgments are unfortunately ruled out. He would also like to reaffirm his gratitude to the following persons who read the original manuscript or major portions of it and who contributed suggestions: Dr. Bjornar Bergethon, Dr. J. Frank Elsass, Harvey Biskin, Louis Lane, Mrs. Janet McGaughey, Dr. Paul Pisk, Karl Van Hoesen, and Clifton Williams. In the preparation of this second edition, similar invaluable help has been received from Gayle and Wayne Barrington, George Frock, Charles Gigante, Dr. Gordon R. Goodwin, Dr. James Riley, LaFalco Robinson, and Andor Toth.

Kent Kennan

SUGGESTIONS
FOR THE USE OF THIS BOOK

Certain changes in the order of material in this book are possible. Some of these are the following:

Chapter 11 (Problems in Transcribing Piano Music) might well be taken up earlier, most logically following Chapter 4. Use of that order has the advantage of preparing students almost from the start for certain problems they will encounter sooner or later in working from piano music. If time is limited and the instructor feels that it is more important to move on to a study of the other instruments than to make actual assignments based on Chapter 11 at that point, he may wish merely to go over the material of the chapter in class; further study of this aspect may be undertaken later if time allows.

Chapters 13 and 14, on percussion instruments, could be introduced after Chapter 9. The same is true of Chapter 15, which is chiefly about the harp.

The section in Chapter 5 on the piccolo, English horn, bass clarinet, and contra bassoon might be delayed until later instead of being presented along with the material on the other woodwinds.

The section in Chapter 4 on string harmonics (always a difficult subject for the student) might also be taken up later as a separate project after the student has had more time to become familiar with the workings of stringed instruments and when he is not so busy absorbing the more basic information.

Chapter 18, on infrequently used instruments, is included chiefly for purposes of reference in the more advanced stages of orchestration study and may be omitted in a first-year course—except for the material on saxophones, which should be covered if Chapter 19 on scoring for high school orchestra is assigned.

Since much of the most important material on orchestration can be learned through a study of symphonic scores, it would seem best to equip the student for score reading as quickly as possible. With that end in mind, the author recommends moving fairly rapidly through the first nine chapters of this book rather than dwelling very long on any one of them. Once the student has acquired enough knowledge of all the instruments to undertake score reading, it is always possible to return to individual instruments or sections for more concentrated work.

As far as the choice of music for score study and listening is concerned, the author feels that shorter works are preferable—at least in beginning orchestration courses, where time is generally at a premium. The student can grasp the essential characteristics of Mozart's orchestration about as well from the Overture to *The Marriage of Figaro* as he can from the C Major Symphony ("Jupiter"), for example, and the choice of shorter works allows for the study of more scores of various styles within the allotted time. As a minimum program of score study, one work from each of the following groups is suggested:

1. Haydn, Mozart, Beethoven
2. Tchaikovsky, Rimsky-Korsakoff, Wagner
3. Debussy, Ravel
4. Richard Strauss

There are, of course, many other composers (including contemporaries such as Stravinsky, Hindemith, and Bartók) whose music may also be included if time permits. Following are a few of the many scores that might be used for class study and listening:

Mozart, Overture to *The Marriage of Figaro*.
Beethoven, *Leonore* Overture No. 3; *Egmont* Overture; *Coriolanus* Overture.
Weber, *Oberon* Overture; *Der Freischütz* Overture.
Tchaikovsky, *Romeo and Juliet*.
Rimsky-Korsakoff, *Capriccio Espagnol*.
Wagner, Prelude to *Die Meistersinger;* Prelude to *Parsifal;* Prelude and Love Death from *Tristan und Isolde;* Overture to *Tannhäuser*.
Debussy, *Prelude to The Afternoon of a Faun*.
Ravel, *Bolero; Le Tombeau de Couperin; Mother Goose* Suite.
Strauss, *Till Eulenspiegel; Don Juan; Death and Transfiguration*
Stravinsky, *Fire Bird* Suite.

In this list, shorter works of the composers represented have been chosen wherever possible, for reasons mentioned earlier. As for longer or more involved works, that would be particularly instructive for score study, a few of the possibilities that come to mind are these:

Berlioz, *Fantastic Symphony.*
Mussorgsky-Ravel, *Pictures from an Exhibition.*
Tchaikovsky, Symphonies No. 4, 5, and 6.
Franck, Symphony in D minor.
Brahms, the Symphonies.
Mahler, the Symphonies.
Debussy, *Ibéria; La Mer; Nocturnes.*
Ravel, *Daphnis and Chloe* Suite No. 2.
Stravinsky, *Petrouchka; The Rite of Spring;* Symphony in Three Movements.
Prokofieff, Symphony No. 5.
Hindemith, Symphony: *Mathis der Maler.*
Bartók, Concerto for Orchestra.
Schönberg, Variations for Orchestra, Op. 31.

At the end of many chapters in this book, suggestions for listening are given. These involve passages from symphonic music that make prominent use of the individual instruments or groups discussed in the respective chapters.

Also valuable for listening purposes are the numerous commercial recordings that give, on one or two disks, characteristic passages for all or most of the orchestral instruments. Some of these recordings are listed here. They (or portions of them) may be presented as they become pertinent to the material being studied.

Britten, *The Young Person's Guide to the Orchestra.* Columbia ML 4197. Variations and fugue by Britten on a theme of Purcell illustrate the various instruments. Liverpool Philharmonic Orchestra, Sir Malcolm Sargent, conductor.

First Chair. Columbia ML 4629. Soloists with the Philadelphia Orchestra, Eugene Ormandy, conductor.

The Complete Orchestra. Music Education Record Corporation, Columbia transcription, XTV 25861–25870. Wheeler Beckett Orchestra of New York, with comments by the conductor.

The Composer and His Orchestra. Mercury, SR-90175. Eastman-Rochester Orchestra, Howard Hanson, conductor and narrator. Examples from Hanson's *Merry Mount* Suite, which is also recorded in its entirety.

Instruments of the Orchestra. Capitol-Angel, HBZ-21002 (mono only), Music Educator's Series. Various artists; commentary by Yehudi Menuhin. For use in elementary and secondary education.

The Instruments of the Orchestra. Vanguard, VRS-1017/8. First desk men of the Vienna State Opera Orchestra, David Randolph, narrator.

Instruments of the Orchestra. Victor, 20522A. Members of the National Symphony, Howard Mitchell, conductor.

Instruments of the Orchestra. Columbia, 19523–4. Bell Telephone Orchestra, Donald Voorhees, conductor.

Meet the Orchestra. Bowmar Records, 122. Sound-Filmstrip Set. Study prints (# 121) and full color posters of instruments (#123) also available. Intended primarily for use in elementary and secondary education.

In planning this book, the author had in mind a year's course in orchestration. When the book is used for a course of only a semester's length, even a cursory covering of all the material in it will probably not be feasible. The decision as to what material to stress and what to pass over lightly (or omit altogether) must rest with the individual teacher and will be determined by the particular needs of his students.

Actual music to be used for the exercises in scoring is not included in this volume but is available in *Orchestration Workbook I* and *Orchestration Workbook II*, also published by Prentice-Hall, Inc.

CONTENTS

xii

THE TECHNIQUE
OF
ORCHESTRATION

Chapter 1

INTRODUCTION

How does one go about learning orchestration? In the first place, there is a certain amount of factual information that must be acquired. Under this heading come the following:

Names of instruments and orchestral terms (including Italian, French, and German equivalents, because many scores are printed in these languages);
Order of instruments on the page;
Ranges of instruments;
Proper notation, including transpositions and special clefs;
General technical abilities and limitations of each instrument (although this does not necessarily involve the ability to *play* the instruments);
Principles of combining and of balancing instruments;
Characteristics of various "schools" of scoring.

This material can be learned from classroom explanations, from books, from talks with orchestral players or demonstrations by them, and from a close study of orchestral scores.

But there is another type of information, which can be learned only by careful and frequent listening (along with score-reading) over a considerable period of time. In this category might be listed a knowledge of these things:

The characteristic tone quality of each instrument;
The sound of various instruments in combination;
The sound of special effects.

The point here is that tone colors cannot really be described adequately in words. It is all very well to read in an orchestration book that the clarinet is "dark" in its lower register, but until one has actually heard the sound in question and impressed it on his "mind's ear," he has no real conception of that particular color for purposes of orchestration. Not everyone seems to be equally endowed in the matter of aural memory and aural imagination, but these qualities can be sharpened by practice.

Once this information has been acquired, it must be applied in actual exercises in scoring—transcriptions of piano or organ music or of music for instrumental groups, and so on. Students who are composers will want to go on and write directly for orchestra. That is obviously the ideal situation, in that the musical ideas are conceived with the orchestral instruments in mind, but we cannot very well expect all students to be composers. Besides, the ability to *transcribe* for orchestra is one of the most usable and important skills to be gained from an orchestration course.

It is assumed that students who are studying orchestration from this book have already had a thorough training in harmony. The writer's experience indicates that poor scoring on the part of students is more often the result of a failure to understand harmonic and general musical structure than of a faulty knowledge of orchestration. Unless the principles of good voice-leading, spacing, and doubling are applied in an arrangement, no amount of clever orchestration will make it sound well; and without an understanding of harmonic content and form, intelligent scoring is impossible. In orchestrating, it is of the greatest importance to think in terms of *lines* rather than in terms of isolated notes. Otherwise the total result will be confused and the individual players' parts will be unmusical and ungrateful to play.

Finally, it cannot be stressed too strongly that accurate workmanship, attention to detail, and a practical approach are all parts of successful orchestration. Anyone who has witnessed an orchestra rehearsal where time was wasted and tempers strained because of mistakes in the players' parts will know how costly and serious inaccuracy can be. As for attention to detail, there are a thousand small points involved in scoring—points that may seem trivial but that, taken all together, make the difference between scoring that comes off in performance and scoring that does not. This all ties in, of course, with a practical approach, which involves the ability to achieve the maximum effect with the simplest means. Orchestration is not a nebulous sort of business conditioned sheerly by "artistic inspiration" but, to a large extent, an intensely real and down-to-earth technique.

Although the terms *orchestration* and *instrumentation* are sometimes used synonymously, it might be well to point out a distinction in meaning that is generally made by musicians and that is observed in this book. Orchestration has to do with the actual process of scoring music for orchestra. Instrumentation, on the other hand, usually refers to a study of individual instruments—their construction, history, abilities, and so on. Sometimes the word is also used in connection with the list of instruments required for a particular piece of music, as when we speak of "the instrumentation" employed in an orchestral work. Of course, anyone who sets out to learn orchestration must, in the process, learn a good deal about instrumentation. There is, then, a certain amount of overlapping between the two terms, in the sense that the second is included (at least partially) in the first.

In order to gain a general perspective before concentrating on individual instruments and sections of the orchestra, we are going to take time in this chapter for a brief look at the orchestra as a whole. "Orchestra" here means symphony orchestra but even that term is rather lacking in precision, because symphonic groups vary considerably in size and make-up. The table that follows lists the orchestral instruments and shows approximately how many of each are likely to be found in orchestras of various sizes. Parentheses around a number mean that the instrument in question may or may not be included.

The celesta and piano, though not regular members of the orchestra, may be used with any of these groups and, like the harp, are "extras," which do not belong to any one of the four sections shown.

		Small Orchestra	Medium-sized Orchestra	Large Orchestra	
	Piccolo		(1)	1	
	Flute	1	2	2	3
	Oboe	1	2	2	3
Woodwind	English Horn			1	
Section	Clarinet	1	2	2 or 3	
	Bass Clarinet			1	
	Bassoon	1	2	2	3
	Contra Bassoon			1	
	(French) Horn	1 or 2	4	4 to 6	
Brass	Trumpet	(1)	2 or 3	3	
Section	Trombone	(1)	3	3	
	Tuba		1	1	
Percussion Section	Percussion	2*	3*	4 or more*	
	Harp	(1)	(1)	(1) or (2)	
	1st Violins	4 to 8	8 to 12	12 to 16	
	2nd Violins	3 to 6	6 to 10	10 to 14	
String Section	Violas	2 to 4	4 to 8	8 to 12	
	Cellos	2 or 3	3 to 6	6 to 10	
	Double Basses	1 to 3	3 to 6	6 to 10	

* These figures indicate the number of percussion players, including the timpanist.

Orchestras even larger than the "large orchestra" described here are sometimes called for (by Stravinsky, Strauss, and Mahler among others). In such cases, woodwinds in fours are generally required: piccolo, three flutes; three oboes, English horn; E♭ clarinet, two B♭ clarinets, bass clarinet; three bassoons, and contra bassoon. In order to supply this instrumentation, most of the major orchestras in this country have extra woodwind players on call.

Each section may play by itself or be combined with one or more of the other sections. When sections are combined, they may take the same musical material or different material. Sometimes only one instrument of a section is used, along with part or all of another section. If all the instruments of the orchestra, or most of them, play, the combination is known as a *tutti* (the Italian word for "all").

The fourth section, the percussion, is most often used for rhythmic support of other instruments, although now and then it can perform on its own to good effect.

The order in which the instruments are listed above is a standard one, which is always employed in modern scores. If an instrument is not included in a score, it will not be listed on the page, but those instruments which *are* used will still follow the standard order. In most scores, all the instruments to be used are included on the first page, whether they play at that point or not, but on succeeding pages, instruments that do not play may be omitted from the listing. When a solo instrument is involved (as in a concerto), its part is normally placed directly above the strings. The same is true of piano, celesta, and choral parts. The examples in Chapter 16 show the appearance of a page of orchestral score.

A note of explanation is necessary concerning the system used in indicating ranges throughout this book. The limits of the extreme possible range are shown in open notes, the limits of the practical or commonly used range in black notes. The reason for this distinction is that nearly every one of the orchestral instruments has notes at the bottom and/or the top of its range that, because of technical difficulties or doubtful intonation or both, are little used and then only under certain conditions. It must be remembered, though, that there is no sharp dividing line between the practical registers and the extreme possible registers, particularly since players and instruments vary. Consequently it is extremely difficult to fix exact limits for each practical range.

Although the historical development of the orchestra is not within the scope of this book, a few brief comments on that subject may help to put the present-day orchestra into better perspective.

Before the seventeenth century, composers for instrumental groups did not specify particular instruments for the respective parts. Among the first to do so were Giovanni Gabrieli (ca. 1557–1612) and Monteverdi (1567–1643); the latter was also an innovator in the use of special orchestral effects. By Bach's time it was usual to specify the instruments involved, but little or no distinction (apart from that of range) was made between them or, for that matter, between parts for instruments and parts for voices. Furthermore, there was as yet no standardized instrumentation; that concept was not fully in evidence until the Classical period. By the early nineteenth century, the orchestra had evolved into a more or less standard group: two flutes, two oboes, two clarinets, two bassoons, two horns, two trumpets, two timpani, and strings (the latter subdivided as they are today but fewer in number).

SUGGESTED ASSIGNMENT

Know:

1. the four sections of the orchestra.
2. the names (in English) of the instruments included in each section.
3. the number of each instrument commonly included in the "medium-sized" orchestra.
4. the format used in indicating ranges throughout this book.

Chapter 2

THE STRINGS

THE VIOLIN

Italian:	Violino	*French:*	Violon	*German:*	Violine
(Plural)	Violini		Violons		Violinen

Ex. 1

Range[1]

The violin's four strings are tuned to the following pitches:

Ex. 2

These are known as the "open" strings, that is, the strings as they are when not stopped by the fingers. A chromatic scale upward is obtainable on each string by stopping the string at the appropriate points. Normally a note is

[1] All the string ranges given in this chapter may be extended upward by the use of harmonics.

played on the nearest string below it; for example, the note would usually be played on the D string. However, the G string might be chosen in certain cases in order to maintain the particular color of that string throughout a passage or to avoid a change of position. This same principle is sometimes used in connection with the D and A strings. Although notes more than a 10th above the pitch of each open string are seldom used on any one of the three bottom strings, the top string is necessarily called upon for very high notes.

Normally, the choice of string rests with the player, a particular string being indicated only in cases where a choice other than the normal one is involved. The strings are sometimes designated by Roman numerals, starting with the E string as "I" and working down. Thus, "on the G string" is often indicated by "IV" placed above the first note to be taken on that string and followed by a dotted line to show how far the direction is to apply. Another way of indicating the same thing is to write *sul G* (literally, in Italian, "on the G") above the passage. The German equivalent is *G Saite*, *Saite* meaning string.

As for the colors of the various strings, the G string is characteristically

full, rich, and rather dark in quality. From about  upward, its

tone becomes curiously intense, as if charged with emotion. The D string is less dark and full, the A considerably brighter, and the E especially brilliant and penetrating.

Each of the following examples illustrates the use of a particular string of the violin. Of course not all melodies lie entirely on one string, as these do; the great majority, in fact, require changes from one string to another.

EXAMPLES SHOWING THE USE OF PARTICULAR STRINGS OF THE VIOLIN

Ex. 3

(a) E string: *Classical Symphony*

(b) A string: Third Symphony

Hanson

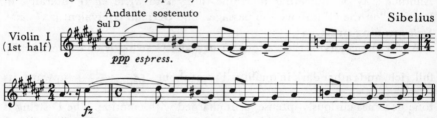

Eastman School of Music Publication; Carl Fischer, Inc.

(c) D string: Second Symphony

Sibelius

Copyright, 1903, by Breitkopf & Haertel. By permission of Associated Music Publishers.

(d) G string: First Symphony

Brahms

Stringed instruments may be either bowed or plucked. For these two effects the Italian words *arco* (bow) and *pizzicato* (picked or plucked) are used. *Pizzicato* is usually abbreviated to *pizz.* and written above the staff, over or near the first note of the passage concerned. When the player is to return to the use of the bow, the word *arco* is written in above the staff. These directions are important and must be included by the orchestrator. However, since the normal method of tone production on stringed instruments is by means of the bow, *arco* need not be included unless there has been a pizzicato passage just previously. For example, if a work starts out with a bowed passage, no *arco* direction is needed. It is not customary to use dots (to indicate short notes) in pizzicato passages; if the pizzicato direction is there, the notes will automatically be short to some degree although (particularly in the case of the double basses and the cellos, with their greater resonance) notes that are not too high can be made to ring somewhat, especially if *vibrato* is used. Under normal circumstances, the easiest notation of time values is employed, rests being omitted wherever possible; for instance,

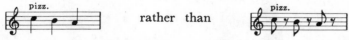

rather than

But the second notation, accompanied by the direction *secco*, might be used if an extremely short, dry pizzicato were desired. And in passages involving longer values where the notes are to be allowed to ring, half notes or even whole notes would be helpful in suggesting that effect. (Usually the direction *vib.* is included in such cases.) As a rule, it is best not to write pizzicato passages for the violin above about ░░░ ; higher notes played pizzicato are so thin and lacking in resonance as to be ineffective for ordinary purposes. It is important to remember that there is a limit to the speed with which successions of pizzicato notes can be performed, and that very rapid changes from arco to pizzicato (or vice versa) are awkward, even impossible beyond a certain speed. Changes of this sort that must be made with scarcely any rest between the last arco note and the first pizzicato note are somewhat easier if the last arco note can be taken "up-bow" so that by the end of the bow-stroke the player's hand is close to the strings and in position to play in pizzicato fashion. Lefthand pizzicatos, though not uncommon in solo violin literature, are seldom used in orchestral parts. The usual indication is a small cross above the note.

A few names for particular parts of stringed instruments come up frequently in orchestration work. The *fingerboard* is the part of the instrument on which the fingers stop the strings. The *bridge* is a small piece of wood that keeps the strings raised and in place above the main body of the instrument. Parts of the bow that are often referred to are the *frog* (or *nut* or *heel*), which is the portion nearest the player's bow hand, and the *point* or *tip* at the opposite end. Special effects involving these and other terms are discussed later on.

A *vibrato* is normally used in playing stringed instruments and is produced by an oscillating motion of the hand on the fingerboard. Without a vibrato the tone is "white" and lacking in expressiveness and warmth (although this very sound is occasionally used for a particular effect in orchestral music). Because a vibrato cannot be produced on an open string,[2] players usually

Double Bass   Viola   Violin   Violoncello

[2] Except by artificial methods, usually involving sympathetic vibration between the open string and another string fingered with vibrato at the pitch of the open string.

avoid the open strings in slow, *espressivo* passages where the difference in tone quality would be too apparent. A further disadvantage in such cases is that the open strings tend to ring and to be louder than stopped tones. The alternative to playing an open tone is to take the same pitch as a stopped tone on a lower string, though this is obviously not possible with the lowest open string of each instrument. The symbol for an open string is an "O" above the note (not to be confused with the symbol for a natural harmonic, which is smaller and perfectly round; harmonics will be discussed in a later chapter). The numbering of the fingers in string writing may be mentioned in passing, because it is invariably confusing to pianists. The index finger is "1"; the middle finger is "2"; and so on. Since the thumb does not figure in the stopping of the strings, no symbol is needed for it.

One frequently hears string players speak of taking a passage "in first position" or in some other position. Perhaps a few examples will serve to explain this concept of position, which is basic to string technique. If the player's left hand is placed on the D string with his first finger on E and the other fingers ready to play F, G, and A (or F♯, G, and A, or other chromatic variations of these basic pitches), he is said to be "in first position on the D string." If he were in first position on the A string, his first finger would rest on B (or B♭, or in rare cases B♯). For second position on the E string, the first finger would rest on G; for third position on the G string, it would be on C, in each case with the other fingers on (or over) the three notes immediately above. The first, third, and fifth positions are easier and more natural than the second and fourth and are consequently chosen more frequently. Positions higher than the fifth are seldom used on the three lower strings (except in solo writing), but higher positions are often needed on the E string. Although players can shift rapidly from one string to an adjacent one or from one position to another, sudden or repeated jumps *across* strings make for awkward string writing, as do sudden or repeated changes from one position to a distant position. A fingering chart for first position on the violin is given on page 12.

A point to remember, especially in writing for players of limited ability, is that the higher the player goes on a string, the closer together the notes lie on the fingerboard and the harder it is to play perfectly in tune. Because higher positions are not so often necessary on the three lower strings, the chief point of difficulty is in passages high on the top string. These can be written with safety for a professional group, but they are an almost certain invitation to disaster in a school orchestra. As a general rule it is safest not to go beyond third position in scoring for school groups. (See Chapter 19 for further comments on this subject.)

FIRST POSITION ON THE VIOLIN

Fingering indi-
cations on this
side apply to
G and D strings

Fingering indi-
cations on this
side apply to
A and E strings

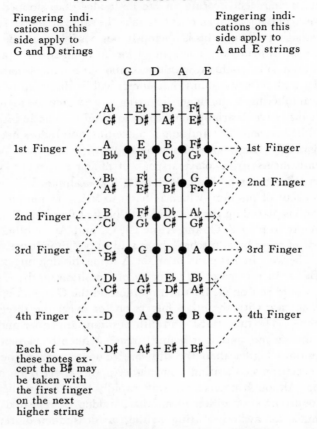

FINGERBOARD OF THE VIOLIN

Double, Triple, and Quadruple Stops

Although the violin is predominantly a single-line instrument, it is capable of playing two, three, or four notes at a time, provided that each note can be taken on a separate string and that the pitches involved can be fingered at once. If any of the notes can be played on open strings, that will make the fingering problem much easier for the player. It is obvious that two pitches cannot be played at the same time on the same string. For example, is impossible as a double stop on the violin because both notes would have

to be taken on the G string. But [musical notation] is quite easy, since the A can be

played on the G string and the F♯ on the D string, the bow being drawn

across both strings at once. The double stop [musical notation] is even easier,

because the D can be played on the open D string and the B on the A string. Of course the notes of a double stop must be playable on *adjacent* strings. The following may be considered practical upward limits for double stops involving intervals up to an octave (practical, that is, for the professional orchestra violinist of average ability):

Ex. 4

2nds	3rds	4ths	5ths	6ths	7ths	8ves
maj. min.	maj. min.	perf. aug.	dim. aug. perf.	maj. min.	maj. min.	

Of these intervals, 6ths are probably the most successful as double stops. Octaves, 5ths, and 4ths present a certain problem of intonation, since the slightest deviation from the correct pitch in either note is more apparent to the ear than it would be in such intervals as the 6th and 3rd, where the mathematical ratio between notes is more complex. Perfect 5ths, by the way, are played with one finger stopping both strings (assuming that open tones are not involved). Unisons, though rare, are possible and are sometimes introduced for the sake of added resonance and volume. They almost always involve an open string; that is, they are generally written on one of these

three pitches: [musical notation] For example, in [musical notation] one of the A's

would be played on the open A string, the other on the D string.

Double stops involving intervals larger than an octave are also possible in certain cases. Sometimes even such widely spaced double stops as

[musical notation] are used. Unwieldy as this may look to the pianist's eye, it is

actually very simple, for the A is an open note and the D presents no problems. For purposes of orchestral writing, quick successions of double stops are generally impractical, though short successions of 6ths or 3rds are not out of the question. Usually, however, such passages are better arranged *divisi* (with the string group divided).

As for triple and quadruple stops, those which include at least one open string are the easiest and the most resonant, but certain other chord arrangements that contain no open note are also possible. Because of the curvature of the bridge, four notes cannot be played at exactly the same time. However, in quadruple stops the bow can be drawn so quickly over the strings that the effect is that of a four-note chord only slightly arpeggiated or broken. Examples 7 and 8 show the more commonly used three-note and four-note chords playable on the violin. (According to Forsyth, a complete catalog of all the chords possible on the violin would amount to nearly 1500 combinations!) The method used here in listing chords that contain no open notes may need a word of explanation. Instead of writing out all the possibilities in connection with each chord pattern, we have merely indicated them in the following manner:

Ex. 5

This particular example means that three-note chords arranged in this pattern are playable on every half-step within the limits shown:

Ex. 6

This and other upward limits given must not be thought of as hard and fast points above which the chords become impossible. All the patterns are possible in still higher positions, but at that level they become so difficult as to be impractical for normal orchestral use. The limits shown here are therefore intended merely as guides for practical usage.

Notice that the predominant intervals in these chord arrangements are 5ths and 6ths. Notice, too, that four-note chords which contain open notes in the middle with stopped notes on the outside are generally impractical and are therefore not included.

THREE-NOTE CHORDS FOR THE VIOLIN (PARTIAL LIST)*

Ex. 7

(Chords containing two open notes)

(Chords containing one open note)

(Chords containing no open note)

Note: Accidentals are written separately for each chord.

* This list has been limited to major and minor triads and dominant-type seventh chords (or incomplete forms of these chords).

FOUR-NOTE CHORDS FOR THE VIOLIN (PARTIAL LIST)

Ex. 8

(Chords containing three open notes)

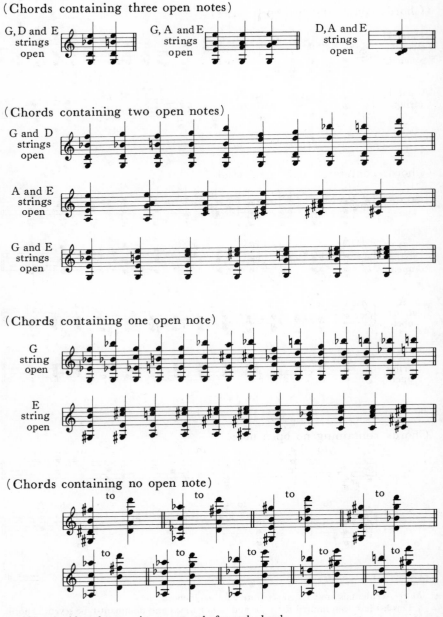

(Chords containing two open notes)

(Chords containing one open note)

(Chords containing no open note)

Note: Accidentals are written separately for each chord.

Although double stops may be used effectively in sustained chords and at a low dynamic level, there is not much point in writing triple and quadruple stops except in fairly loud passages, usually in sharply detached chords where an extra degree of volume or accent is wanted. It is, however, possible to sustain the top note or the two top notes of a three-note or four-note chord:

Ex. 9

Even inner notes may be sustained, though that possibility is not of much practical use. Since the main objective in triple and quadruple stops is usually added resonance, those that contain one or more open tones are ordinarily the most effective, besides being the most comfortable to play.

Certain other string effects, although not technically triple or quadruple stops, depend on the same principle. For instance, in these passages,

Ex. 10

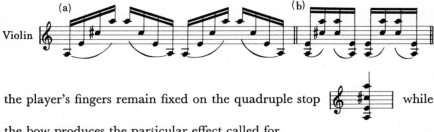

the player's fingers remain fixed on the quadruple stop ♩ while the bow produces the particular effect called for.

Examples 12(b) and (h) at the end of Chapter 3 illustrate the use of "multiple stops" (a term that may conveniently be used to apply to double, triple, and quadruple stops).

EXAMPLES OF PASSAGES FOR THE VIOLIN

Ex. 11

(a) G minor Symphony

(b) Third Symphony

Adagio assai
sotto voce

Beethoven

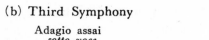

(c) Overture to *Oberon*

Allegro con fuoco

Weber

(d) *Capriccio Espagnol*

♩.= 66 *sempre non div.*

Rimsky-Korsakoff

(e) Fifth Symphony

♩.=66

Tchaikovsky

fff con desiderio e passione

(f) *Death and Transfiguration*

Allegro

Strauss

ff marcato

(g) *The Rite of Spring*

Vivo

Stravinsky

THE VIOLA

Italian:	Viola	*French:*	Alto	*German:*	Bratsche
	Viole		Altos		Bratschen

Ex. 12

Range   Open Strings

If the material on the violin has seemed lengthy and detailed, there may be some consolation in the thought that much of it applies to the other stringed instruments as well. In the case of the viola, the chief differences to be considered are: (1) its greater size as compared with the violin; (2) its characteristic tone color; (3) its range; and (4) the use of the alto clef (viola clef).

It is not surprising that the uninitiated concert goer is apt to confuse the viola with the violin. Although the two look quite similar from a distance, the viola is somewhat larger and heavier,[3] and the distance between notes on the fingerboard is slightly greater than in the case of the violin. As for the characteristic quality of the instrument, someone once commented that the sound of the viola is to the sound of the violin what the flavor of duck is to the flavor of chicken. It is unfortunate that this attractive gaminess of tone is sometimes minimized in an effort to make the viola sound like the violin; there is no reason why the viola should not be allowed to assert its own distinctive personality.

For those who have not used the C clefs before, a note of explanation is

necessary here. The alto clef, ![alto clef], puts middle C on the middle line

of the staff. The open strings of the viola, then, are C, G, D, and A, reading from bottom to top. Since the viola's normal register is from an octave below middle C to about a 12th above it, the use of the treble clef would require frequent ledger lines below the staff, while writing in the bass clef would involve an even more terrifying array of ledger lines above the staff. The alto clef provides a solution to the problem by placing middle C in such a location that the average viola part can be kept within the staff. If the part goes unusually high and stays there for some time, the treble clef is usually used. As a rule, it is not wise to change clef for the sake of one or two

---

[3] There is more variation in size among violas than among the other stringed instruments. Many violas are slightly larger than the one shown on page 10.

notes; players prefer to read a few ledger lines rather than shift their thinking from one clef to another too often. Viola parts in scores intended for high

school use should not go above about

What has been observed about the quality of the strings in the case of the violin applies in a relative way to the viola. There are the same darkness and body to the lowest string, the same comparative brilliance to the top string, and the same gradations between these extremes in the two middle strings.

Too often in orchestral scoring the violas are given rather undistinguished parts: chordal figurations, sustained harmony tones, afterbeats, and the like. (This is particularly true in older music.) They are capable, however, of doing everything the violins can do, discounting differences of range, of course. As we move on to a view of the string group as a whole, it will become more apparent how valuable the viola is as a bridge between the violin and the cello.

The same patterns available as multiple stops on the violin are possible on the viola a 5th lower. However, quadruple stops in the higher positions are a bit more difficult and less effective than on the violin and are better avoided. Examples 13 and 14 show the more usable triple and quadruple stops on the viola.

THREE-NOTE CHORDS FOR THE VIOLA (PARTIAL LIST)*

Ex. 13

(Chords containing two open notes)

Note: Accidentals are written separately for each chord.

* This list has been limited to major and minor triads and dominant-type seventh chords (or incomplete forms of these chords).

FOUR-NOTE CHORDS FOR THE VIOLA (PARTIAL LIST)

Ex. 14

(Chords containing three open notes)

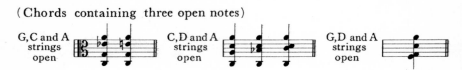

(Chords containing two open notes)

(Chords containing one open note)

(Chords containing no open note)

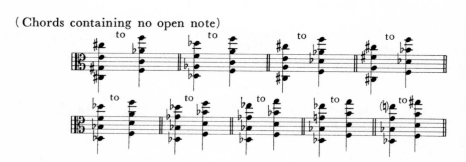

Note: Accidentals are written separately for each chord.

EXAMPLES OF PASSAGES FOR THE VIOLA

Ex. 15

(a) Prelude to *Tristan und Isolde*

Langsam und schmachtend
zart*(dolce)*   Wagner

(b) *Romeo and Juliet*

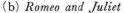

Allegro giusto   Tchaikovsky
con sord.

In unison with
English Horn

(c) Fifth Symphony

♩=138   Tchaikovsky

(d) *Till Eulenspiegel*

Gemächlich   Strauss
div.

In unison with
Bassoons

(e) *Daphnis and Chloe* Suite No. 2

Lento   Ravel

In unison with
Clarinet

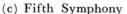

Permission for reprint granted by copyright owner, Durand et Cie, Paris, France; Elkan-Vogel, Co., Inc., agents for the U.S.A.

THE VIOLONCELLO (CELLO)

| *Italian:* | Violoncello | *French:* | Violoncelle | *German:* | Violoncell |
| | Violoncelli | | Violoncelles | | Violoncelle |

Ex. 16

Range   Open Strings

The complete name violoncello (not viol*i*ncello) has been more or less abandoned today in favor of the shortened form, cello. Although the instrument is too large to be held as the violin and viola are and must rest on the floor (secured by an adjustable peg at the bottom), it operates on basically the same principles. as the smaller stringed instruments, except for some differences in fingering necessitated by the fact that the notes are farther apart on the fingerboard. The open strings have the same letter names as the open strings of the viola but are an octave lower.

The normal clef for the cello is the bass clef. However, in order to avoid the use of many ledger lines in passages that lie in the upper part of the compass, the tenor clef, , is often used. This clef places middle C on the fourth line and must not be confused with the alto clef, which is never used by the cello. If the part goes so high as to require the continuous use of ledger lines even in the tenor clef, then the treble clef will probably be substituted. One might argue that bass and treble clefs would be sufficient. That is perfectly true. But when a passage lies between the F below middle C and the F above middle C, for example, the tenor clef will keep the notes on the staff, whereas either bass or treble clef would require ledger lines. In any case, tradition and common practice dictate that the cello shall use the tenor clef for most of its higher passages. An old and fortunately obsolete custom ruled that when the treble clef was used immediately following the bass clef, the notes in the treble were to be written an octave higher than the sounds desired. Such a system appears completely pointless. It is mentioned here only because it occasionally turns up (as late as Tchaikovsky and Dvořák) and proves confusing to the uninitiated score reader.

The cello has a reputation, amply deserved, for mellowness and warmth of tone. The two bottom strings (the C string in particular) are rich and full-bodied; passages played on them have a way of sounding grave and somehow reflective. The D string is brighter, with a warm and ingratiating quality, while the A string possesses a vibrant, singing tone all its own. Melodies played on it take on a strongly *espressivo*, almost passionate, quality that becomes more intense and poignant as one goes higher on the string.

The upper limit of use is particularly hard to fix here. Virtuoso solo work occasionally calls for notes even higher than the top G given as the highest

possible note, but for orchestral use it is best not to write above ;

even notes in that area are rather difficult from the standpoint of intonation. In school orchestras, the cello section had better not be written above

Much of the time, the cellos constitute the bass voice of the string group (often with the double basses sounding an octave lower). However, they may be used as a tenor or baritone voice, or even on the melody if it does not go too high.

There are two small limitations concerning double stops on the cello: Avoid 2nds and octaves unless one of the notes is open. Triple and quadruple stops based on the following patterns are all practical as long as the top note

is no higher than 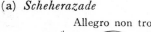 .

Ex. 17

This is by no means an exhaustive list but includes the chord arrangements most frequently encountered in orchestral cello parts.

The cello section is frequently called upon to play broken-chord patterns such as the following, which (like those on page 17) are simply multiple stops in which the notes are sounded consecutively instead of at approximately the same time.

Ex. 18

(a) *Scheherazade*

(b) Symphony in D minor

26

(c) Fourth Symphony   Mahler

Cello

fff

EXAMPLES OF PASSAGES FOR CELLO

(See also the double bass examples, which include passages for cellos and basses sounding in octaves.)

Ex. 19

(a) Third Symphony

Allegro con brio   Beethoven

p   *cresc.*

(b) Fifth Symphony

Andante con moto   Beethoven

(In unison with Violas)

p dolce

f   *p*

(c) Fourth Symphony

Andante moderato   Brahms

p espress.

(d) *Don Juan*   Strauss

♩=76
senza espr.

p

(e) Third Symphony

Con moto   Harris

f

THE DOUBLE BASS

Italian: Contrabasso   *French:*   Contre basse   *German:*   Kontrabass
             Contrabassi   Contre basses   Kontrabässe

Ex. 20

Range   Open Strings   Sounding an 8ve lower.

The double bass is known by a variety of other names: contra bass, string bass, bass viol, or simply bass. ("Bass violin" is an amateurish misnomer.)

We now encounter for the first time an instrument that does not sound as written. The double bass sounds an octave lower than written, or, to state the case conversely, the notes must be written an octave higher than they are intended to sound. A glance at the lower range of the instrument will explain the need for such an arrangement. If the part were written at actual or "concert" pitch, ledger lines would be in continuous use, and the result would be cumbersome to write and awkward to read.

The double bass in standard use today has four strings, which are tuned in 4ths rather than in 5ths. The five-string bass, which is still much used in Europe but is rarely seen in the United States, tunes its fifth string to a C below the low E. In this country, the device commonly used for making these low notes possible is an extension to the fingerboard of a four-string bass. The bottom string can then be tuned down to C instead of E. In most professional orchestras, at least two or three basses have this extension, and in some orchestras the whole bass section is equipped with them. School orchestras, on the other hand, seldom include a bass with an extension. Fortunately, notes below the low E do not occur very often; where they do, they can often be played an octave higher without any serious damage to the effect. This "extended" low register of the instrument is valuable for dark color effects and for finishing out phrases that dip below the low E. But as a general rule, the double bass sounds much better when it is not kept too low. It has more incisiveness, more sense of definite pitch, in its upper and medium registers. Then, too, it has a way of sounding low even when the part appears to be moderately high. The tenor clef or the treble clef may be used in very high passages.

Because of its great size and the ponderousness of its technique, the instrument has some limitations of performance as compared with its smaller relatives. For one thing, it is less agile. Though rapid running passages are possible, they should not be too long or too frequent. Besides being strenuous for the player, they are apt to sound strangely "fuzzy" and unsatisfactory. In order to ease the technical problem and make for a clearer effect, the basses are sometimes given a simplified form of what the cellos—and possibly the lower woodwinds—are playing:

Ex. 21

Cellos

Double Basses
(Sounding an
8ve lower)

Of course it is not necessary, or even advisable, that the basses play constantly; in fact, their effectiveness is generally in inverse ratio to the amount they play. Therefore, a possible solution, in case the passage at hand seems unsuited to their technique, is simply to give them a rest.

One point to remember in writing for the double bass is that triple and quadruple stops are completely out of the question. A few double stops—those involving one or two open strings—are possible. Usually, however, it is better to divide the section when two notes must be played by the basses. Most of the other effects discussed in connection with the violin, viola, and cello are possible on the double bass. Pizzicato passages are frequent and especially effective, because they provide support without heaviness and give a welcome relief from the bowed sound.

The basses are seldom called upon to play alone. Their tone is apt to be a bit dry and lacking in focus, and they do not have the *espressivo* possibilities of the cellos. But they frequently take melodic passages an octave below the cellos. Their lower register is dark, almost ominous, in quality, while the upper two strings are somewhat clearer and brighter in color.

EXAMPLES OF PASSAGES FOR DOUBLE BASS

(Since the double bass sounds an octave lower than written, passages in which the cellos and basses are *written* in unison will sound in octaves.)

Ex. 22

(a) Fifth Symphony

Allegro   Beethoven

Cellos,
Basses

(b) Symphony in B minor (*Unfinished*)

(c) *The Elephant* (from *The Carnival of Animals*)

Permission for reprint granted by copyright owner, Durand et Cie, Paris, France; Elkan-Vogel Co., Inc., agents for the U.S.A.

(d) *Death and Transfiguration*

(e) *Daphnis and Chloe* Suite No. 2

Permission for reprint granted by copyright owner, Durand et Cie, Paris, France; Elkan-Vogel Co., Inc., agents for the U.S.A.

(f) *Symphonic Metamorphosis of Themes by C. M. von Weber*

Lively (♩=96)   Hindemith

Reproduced by permission of Schott & Co., Ltd., London.

So far we have discussed only the more elementary material on the individual stringed instruments. It should be apparent even from this brief discussion, however, that writing for strings is a special technique. What looks easy to the pianist may prove surprisingly awkward for the string player, while there are fine string parts that would be totally impractical for woodwind or brass instruments. There is a good deal to be learned not only about combining the stringed instruments to make up a string orchestra, but also about matters of bowing and special effects. These are the subjects to be taken up next.

SUGGESTED ASSIGNMENT

Know:

1. open strings and ranges (possible and practical) of the stringed instruments.
2. correct notation in alto and tenor clef.
3. transposition used by the double bass.
4. indications for the use of a particular string.
5. general principles involved in writing double, triple, and quadruple stops.
6. Italian, French, and German names for the stringed instruments.

SUGGESTED LISTENING

Because passages for the violins are so abundant and familiar, and because the violins are heard prominently in the music for suggested listening given at the end of Chapter 4, they are not included here.

Violas

Wagner, Prelude to *Tristan und Isolde*, meas. 90.
Tchaikovsky, *Romeo and Juliet*, letter G;[4] Fifth Symphony, 3rd movt., letter E.
Strauss, *Don Quixote*, measure 18, etc.; *Till Eulenspiegel*, meas. 179 (*Gemächlich*).
Ippolitov-Ivanov, *Caucasian Sketches: In the Village*.
Ravel, *Daphnis and Chloe* Suite No. 2, figure 158.
Bartók, *Music for String Instruments, Percussion and Celesta*, beginning; 3rd movt., meas. 6.
William Schuman, *American Festival Overture*, 5 bars after figure 80.

[4] Throughout the "Suggestions for Listening" in this book, only the *beginning* point of each passage is indicated, by means of a measure number or a rehearsal letter or figure

Cellos

Beethoven, Third Symphony (*Eroica*), beginning.
Schubert, Symphony in B minor (*Unfinished*), 1st movt., 2nd theme.
Brahms, Third Symphony, 3rd movt.; Fourth Symphony, 2nd movt., meas. 41;
   Piano Concerto No. 2, 3rd movt., beginning.
Saint-Saëns, *The Swan* from *The Carnival of Animals* (solo cello).
Wagner, *Tristan und Isolde*, beginning of Prelude; *Love Death*, meas. 9.
Glinka, Overture to *Russlan and Ludmilla*, 2nd theme, meas. 81.
Strauss, *Don Quixote*, Variation 5.
Elgar, *Enigma Variations*, Variation 12.
Mahler, Fourth Symphony, 3rd movt., beginning and at figure 9.
Harris, Third Symphony, beginning.
Hanson, First Symphony, beginning.
Villa-Lobos, *Bachianas Brasileiras* No. 1, for eight cellos.
Bloch, *Schelomo* (virtuoso writing for solo cello with orchestra).

Double Basses

Since the double bass section seldom takes a musical idea entirely by itself, most of the examples that follow involve octave or unison doublings with other instruments.

Beethoven, Fifth Symphony, 3rd movt., beginning; also beginning of Trio; Ninth
   Symphony, 4th movt., meas. 8.
Franck, Symphony in D minor, beginning.
Saint-Saëns, *The Elephant* from *The Carnival of Animals*.
Goldmark, *Rustic Wedding* Symphony, beginning.
Strauss, *Also Sprach Zarathustra*, fugue in the "*Von der Wissenschaft*" section (involves
   four desks of basses, each desk playing a separate part); *Death and Transfiguration*,
   16 bars after letter D.
Mahler, Fourth Symphony, 3rd movt., figure 9 (basses playing *pizzicato* notes);
   First Symphony, 3rd movt., beginning (solo bass with mute).
Stravinsky, *The Rite of Spring*, 1 bar after figure 121.
Respighi, *Pines of Rome*, beginning of Part IV (*Pines of the Appian Way*) (bottom
   string tuned down to low B).

Chapter 3

THE STRING
ORCHESTRA

There are a good many reasons why the strings may well be considered the most important section of the orchestra:

1. As a group they possess an enormous pitch range; the orchestrator has at his command the entire compass from the highest note of the violin to the lowest note of the double bass.

2. Strings are very versatile technically. Rapid scale passages, slow *cantabile* melodies, short detached notes, long sustained tones, skips, trills, and chordal figurations are all practical and effective.

3. The vibrancy and warmth of the string tone make it especially useful. The strings can produce a particular *espressivo* quality not obtainable in the other choirs of the orchestra. And the tone is one that does not pall easily.

4. There are fewer problems of *blend* in the string section than in the other sections of the orchestra.

5. The *dynamic* range of the string section is unusually wide. Although neither strings nor woodwinds can equal the brass in the matter of sheer power, a full string section is able to produce a good, resonant *fortissimo*. At the other end of the dynamic scale, the string choir can reduce its tone to an almost inaudible *pianissimo*.

6. Unlike the woodwind and brass instruments, which must be given rests from time to time in order to allow the players to breathe and rest their lips, the strings are able to play continuously for longer periods if necessary. This is not say that they should be asked to play indefinitely without resting, but the problem is not nearly so acute as in the case of the wind instruments.

7. The strings are sometimes spoken of as "the backbone of the orchestra."

This description is based in part on the points listed above but also on traditional usage. Since the early days of the orchestra, the strings have been called upon to carry the greatest burden of the playing. That is, if one were to count the number of measures played by the woodwind, brass, and string sections, respectively, in a large number of scores, he would find that in each work the strings played the greatest number of measures, with the woodwind section ranking second, and the brass ranking third.

The number of players in each string group is not specified in scores, except in rare cases where an extra-large string section is called for. Ordinarily the full complement of strings is implied, that is, 16 first violins, 14 second violins, 12 violas, 10 cellos, and 8 to 10 double basses. But in actual practice a good many orchestras do not include this many string players, as the table on page 3 has indicated. When scores written especially for "small orchestra" are played, the size of the string section is reduced. Also, because the orchestra of Haydn and Mozart's day included fewer string players than our modern orchestra does, many conductors prefer to use only a portion of each string group in performing music of the Classical period.

Normally, the members of each string group play a single melodic line in unison. But it is possible to divide each group into two or more parts, each part playing different notes. In that case the Italian word *divisi*, usually shortened to *div.*, is placed next to the passage, most often above the staff. In the case of division into more than two parts, the number of parts is indicated as follows: *div. a 3* or *div. a 4*, etc. (See Appendix A for the equivalents of these terms in other languages.) Ordinary *divisi* passages (two parts) are very frequent; more than two parts are less often used, while the use of more than four is apt to be risky if one is writing for anything less than a full string section or for players of limited ability. In ordinary *divisi* writing, the two parts can usually be written on the same staff. If they involve the same time values, a single stem may be used for both—provided, of course, that the *div.* indication is present so that the two notes will not be taken for a double stop. But if the time values in the two parts are different, then separate stems will be necessary, that is, stems up for the upper part, stems down for the lower part. When the two parts cannot conveniently be written on the same staff (for example, when they cross repeatedly) two staves are used. In that case, the *divisi* direction is sometimes put at the edge of the page, preceding the divided part. (All these points are illustrated in the examples of string scoring that follow.) With divisions into three or more parts, the parts may be arranged in whatever way is most convenient—two or more to a staff or each part on a separate staff. Any or all of the string groups may be divided, though the basses are divided less often than the other string groups. After a *divisi* passage, when the string group is to play in unison again, the expression *unisono*, shortened to *unis.*, is used. *Non divisi* (*non div.*) is commonly written above passages that could be played *divisi* but are meant to be played by the use of double stops.

Dynamics must be indicated below each staff. This is extremely important and sometimes difficult to impress upon the beginning orchestrator. Whereas the pianist can gain a complete idea of the music he is playing from the page before him and can adjust dynamics and the weight of individual voices accordingly, the orchestral player sees only his own part. He cannot tell from it whether he is playing an important musical idea that should be brought out or a subordinate voice that must be kept in the background. Therefore, he must be told exactly how loudly to play at all times. It is quite possible that while he is playing *ff*, another instrument in the orchestra will be marked *mf* or even *pp* in order to achieve the proper effect. Crescendos, diminuendos, and any other dynamic changes, along with such directions as *espressivo* or *marcato*, must likewise be written in beneath each part they apply to.

Since matters of *tempo* normally apply to all the instruments at the same time, one tempo marking at the top of the page, above the woodwinds, and one lower down, just above the strings, are usually sufficient in the score. But these tempo indications (including any *ritardandos, accelerandos*, or similar markings) are included by the copyist in each part, when the players' parts are extracted from the score.

A brief reminder on a few points of notation may be in order here. Notes below the middle line of the staff have stems up; those above the middle line have stems down; notes *on* the middle line may have stems either up or down. In groups such as eighths or sixteenths, the direction of the stems is determined by the position of the majority of the notes in the group. Notice that in orchestral writing, instrumental rather than vocal notation is used. (See Ex. 1.)

Ex. 1

(a)

not

(b)

Notice, too, that it is unnecessary to have a separate bar-line for each staff. Simply draw one long bar-line through all the parts of each section. Be sure to line up the parts so that the notes which are to sound together are in a straight line, vertically, on the page. Whole notes go at the beginning of the measure, but whole rests should be placed in the middle. Nowadays,

the whole rest ⊏___▬___⊐ may be used with any meter signature to indicate

a full measure of rest.

On the first page of a score, the names of instruments are normally written out in full; after that, abbreviations are commonly used. In the case of strings, those most often seen are: "Vl." or "Vln." or just "V." for Violin (followed by "I" or "II" for "first" or "second"); "Vla." for Viola, or "Vle." (the Italian plural abbreviated) for Violas; "V-Cello" or "Vc." for Violoncello; and "D. Bass," "D.B.," "C.Bass," or "C. B." for Double Bass. The usual method of bracketing the violins and the whole string section can be observed in the examples that follow.

POSSIBLE ARRANGEMENTS IN SCORING FOR STRING ORCHESTRA

In order to make our first work in scoring for strings as uncomplicated as possible, a short phrase from a Bach chorale[1] has been chosen as an example:

Ex. 2

Jesu, meine Freude

Bach

Certain obvious arrangements of the strings suggest themselves immediately: first violins on the melody, second violins on the alto part, violas on the tenor, and cellos on the lowest voice. The double basses may either rest or be given the same *written* part as the cellos, which means that they

---

[1] This chorale excerpt is from an *a cappella* motet. Of the arrangements shown in Examples 3–11, only Example 3 corresponds with Bach's own practice as seen in his cantatas.

will sound an octave lower than the cellos. Using the latter choice, the scored version would look like this:

Ex. 3

This is the most frequent arrangement of the strings and one which will sound very satisfactory, either with or without double bass.

The range of a voice is obviously a factor in deciding what instrument shall take it. For example, in this Bach excerpt the tenor line could not be taken by violins because it goes down to an F♯, one half-step lower than the violins can play. Nor could the bass voice be taken by viola, because of the notes that fall below the viola's low C.

Since no dynamics or tempo indications are included in the original Bach version, we have had to supply our own. Dynamic markings could be anything from *ppp* to *fff*, depending on the mood and general conception we give to the excerpt. Various dynamic levels have been used in the scorings shown and a tempo marking of *Adagio* chosen arbitrarily. We might decide that the music should be either *legato* or *molto marcato*; but that question will have to be put aside temporarily, for it involves problems of bowing which are being reserved for the next chapter.

Suppose we feel that the chorale melody (the upper part) in *Jesu, meine Freude* should be brought out a bit in relation to the other voices. The effect could be achieved very easily by marking the first violins a little louder than the other instruments. Or, we could arrive at an effect of greater weight and resonance on the melody by giving it to both first and second violins. In that case, we have a new problem: The three remaining voices must somehow be taken by *two* sections, the violas and the cellos. (It seems best to use the double basses only for the part they played in the first version.) The obvious solution here is to divide either the violas or the cellos to give two parts. If we divide the violas, the arrangement is as follows:

Ex. 4

With a full viola section this version would sound well; but in school and other nonprofessional groups, viola sections are apt to be "understaffed," and when they are divided in half there is simply not enough body in each half to balance the rest of the strings. In such a case, the balance could be improved by marking the violas a degree louder than the other sections, as shown in parentheses.

The other solution is to divide the cellos:

Ex. 5

In this version the division is somewhat compensated for by the fact that the upper cellos are in their high, vibrant register where they will come through rather prominently. If this upper part stayed high, it might well be written in tenor clef, in which case separate staves would be used for the two halves of the cello section, as in Example 6.

In case the particular color of violas were wanted on the melody, such an arrangement could be used. Because the tenor part in our example is too low for violins, the alto is the only line left that they could play. First and second violins together would be too heavy for the alto, so that either first or second violins should be given rests in this case. There is nothing wrong with letting a section rest, but a more effective solution might be to put violas and first violins on the melody (in unison) for greater weight and for mixed color:

Ex. 6

Half the cellos doubled in unison with violins on the melody would add poignancy and intensity to the tone. That would take the upper half of the cellos rather high, but not unreasonably so for a professional group. It should be pointed out, though, that this arrangement of the strings is by no means a common one, and that in many pieces of music it would be inappropriate or impractical (or both) to give the cello the melody, particularly at its original pitch. In fact, the high cello part in Example 7 is open to question as being too lush and romantic in this context; it is included here more with the idea of exploring various possibilities than with any implication of stylistic appropriateness. (One might add, however, that there is considerable divergence of opinion as to what *is* stylistically appropriate in scoring music of given periods.)

Ex. 7

Of course it would be possible to use all the cellos on the melody, but in that case the double basses would have to play the bass at its original pitch by themselves. While that arrangement might be satisfactory if the bass section were large, it is much safer to retain half the cellos on the bass line and to write the double bass part so that it will sound an octave lower. One might suppose that dividing the double basses in octaves (on the bass and its doubling an octave lower) would work out well. In actual practice it does not; the effect is disappointing and is almost never used in orchestral scoring.

VERSIONS USING OCTAVE DOUBLINGS
OF THE THREE UPPER VOICES

In having the double basses play the bass voice an octave lower than in the original, we amplified the original version slightly. Similarly, the top voice (when it is the melody) may be doubled an octave higher than in the original. The effect is somewhat more brilliant. It is also possible to fill in the octave at the top by doubling the alto and tenor voices an octave higher as well. These two versions are shown in Examples 8 and 9, respectively.

Ex. 8   **Ex. 9**

As a rule, the effect of doubling only the alto or only the tenor an octave higher is not good because of the gaps of open 4ths and 5ths that often result. In other words, it is normally best to double both alto and tenor or neither, at the octave, in scoring a four-voice composition of this sort. Doubling of inner voices an octave *lower* than the original is usually out of the question because of the muddiness that results when voices are spaced close together low in a chord.

In some music, the same objection would apply to a doubling of the melody an octave lower. In our Bach example, however, the effect of doubling it at the lower octave is not too thick; in fact, that arrangement actually improves the spacing by filling in some unnecessarily wide gaps between the tenor and bass voices. This possibility is demonstrated in Examples 10 and 11.

Example 11 also makes use of upper-octave doublings of the soprano, alto, and tenor voices; as in the preceding versions, the double basses have been written to sound an octave lower than the bass in the original. Although the layout of the divided violin sections is different in Examples 9 and 11, respectively, the sound of the combined violin sections will be approximately the same in each case.

Ex. 10   **Ex. 11**

The last version is obviously the fullest, the most resonant. This is not to say that it is therefore preferable to the others, however. There are generally many effective ways of scoring a given passage, and the way chosen will be the one that seems the most telling and appropriate in context.

Example 12 shows excerpts from symphonic literature that involve the string section prominently. In (c), (d) and (g) only the strings are playing; in the remaining examples other instruments not shown here are also playing, but in each case the strings give a fairly complete idea of the musical substance. In (b) note the use of multiple stops in which the top note is held. In (c) and (g) the effect is extremely rich and warm, partly because of the harmonic fullness afforded by the division of one or more string groups, partly because the melody is taken by violins playing high on their G string. Concerning (d), the speed of the notes is about the maximum at which successive pizzicato notes can be played comfortably. Example (e) makes use of the very high register of the violin, where the quality is bright, singing and intense. In (f) harmonic background is supplied through some characteristic and effective string arpeggios based on multiple-stop patterns. In (h) the effect is heavy and savage. Woodwinds, horns, timpani and bass drum are also playing.

EXAMPLES SHOWING VARIOUS POSSIBILITIES
IN ARRANGING THE STRINGS

Ex. 12

(a) C major Symphony (*Jupiter*)

Mozart

(b) Fifth Symphony

Beethoven

(c) Fourth Symphony

(d) Fourth Symphony

(e) Second Symphony

Schumann

(f) Symphony in E minor (*New World*)

Dvořák

(g) Ninth Symphony   Mahler

Sehr langsam und noch zurückhaltend. a tempo (*Molto adagio*)

(h) *The Rite of Spring*

Stravinsky

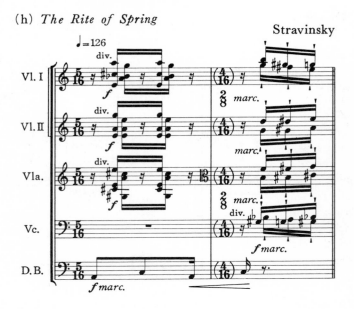

REMARKS ON SPACING, DOUBLING, AND VARIOUS TEXTURES

Students who are using this book as a text will normally embark on their first project in scoring for strings after reading this chapter, and there are some points concerning spacing and doubling that they will need to keep in mind. Although these are points that they will presumably have covered in their harmony courses, the author has found that a brief review of them is often helpful.

Since we shall want to refer to the overtone series presently in connection with spacing and with string harmonics and at many other points later on in connection with wind instruments, a short commentary on that subject seems in order here.

All musical instruments make use of a vibrating body (a string, an air column, etc.), which vibrates not only as a whole, to produce the main tone or "fundamental," but in halves, thirds, fourths, and so on. These fractional vibrations produce pure sounds of higher pitch and much weaker intensity than the fundamental, the pure sounds normally being heard as part of the composite tone. Example 13 shows a fundamental (C) with its first fifteen overtones.

Ex. 13

(Notes that do not correspond exactly with our equally tempered scale are shown in black.)

The terms "partials" and "harmonic series" are often used in connection with overtones, but they include the fundamental, whereas the term "overtone" does not. The first overtone, then, is the second partial. In Example 13 the notes have been numbered on the basis of partials; that is, the fundamental is numbered "1," and so on. Certain partials come out more strongly in some instruments than in others, with consequent differences between the respective tone qualities of the various instruments.

Normally, spacing of harmony is modeled in a general way on the harmonic series: the wide intervals are put at the bottom, the smaller intervals in the upper part of the chord. Usually it is best to leave a clear octave at the bottom, although if the chord is not too low it may be possible to begin with a 5th at the bottom:

Ex. 14

If notes are put close together in the lower portion of a chord, a thick, muddy effect results; therefore, avoid putting the 3rd of the chord too low—

say below  (assuming the chord to be in root position).

In scoring music written originally in open spacing, it is often a wise idea to fill in the gaps between the upper parts by means of octave doublings, in effect to convert the open structure to close. For example,

Ex. 15

might become

While open spacing is frequently used for the strings and is not out of the question for the other instruments, close spacing is, as a general rule, more effective in the orchestra.

Even in music written in close structure it sometimes becomes necessary to add a "filler" part; that is, an extra voice introduced in order to fill in gaps between voices (most often between tenor and bass). Such a voice may double other voices part of the time, then branch off to fill in gaps where necessary; or it may take an independent line of its own, doubling chord tones at times but not actually playing the same line as any of the other voices. In the following excerpt from "America" a possible filler part is shown in small notes:

Ex. 16

However, students will probably do well to avoid fillers except in cases of absolute necessity. Such parts are usually not very strong or interesting from a linear standpoint, and if used indiscriminately they tend to detract from the clarity of the other voices and to bring about a muddy texture. Besides, beginning orchestrators often have difficulty in maintaining good voice-leading in the orchestral parts, and the addition of an extra voice that may rove at will only complicates the problem.

Sometimes the top voice of a closely spaced chord is doubled an octave higher, leaving a gap of an octave at the top (as in Example 8). In such cases the effect is good, and there is no objection to the octave gap.

As a rule, when a primary triad (I, IV, or V) is in first inversion, the bass should not be doubled in the upper parts. The same applies to 7th chords in any inversion:

Ex. 17

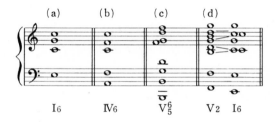

(Of course the bass may always be doubled an octave *lower*.) Notice that in (d), above, proper voice-leading demands that certain notes be doubled in the tonic chord. When an "active" tone (such as the seventh scale degree) is taken by a particular instrument, the resolution of that tone must obviously occur in the same instrument.

It should perhaps be added that this material on spacing and doubling does not always apply in twentieth century music. Certain composers, Stravinsky in particular, have achieved fresh and intriguing effects by a deliberate use of unusual spacings and doublings (see page 292).

What has been said here so far applies chiefly to harmonic (chordal) music. Homophonic and especially polyphonic textures will involve different approaches. These musical situations are discussed at some length in later chapters but a few comments on them at this point may be helpful.

In scoring homophonic music, it is normally desirable that the melody stand out from the background. This may be achieved by presenting it in a contrasting color, by giving it extra weight, by marking it louder, by doubling it in octaves, or by using a combination of any of these means. Homophonic music for the piano often involves idiomatic accompaniment figures (such as wide arpeggios), which may have to be changed to patterns better suited to the instruments concerned; and certain notes may have to be sustained in the orchestral version to approximate the effect of the piano's sustaining pedal. In general, wide gaps between the notes played by the two hands should be filled in, at least partially.

In polyphonic music, the chief objectives are balance between voices (or a calculated emphasis on one when that is appropriate) and linear clarity. The most effective way to make the voices stand out sharply from each other is to give them to different timbres. But that approach is by no means always necessary, nor is it always possible (as, for example, in scoring for one section of the orchestra alone). Concerning doublings, the upper voice can generally be doubled an octave higher and the bottom voice an octave lower without damaging the clarity of the texture; occasionally the upper voice may be doubled an octave lower. Lower-octave doublings of the inner voices are usually out of the question because of the thickness and the overlapping of the bass that may result; even upper-octave doublings of these voices may produce linear confusion.

SUGGESTED ASSIGNMENTS*

A. Know:

1. number of players in each string group (in a full orchestra).
2. order and arrangement of the strings on the page.
3. customary abbreviations of names of stringed instruments.
4. directions for the division of a string group into two or more parts.
5. proper placing and use of indications for dynamics and tempo.
6. principles of good spacing and doubling.

B. Select a short four-voice chordal excerpt and score it in six different ways for strings. Bowing need not be indicated.

* *Music for suggested listening is listed at the end of Chapter 4.*

Chapter 4

BOWING
AND SPECIAL EFFECTS

The term "bowing" may mean the actual motion of the bow over the strings, or it may mean the indications in a string part which tell the player how the music is to be bowed. Using the word in the latter sense, bowing includes: (1) slurs over each group of notes to be taken in the same bow; (2) down-bow marks (⊓) or up-bow marks (∨) at points where the use of one or the other is preferable; (3) such indications as dots or accent marks over the notes to suggest the type of bowing appropriate; and (4) actual words, such as *spiccato*, to indicate the exact type of bowing to be used. The directions *arco* and *pizzicato*, which have been discussed earlier, might also be listed under the heading of bowing.

Beginning students of orchestration invariably feel "put upon" when they are asked to include bowing in their scores. Their usual reaction is, "Why not let the string player worry about that problem? He knows more about it than we do." There are several answers to this attitude. One is that a passage may be given a number of different interpretations depending on how it is bowed; although the player may know more about bowing than the budding arranger, he does not know, without bowing marks, just what effect the arranger intended. In other words, bowing is an integral part of the music and should not be left to chance. A glance at any orchestral score will confirm the fact that slurs to indicate bowing are always included, simply as a matter of standard practice. It may be objected that the conductor or the players will probably make some changes in the bowing anyway. That is true, even in the case of standard symphonic literature. Nevertheless, the original bowing will give an idea of the basic conception of the music. Another answer is that planning of the bowing for all the groups of the string section at the same time brings about a uniformity of effect that is very important and that would be hard to achieve if each group were allowed to choose its own bowing.

There is a point that needs to be clearly understood at the beginning: in string music the slur does not normally indicate broad phrase outlines as it does in piano music; instead it is used to show which notes are to be taken on the same bow. For instance, in Example 1 the first four notes are taken on one bow; then the bow reverses direction to take the next two notes and again to take the last three.

Ex. 1

The same passage might have been bowed in several other ways, three of which are shown here:

In the last version, where no slurs are shown, the player would use a separate bow (that is, change the direction of the bow) for each note. It should be emphasized that no break in sound need occur when the bow changes; however, a separation between notes *may* be made if desired.

There are a few scores in which phrasing rather than bowing is indicated at certain points in the string parts, usually in long, sustained melodic lines. In such cases the bowing to be used is decided upon by the conductor or the players. Occasionally phrase marks are included in addition to bowing slurs in order to insure an even, connected effect, but the vast majority of scores rely solely on bowing slurs to project the musical structure of the string parts.

Some factors that influence bowing are the dynamics and tempo involved, the general effect desired, and such technical considerations as the need for a down-bow or an up-bow at certain places.

As for dynamics, the amount of bow "used up" varies in a general way with the volume of tone produced. Consequently, the player can take more notes per bow in a soft passage than in a loud one. But that does not mean that all soft passages should be slurred in long groups and all loud passages played with separate bows. It is perfectly possible to change bow frequently in a soft passage, even to the point of playing rapidly moving parts with a bow to a note:

Ex. 2

Overture to *The Marriage of Figaro*

Mozart

And a reasonable number of notes may be taken on one bow even in a *fortissimo*:

Ex. 3

Symphony: *Mathis der Maler*

Hindemith

Reproduced by permission of Schott & Co., Ltd., London.

The influence of tempo on bowing is fairly obvious. The faster the tempo, the more notes the player can take comfortably on each bow.

In describing the difference between a slurred effect and a separately bowed effect, it might be said that the first is smoothly flowing, while the second gives a greater sense of articulation to each note. Fast running passages in which each note is separately bowed are particularly vigorous and sparkling. Of course, a passage need not be all bowed or all slurred. Interesting combinations of the two effects are illustrated in Example 4.

Ex. 4

(a) First Symphony

Allegro molto   Beethoven

(b) C major Symphony (*Jupiter*)

Allegretto   Mozart

In plotting bowing, it is often necessary to bring the player out on a down-bow or an up-bow at a particular point. For example, down-bows are in order for heavily accented notes and are even preferable for strong beats in a measure. On the other hand, an anacrusis (up-beat) is best given to an up-bow, in order that the strong beat that follows may be taken down-bow. Crescendos are somewhat easier on an up-bow. A "group-staccato" bowing, to be described presently, is mainly an up-bow stroke, while the *jeté* is normally performed on a down-bow. The signs for up-bow and down-bow (∨ and ⊓) are put in, above the notes, only at points where the player would not be likely to choose that bowing automatically. For instance, it is a convention that the first note of a passage will be taken down-bow unless an up-bow mark is shown, or unless the first note is obviously an up-beat requiring an up-bow. But in any case where the proper bowing cannot be anticipated at a glance, it should be clearly indicated at the beginning of the passage. Usually it is superfluous to include alternate down-bow and up-bow signs throughout a passage, since the player must change from one bow to the other of necessity, and the slurs will tell him where to change. The important thing is to get him started on the right bow, and the rest should follow automatically.

There is another small technical point that influences bowing: if a jump from one string to a nonadjacent string is involved, the notes in question obviously cannot be taken *legato*.

TYPES OF BOWING

Perhaps no aspect of orchestration offers more chance for controversy than does the labeling of various types of bowing. There is disagreement on this subject not only among orchestration books but among players themselves. In the first place, the terminology involves a hodge-podge of languages, and there are sometimes two or three different names in each language for a particular type of bowing. To complicate matters still further, descriptions of certain bowings differ from book to book and from player to player. It should be pointed out, too, that the period and style of the music influence the interpretation of bowing marks. For example, dots over the notes in a passage by Haydn might call for one type of bowing, while the same indication in a contemporary score might suggest another type.

As a result of all this confusion, it is very difficult to write in an authoritative way on the subject of bowing types.

It is suggested that the student consult with string players in order to gain a more intimate knowledge of bowing possibilities. The list given here is a highly simplified one; many combinations and subtle variations are possible.

The chief bowing types may be broken down into two main categories:

those in which the bow stays on the string and those in which it leaves the string.

ON-THE-STRING BOWINGS

Legato

Groups of notes are slurred together; the total effect is as smooth as possible.

Ex. 5

Don Juan

Détaché

Each note is bowed separately. Although the word *détaché* suggests a break between the notes, that is not normally implied in the term as it is used by most string players in this country today. Successive notes taken *détaché* may be joined together smoothly, or the connection may be made less smooth by emphasizing the articulation that goes with the changing of the bow. An accented *détaché* is possible and effective. *Détaché* bowing can be executed at practically any speed and dynamic level. At slower tempos (especially in a *forte*), full bows may be used; at medium or faster speeds the middle or upper portion of the bow is normally involved. The point may be used for a delicate effect or, less often, the frog for a heavy one. As a rule, there is no special indication for the use of *détaché* bowing, apart from the absence of slurs. But sometimes in older music (particularly in passages where slurred and *détaché* groups alternate) dots are used to signify the *détaché* (as in Ex. 4 [a]).

Ex. 6

(a) Prelude to *Die Meistersinger*

(b) Fourth Symphony

Martelé (martellato)

The description "hammered," which has commonly been applied to this type of bowing because of the literal meaning of *martelé*, is perhaps misleading; the bow does not strike the string from above but begins and remains on it, moving very quickly and stopping abruptly at the end of each stroke so that there is a clean-cut separation between notes. The *martelé* is most often done at the upper part of the bow but may also be done at the frog to produce a more robust effect. The indication for it may be dots, arrowheads, accents, or a combination. Occasionally the word *martelé* is written in, sometimes followed by a direction for the specific use of the frog or the point (see Appendix A for these terms in foreign languages). More often, however, the player simply chooses the *martelé* bowing as being appropriate to the music at hand. Obviously, this type cannot be used when the notes move along too swiftly; beyond a certain speed, the stopping of the bow between strokes becomes an impossibility.

Ex. 7

Fourth Symphony

Staccato

Employed in a generic sense, the word *staccato* can be applied to any bowing (off-the-string or on-the-string) in which the notes are separated from each other. However, when used as part of the term *slurred staccato*, it refers specifically to an on-the-string bowing in which a series of notes is taken (generally up-bow) with a separate "push" for each note. If many notes are involved, the stroke is so difficult as to be impractical for orchestral playing. But in a limited form, often called *group staccato*, it figures constantly in orchestral string parts. Two types may be cited. The first is primarily an up-bow stroke and consists of three or four notes (occasionally more) which are made to sound separately under the same bow, as at the beginning of Example 8.

Ex. 8

Eighth Symphony

The second type (Example 9) can be performed on either an up-bow or a down-bow. It consists of two repeated notes with a separation between that is produced by a momentary stopping of the bow. Illogically, the notation usually involves a dot above or below the *second* of the two notes, although the first is actually the one that is shortened in performance. Versions (a), (b), (c), and (d) will all sound approximately alike.

Ex. 9

Louré (portato)

This bowing is used chiefly in music of a slow, *espressivo* character. Two or more notes (seldom more than four) are taken on one bow, with a separate pressure and a slight initial swelling of the sound on each note. As applied in some music, the *louré* may involve an almost imperceptible break between the notes.

Ex. 10

Copyright, 1903, by Breitkopf & Haertel. By permission of Associated Music Publishers.

OFF-THE-STRING BOWINGS

Spiccato

This is normally a light, middle-bow stroke in which the bow bounces off the string, taking one note to each bow. It is used very frequently in orchestral playing but is not generally practical if the dynamic level is to be louder than about *mf*. However, in passages that are not too rapid, a heavier type of spiccato done at or near the frog may be employed in case more sound is wanted. The usual indication for *spiccato* bowing is simply dots; or the word *spiccato* may be written in.

Ex. 11

(a) Second Symphony

In ruhig fliessender Bewegnung
spring. Bogen
Mahler
Vl. I
pp

(b) First Symphony

Allegretto ♩=152
Shostakovich
Vl. I
p

The term *sautillé* (from the French verb "to leap") is often used interchangeably with *spiccato*. But it is better reserved for a very fast, light and delicate type of *spiccato* bowing in which the jumping of the bow results chiefly from the resilience of the stick rather than from an individual drop-and-lift motion for each note. (See Ex. 11[c].)

(c) *Midsummer Night's Dream*, Overture

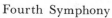

Allegro di molto
div.
Mendelssohn
Vl. I
pp

Group Spiccato

Although this term has been little used, it seems a logical one to describe a bowing similar to the group *staccato* but *off* the string. Instead of reversing direction for each note as in the ordinary *spiccato*, the bow picks up a series of short notes, usually on an up-bow. This stroke is sometimes referred to as *staccato volante* or "flying *staccato*." However, the *spiccato* designation seems to offer less chance for confusion in terminology.

Ex. 12

Fourth Symphony

Moderato
Mahler
Vla.
pp legg.

Jeté (ricochet, saltando, sautillé)

In the *jeté* (meaning "thrown" in French) the bow, in its upper half, is made to bounce on the string very rapidly with a down-bow stroke, in such a way as to sound a group of two to six notes—most often repeated notes. The notation usually consists of dots under a slur.

Ex. 13

(a) *Capriccio Espagnol*

(b) *Fire Bird* Suite

Successive Down-bows

This device is sometimes used when a very decided break between notes is in order. Since the bow must be lifted and returned to the string between each two notes, the separation comes about automatically. This type of bowing is seldom employed for more than a few notes at a time, and it is not practical when the notes move along too quickly. The effect of successive down-bows is vigorous, sometimes almost savage, especially on the lowest string of each instrument.

Ex. 14

(a) *Petrouchka*

(b) *Fifth Symphony*

Successive Up-bows

This bowing also produces a clear separation between notes, but it is useful chiefly for a more delicate effect at softer dyanmic levels. (Compare Ex. 14[b] and 15[a].)

Ex. 15

(a) Fifth Symphony

(b) Classical Symphony

SPECIAL EFFECTS

Tremolos

Although tremolos are often included under the heading of bowing-types (of the on-the-string variety), they are not actually *types* in the sense that the bowings described in the preceding pages are. The bowed tremolo is, after all, simply an accelerated version of the *détaché*, and the fingered tremolo makes use of ordinary slurred bowing while the fingers produce the distinctive effect. Furthermore, because the function of tremolos is essentially a coloristic one, there is considerable reason for grouping them with the other devices to be discussed in this section.

Bowed tremolo:

(a) Unmeasured

Ex. 16

In the unmeasured form of the bowed tremolo, the bow is moved back and forth over the string as rapidly as possible. Three bars through the stem are ordinarily interpreted to mean an unmeasured tremolo, though sometimes in very slow tempo four bars through the stem are used to insure that the notes are not played as measured thirty-seconds. It is best to write in the word *tremolo* (abbreviation, *trem.*) in doubtful cases. The expression "at point" or *punta d'arco* in tremolo passages signifies that the tremolo is to be made at the point of the bow in order to achieve a delicate, wispy sound. In some passages the unmeasured tremolo gives an effect of energy and excitement; at other times, especially when used high and softly, it can produce a shimmering, ethereal effect.

EXAMPLES OF BOWED TREMOLO (UNMEASURED)

Ex. 17

(a) *Tristan und Isolde*

(b) Second Symphony

(c) *Prelude to The Afternoon of a Faun*

(b) Measured

Ex. 18

The measured tremolo, as its name implies, calls for a definite number of repeated notes, the number being shown by the notation. One line through a quarter-note or half-note stem means eighth notes; two lines, sixteenths. One line through an eighth-note stem means sixteenths; two lines, thirty-seconds; and so on. Triplets are indicated by a figure three above each note, or occasionally by three small dots placed next to the note head. Probably the safest way is to write out the actual notes involved in a measured tremolo for one measure at the beginning of the passage; after that, the simplified notation may be used. This method is shown in Example 19(a).

Tremolos (particularly the unmeasured variety) have been so over-exploited in romantic music that they have lost a good deal of their effectiveness and had better be used sparingly today.

EXAMPLES OF BOWED TREMOLO (MEASURED)

Ex. 19

(a) Sixth Symphony

(b) *Fantastic Symphony*

(c) Symphony in D minor

(d) Fifth Symphony

1st Vl.

Sibelius

With special permission from Wilhelm Hansen, Copenhagen.

Fingered tremolo (slurred tremolo):

Ex. 20

Vl.

In the fingered tremolo, which is usually unmeasured and which ordinarily involves two notes on the same string, one finger remains fixed on the lower of the two notes while another finger alternately plays and releases the upper note very rapidly so that a kind of trill between the notes results. The bow moves over the string in the normal way rather than quickly back and forth as in the bowed tremolo. The two notes involved are most often a 3rd apart, though intervals up to the diminished 5th are possible on the violin. On the viola, the limit had better be a perfect 4th, and on the cello a major 3rd. In notating fingered tremolos, each note is given twice the value it should have, mathematically speaking. Presumably, the theory is that the two notes of each pair sound so nearly at once that each note can be given full value. Frequently, fingered tremolos are written this way:

Ex. 21

That is, the two notes of each pair are crossed with themselves. Forsyth comments that this is merely "a pretty arrangement for the eye of the score-reader" and that with a whole group of strings the same sound results whether the intervals are written upward or downward. It would appear, then, that a single-line part like the fingered tremolo in Example 20 is sufficient. The fingered tremolo gives a delicate rustling effect that is elusive and attractive. It is most often used as a background for solo passages played

by woodwinds or horn. Fingered tremolos involving notes on two different
strings are possible but not very satisfactory. They are better avoided.

EXAMPLES OF FINGERED TREMOLO

Ex. 22

(a) *Prelude to The Afternoon of a Faun*   (b) *Fingal's Cave* Overture

*Example 22 (a): Permission for reprint granted by Editions Jean-Jobert of Paris, France, Copyright
Owners; Elkan-Vogel Co., Inc., of Philadelphia, Pa., Sole Agents in the United States.*

Other Special Effects

Muted (Italian: *con sordino* [*sordina*], abbrev., *con sord.;* French: [*avec*]
sourdine[*s*]; German: *mit Dämpfer*[*n*]).

The mute, a small clamp of wood, metal, rubber, leather, or plastic which
fits onto the bridge, reduces the volume of tone and gives it a veiled quality.
At least two bars of moderate 4/4 time (preferably more) should be allowed

for putting on mutes and at least one bar for taking them off.[1] It is usually wise to write, in the players' parts, "Put on mutes" in the rest preceding the muted passage and "Take off mutes" in the rest following it, so that players will be prepared in plenty of time for the passage to follow. A little-used effect calls for the mutes to be put on or taken off one desk at a time over a given number of measures. ("Desk" or "stand" is used to describe each group of two players; that is, the two who sit side by side and read from the same music.) The double bass uses a mute less often than the other stringed instruments, since the unmuted bass tone can be reduced to a whisper and can be made to blend fairly well with the other strings muted.

Playing with the bow at or near the bridge (Italian: *sul ponticello;* French: *sur le chevalet;* German: *am Steg*).

The resulting sound is glassy and eerie in quality. The intensity of this distinctive color varies with the proximity of the bow to the bridge. The device is probably most effective when used with a bowed tremolo. Examples can be seen near the beginning of Bartók's Concerto for Orchestra, at measure 219 of the first movement, and at measure 482 of the fifth movement. In the last instance the player is directed to return gradually to the normal sound in the course of measures 529 to 533.

Bowing over the fingerboard (Italian: *sul tasto* or *sulla tastiera;* French; *sur la touche;* German: *am Griffbrett*).

The sound is softer and less resonant. This is an effect which appears frequently in French impressionist scores. (See Ex. 22[a].) The term *flautando* directs the player to bow only very slightly over the fingerboard.

Playing "with the wood," that is, the back of the bow (Italian: *col legno*; French; *avec le bois;* German: *mit Holz*).

This is a rarely used effect and one which is generally confined to repeated-note figures, though there are a few instances of its use with legato and tremolo bowing. The sound is brittle and dry, and little volume is possible. Three examples that might be cited occur in Bloch's *Schelomo* at figure 6, in Bartók's *Music for String Instruments, Percussion and Celesta* at measure 90 of the fourth movement, and at the beginning of Holst's *The Planets.*

The direction for cancelling any of these special effects is *modo ordinario* (or simply *ord.*), meaning "in the ordinary way."

---

[1] The Heifetz Mute is so constructed that it can be clamped to one of the strings in the unused area below the bridge when not in use. Therefore, it can be put on and taken off more quickly than the ordinary mute.

Abnormal tuning (Italian: *scordatura*).

The player is directed to tune one or more strings higher or lower than usual. The most frequent purpose of this arrangement is to extend the range of an instrument downwards, as in Part IV of Respighi's *Pines of Rome*, where half the cellos and half the basses tune their bottom string to a low B. *Scordatura* may also be used to allow a particular pitch to be played as an open note, as in the last measure of Stravinsky's *The Rite of Spring*, where the cellos tune their A-string down to a G♯ which is then played as part of a quadruple stop. Or, rarely, the device may be employed for reasons of color: in the second movement of Mahler's Fourth Symphony the score calls for a solo violin with all four strings tuned a whole tone higher than usual, the object being to simulate the sound of a "cheap fiddle."

Glissando.

Two notes connected by a line

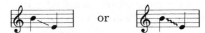

are played in such a way that the notes in between sound as a *glissando;* that is, the finger slides along the string instead of stopping each note separately. The glissando effect may be made very pronounced or may be reduced to an almost imperceptible connection between the notes. In the more moderate form, it is sometimes known as a *portamento* and is quite often introduced by the player, even where no direction is present, in order to give an extremely legato effect.

Half (of a string group) (Italian: *la metà;* French: *la moitié*; German: *die Hälfte*).

Occasionally the sound of a smaller-than-normal string group is wanted. In such cases the score may specify that only half of a particular string group is to play ("½ Violins I," or "½ Cellos," etc.). An example as applied to the double basses can be seen at the beginning of Strauss's *Till Eulenspiegel*.

First desk only or first two desks only, etc. (desk — Italian: *leggio;* French: *pupitre;* German: *Pult*).

The sound is reduced still further and approaches the solo quality, especially if only one desk is playing.

Solo strings.

When a more intimate, personal quality is desired, strings may be employed in a solo capacity. The direction in such cases is "1 solo violin" or "2 solo violas" (if two different parts are involved) or "4 solo cellos," as the case may be. Such parts are usually written on a separate staff or staves just above the string group to which the solo instrument belongs, although if the rest of the string group is not playing, a separate staff need not be used (in the case of one solo instrument).

Special pizzicato effects.

In the "snap pizzicato" the string is plucked with such force that it rebounds against the fingerboard. The indication is the sign ⊘ (or ⊘) over each note to be played in this fashion. Bartók is especially fond of this device, and examples of it may be seen in his *Music for String Instruments, Percussion and Celesta* (third movement, measure 49) as well as in his Violin Concerto (first movement, measure 373).

The "nail pizzicato" (indication ⊙ or ◎) involves using the fingernail rather than the fleshy part of the fingertip to pluck the string. The resulting sound is sharply metallic. An example occurs in the Adagio movement of Bartók's Fifth String Quartet at measure 32.

Multiple stops may be played pizzicato with a back-and-forth motion of the hand, the indication being either alternating down-bow and up-bow signs, or arrows. Example 14(i) in Chapter 10 illustrates this effect. Sometimes *quasi guitara* is included. The arpeggiation in pizzicato chords may be accentuated or reduced to a minimum; if the latter effect is desired, *non arpeggiato* should be written in, or a vertical bracket before the chord may be used instead (or additionally).

NATURAL HARMONICS

Harmonics are simply overtones of the strings. They have a flutelike, silvery quality that can be highly effective as a special color. In orchestral writing they are apt to be used for isolated notes or for short melodic lines in a moderate tempo. Rapid successions of them are difficult to perform and should be avoided.

In the remarks at the end of Chapter 3 it was explained that strings, like other sounding bodies, vibrate not only as a whole but in halves, thirds, fourths, and so on at the same time, producing overtones. These are normally heard as parts of the composite tone, but we can isolate them by touching the string lightly at certain points:

1. In the middle (an octave above the pitch of the open string); the result is a harmonic an octave higher than the pitch of the open string.

2. One third of the string length from either end (either a perfect 5th above the open pitch or at the point where the note would ordinarily be played); the result is a harmonic an octave and a 5th higher than the open pitch.

3. One fourth of the string length from either end (either a perfect 4th above the open pitch or at the point where the note would ordinarily be played); the result is a harmonic two octaves higher than the open pitch.

4. One fifth of the string length from either end (either a major 3rd above the open pitch or at the point where the note would ordinarily be played) or two fifths of the string length from either end (either a major 6th or a major 10th above the open pitch); the result is a harmonic two octaves and a major 3rd higher than the open pitch.

Other harmonics above this are possible but are seldom seen in orchestral writing. Even number 4 is used infrequently. Harmonics such as these, which are overtones of an open string, are called "natural" harmonics. Following is a chart showing the natural harmonics available on each of the violin's four strings, along with the notation involved. Notice that in some cases the same pitch occurs as a natural harmonic on two different strings.

NATURAL HARMONICS

Ex. 23

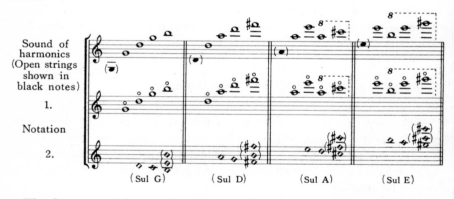

Sound of harmonics (Open strings shown in black notes)

1.

Notation

2.

(Sul G)   (Sul D)   (Sul A)   (Sul E)

The first natural harmonic on each string, the one an octave above the open note, is always notated at actual pitch with a small circle over it. The other natural harmonics may be notated in either of two ways, depending on how they are to be played. As explained earlier, they may be produced by touching the string lightly at either one of two points (more than two in the case of the fourth overtone). Notation 1 in Example 23 is used if the string is to be touched lightly at the point where the note would ordinarily be produced. Notation 2 shows, by means of a diamond-shaped note, another point on the string which can be touched lightly to produce the same harmonic. (The actual pitch of the harmonic usually does not appear in this case, although some composers prefer to include it as well.) The string to be used is often indicated below the note—for example, "sul D" or "D string" or "III."

As a general rule, this second method is somewhat easier than the first in performance. On the other hand, the playing method called for by Notation 1 is preferable in cases where the hand is already high on the string and would have to make an awkward jump to the other end of the fingerboard in order to use the second method. Some writers on orchestration recommend using Notation 1 exclusively for natural harmonics, the player then choosing the easiest method of playing the note. However, Notation 2 appears frequently in scores; consequently the author feels that students should understand it as well.

Although these points, and others in connection with harmonics, have a way of sounding complicated on paper, they can be made quite clear in a few minutes by means of an actual demonstration with a stringed instrument. The writer recommends strongly that such a demonstration be arranged at the time this material is taken up.

ARTIFICIAL HARMONICS

In order to produce as harmonics notes that are not overtones of the open strings, a slightly different procedure is necessary. The string is pressed down firmly by the first finger at a point two octaves below the pitch of the desired harmonic; at the same time, the fourth finger touches the string lightly at a point a perfect 4th higher, which is equivalent to dividing the unstopped portion of the string into quarters. A harmonic two octaves above the firmly fingered pitch results. (This is like number 3 of the natural harmonics, except that a stopped pitch rather than an open one is used as fundamental.)

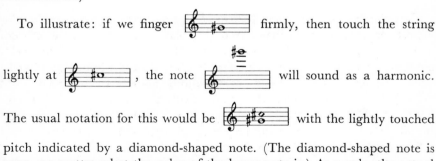

The usual notation for this would be with the lightly touched

pitch indicated by a diamond-shaped note. (The diamond-shaped note is open, no matter what the value of the lower note is.) As a rule, the actual sound is not even shown (though sometimes it is included as well, making three written notes for one sound). A question that students invariably ask at this point is: Why not avoid all these complications by simply writing the passage at actual pitch and marking it "harmonics"? This is what

Forsyth calls "the lazy way," and it is not recommended; it saddles the player with the problem of figuring out the most convenient method for producing each harmonic—a problem that is apt to waste time in rehearsal and one that should rightfully have been solved in advance by the arranger. The same objection applies to the practice of indicating all harmonics by circles over the notes.

Let us go back, now, and review the process of writing a note as a harmonic. The orchestrator should first see whether the note is playable as a natural harmonic. If it is, that way is usually easier and therefore preferable. If the note cannot be played as a natural harmonic, the following procedure can be adopted for writing it as an artificial harmonic: measure down two octaves from the actual pitch desired and write that note (with the proper time value), then write a diamond-shaped note a perfect 4th higher. (Notice that to make a *perfect* 4th, accidentals must often be added.) For example, if the following passage were to be played in harmonics,

Ex. 24

we would write:

Here the last note, A, could be played as a natural harmonic and would almost certainly be taken that way by the player even though it is written as an artificial harmonic. This substitution of the "artificial" for the "natural" notation when number 3 of the natural harmonics occurs in a series of artificial harmonics is a license that has come to be more or less accepted.

Artificial harmonics other than those involving the stretch of a 4th are possible but are seldom used. To give just one example: if the player touches the string lightly with his fourth finger a perfect *5th* above the stopped note, a harmonic a 12th higher than the stopped tone results.

Although two artificial harmonics at a time are occasionally called for in virtuoso solo literature for the violin, that arrangement is generally too difficult for orchestral use, with the exception of two artificial harmonics a perfect 5th apart, which can be played as a double stop by pressing two adjacent strings down firmly with the first finger and touching the two strings lightly a perfect 4th higher with the fourth finger.

What has been said about harmonics on the violin applies equally to the viola. Artificial harmonics are extremely difficult for the cello and out of the question for the double bass except in the higher positions; they should therefore be ruled out for these instruments except in virtuoso solo work. Natural harmonics are practical for both, in orchestral writing, however. Certain composers, notably Stravinsky, have made extensive and highly effective use of natural harmonics in parts for the double basses.

EXAMPLES OF NATURAL HARMONICS

Ex. 25

(a) *Capriccio Espagnol*   Rimsky-Korsakoff

(b) Concerto for Orchestra   Bartók

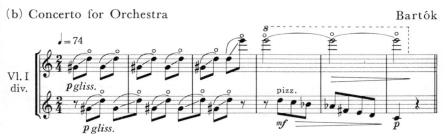

Copyright, 1946, by Hawkes & Son (London) Ltd. By permission of the copyright owner, Boosey & Hawkes, Inc.

(c) *Pictures from an Exhibition*

Mussorgsky-Ravel

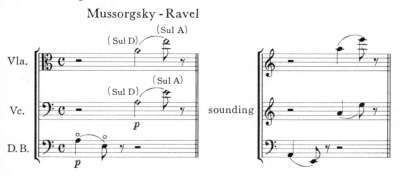

Copyright, 1929, by Edition Russe de Musique. By permission of the copyright owner, Boosey & Hawkes, Inc.

72

(d) *The Rite of Spring*

Stravinsky

(These harmonics are performed by sliding the finger lightly over the C string between middle C and c³. The harmonics shown result automatically.)

EXAMPLES OF ARTIFICIAL HARMONICS

Ex. 26

(a) *Ibéria*

Librement expressif   Debussy

Permission for reprint granted by copyright owner, Durand et Cie, Paris, France; Elkan-Vogel Co., Inc., agents for the U.S.A.

(b) *Capriccio Espagnol*

Rimsky-Korsakoff

SUGGESTED ASSIGNMENTS

A. Know:

1. the various types of bowing, the names commonly used for them, and the indication for each.
2. special effects obtainable on strings and the names for them.
3. principles involved in writing harmonics (natural and artifical).

B. The following are suitable as exercises in scoring for string orchestra. Include bowing indications (slurs and any other markings necessary).

1. Bach, Sarabande from First French Suite.
2. Bach, Fugue III from *The Well-Tempered Clavier*, Vol. I
3. Bach, Fugue XVI from *The Well-Tempered Clavier*, Vol. I.
4. Bach, Fugue in G minor from *Eight Little Preludes and Fugues for the Organ.*
5. Bach, Fugue VII from *The Art of Fugue.*
6. Bach, Fugue IX from *The Art of Fugue.*
7. Mozart, Sonata in B-flat major, K. 498a, 3rd movt.
8. Beethoven, Sonata, Op. 2, No. 1, 2nd movt., meas. 1–16.

9. Beethoven, Sonata, Op. 2, No. 2, 2nd movt., meas. 1–8.
10. Beethoven, Sonata, Op. 10, No. 2, 3rd movt. meas. 1–32.
11. Beethoven, Sonata, Op. 10, No. 3, 3rd movt., meas. 1–16.
12. Beethoven, Sonata, Op. 28, 2nd movt., meas. 1–8.
13. Schubert, Sonata, Op. 147, 2nd movt., meas. 1–28.
14. Schubert, Sonata, Op. 164, 2nd movt., meas. 1–16.
15. Schumann, "Träumerei", from *Scenes from Childhood.*
16. Schumann, "Curious Story" from *Scenes from Childhood.*
17. Brahms, *Romanze,* Op. 118, No. 5.
18. Tchaikovsky, "Morning Prayer" from *Album for the Young.*
19. Prokofieff, Gavotte, Op. 12, No. 2.
20. Bartók, No. 12 from *Fifteen Hungarian Peasant Songs.*
21. Hindemith, "Interludium" between "Fuga Decima" and "Fuga Undecima" from *Ludus Tonalis.*

SUGGESTED LISTENING

Strings

Vivaldi, Concerti.
Corelli, Concerti Grossi.
J. S. Bach, Suites for Strings; Brandenburg Concerti Nos. 3 and 6.
C. P. E. Bach, Symphony No. 3 in C major.
Handel, Concerti Grossi.
Mozart, *Eine kleine Nachtmusik;* Divertimenti.
Tchaikovsky, *Serenade for Strings,* Op. 48.
Arensky, *Variations on a Theme of Tchaikovsky.*
Miaskovsky, Sinfonietta.
Sibelius, Canzonetta.
Schönberg, *Verklärte Nacht.*
Bloch, Concerto Grosso for string orchestra (with piano).
Bartók, *Music for String Instruments, Percussion and Celesta.*
Vaughn-Williams, *Fantasy on a Theme of Thomas Tallis.*
Stravinsky, *Apollon Musagète.*
Barber, *Adagio for Strings.*
William Schuman, *Symphony for Strings.*
Copland, Third Symphony, 3rd movt., beginning.
Persichetti, Symphony for Strings.

Chapter 5

THE WOODWINDS

THE FLUTE

Italian:	Flauto	*French:*	Flûte	*German:*	Flöte
	Flauti		Flûtes		Flöten

Ex. 1

Somehow it is always difficult for the orchestration student who does not play a wind instrument to understand the wide differences in power and quality between the various registers of each woodwind. To complicate matters still more, there is no general principle that applies to all the woodwinds in this respect; some are thick and heavy in their bottom register, thin and light at the top, while others reverse this relationship. In the case of the flute, the bottom octave is weak and somewhat breathy, but it has a velvety, sensuous charm that is shown off to good advantage in such scores as Debussy's *Prelude to The Afternoon of a Faun.* Since little volume is possible in this low register, accompaniment must be kept light if the flute is to come

through. From   the tone becomes progressively brighter

and stronger. The notes above this have considerable strength and a haunt-

ing, silvery brilliance. However, from  upward the tone tends
to be shrill, and the notes are less easy to produce. This extreme upper
register should not be used at softer dynamic levels. Some orchestration
books list C as the top note possible on the flute; but since the C♯ and D
above this can actually be played and are called for in certain scores, it
seems reasonable to include them in the "possible" range. On the other
hand, their quality and intonation are apt to be inferior. Consequently
they are not suitable for sustained tones but are useful chiefly for finishing
out phrases that extend momentarily above the high C. Some flutes are
built to include a B below the bottom C, and that note is occasionally called
for in scores. Obviously, it is better avoided unless one is sure of having a
flute with the low B extension on hand. An important point in favor of the
extension is the fact that it makes the low C stronger and more easily
playable.

The flute is equally at home in sustained melodies or in florid passages.
Because of its lightness and grace, it is especially good at airy, scherzo-like
parts and ornate "filigree" work. Rapid repeated notes, double-tonguing,
triple-tonguing and flutter-tonguing (to be discussed later), rapid scales
and arpeggios are all practical and effective on the instrument. All trills are

possible except those on or above  and the following:

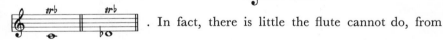 . In fact, there is little the flute cannot do, from
a technical standpoint, in either a legato or a staccato. Although its smaller
counterpart, the piccolo, has the distinction of being the most agile of the
woodwinds, the flute is a very close second.

An important point to remember is that the flute requires a great deal
of breath in playing and that plenty of rests are therefore desirable. Of
course, it is possible for the player to take a breath very quickly (between
phrases, for example), but too much of that sort of thing without a rest is
tiring. Rests give the flutist—or *flautist*, to use the traditional name—a
chance not only to breathe more comfortably but to relax his lips.

The normal fingering for the notes above the second C♯ on the flute
involves the use of harmonics. But the term "harmonics," as applied to
the flute, refers only to those harmonics not normally used. These are occasionally called for, the indication being the same as that for string harmonics—a small circle above the note. They have an odd, "white" quality
useful for a particular effect but tend to be flat in pitch. Now and then
flutists play one or two notes as harmonics in passages where the normal

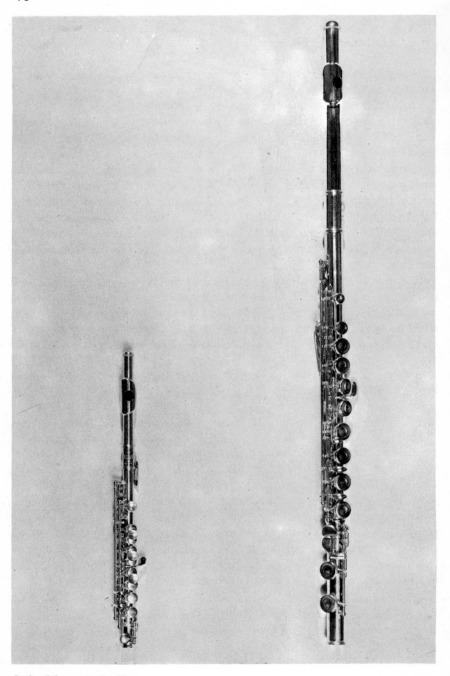

Piccolo   Flute

fingering would be awkward. Example 3 in Chapter 17 includes a succession of harmonics for two flutes.

EXAMPLES

Ex. 2

(a) Third Symphony

Permission for reprint granted by copyright owner, Durand et Cie, Paris, France; Elkan-Vogel Co., Inc., agents for the U.S.A.

(See also the flute parts in the excerpts from Debussy's *Prelude to The Afternoon of a Faun* given in Ex. 17 [c] and 22 [a] in Chapter 4.)

THE OBOE

Italian:	Oboe	*French:*	Hautbois	*German:*	Oboe
	Oboi		Hautbois		Oboen
				Old spelling:	Hoboe(n)

Ex. 3

The oboe, along with the English horn, bassoon, and contra bassoon, belongs to the double-reed branch of the woodwind family. Its spicy, somewhat nasal tone is one of the most distinctive of orchestral colors—one which has a way of cutting through other colors and of standing out against any background. For this reason, the oboe is an ideal solo instrument. It can be poignant or light-hearted, and it is especially well suited to melodies of a pastoral nature. Although not as agile as the flute or the clarinet, it can perform with considerable speed and flexibility if need be, either legato or staccato. This is not to imply that it is valuable only in a solo role, for it is also useful in combination with other instruments. However, one must be careful about giving it a subordinate voice in a lightly scored passage, since its incisive tone may come through too prominently for background. Another point to remember is that the highly colored oboe timbre becomes tiresome to the ear if used for too long at a time.

Below about 𝄞 the oboe tends to sound a bit thick and coarse —"honky," as oboe players sometimes put it. For that reason, these bottom notes, particularly the low B♭, are better avoided in any passage where the oboe is to be heard prominently. Parts that dip down into this lowest register but quickly get away from it are not objectionable; the main point is not to stress these very low notes in solo work. Occasionally, however, they are used intentionally to achieve a special effect, as in Stravinsky's *Symphony of Psalms*, where they give an ultra-reedy, primitive flavor, and in Prokofieff's *Peter and the Wolf*, where they serve admirably to personify the duck.

From 𝄞 is the oboe's most useful and characteristic reg-

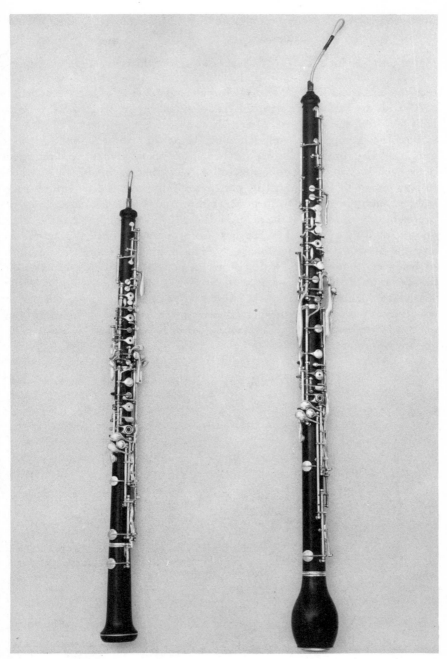

Studio Gilmore, Austin, Texas

Oboe   English Horn

ister. Above that the tone becomes thinner and less pungent, though quite

usable up to about ![music notation] . The notes above this are generally imprac-

tical for orchestral use, the high A, in particular, being extremely difficult.

All trills are available except the half-step trill on the bottom B♭, though trills involving the top F and G are better avoided.

Double-tonguing and triple-tonguing, being very difficult on the oboe, are rarely used, but the instrument is capable of playing fairly rapid repeated notes even with single-tonguing. As intimated earlier, it should not be asked to play extremely fast or intricate passages. Unlike the flute, it requires very little expenditure of breath in performance. But the player has a different problem, that of *holding in* the air until the next breathing point while using only a small amount of it in playing. Consequently, sufficient rests are as essential in oboe parts as in flute parts, if for a different reason. In addition to being an uncommonly taxing instrument, the oboe is a sensitive and somewhat unpredictable one as well. Notes must be humored and cajoled; the reed is delicate and must be "just so"; temperature and atmospheric conditions can produce unexpected and disastrous results. In short, the oboe is something of a temperamental *prima donna*, but an indispensable one in the orchestra.

EXAMPLES

Ex. 4

(a) Third Symphony

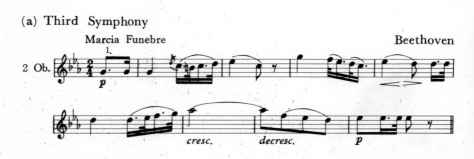

(b) Seventh Symphony

(c) Second Symphony

Permission for reprint granted by copyright owner, Durand et Cie, Paris, France; Elkan-Vogel Co., Inc., agents for the U.S.A.

THE CLARINET

Italian:	Clarinetto	French:	Clarinette	German:	Klarinette
	Clarinetti		Clarinettes		Klarinetten

Ex. 5

In the past, clarinets pitched in various keys were used. Of these, the two chief survivors today are the clarinet in B♭ and the clarinet in A, the first being the more commonly used of the two. Both are transposing instruments; that is, they are not written at actual pitch. In the case of the B♭ clarinet, the part must be written a major 2nd (a whole step) higher than the sounds desired, while the part for the A clarinet is written a minor 3rd higher than the sounds. For the benefit of students who have not had experience with transposing instruments, let us elaborate a bit on this system and give some examples to show how it works.

The B♭ clarinet is so labeled because B♭ is the sound that results when written C is played. That is, when the B♭ clarinet player sees [music notation] on the page, he uses the fingering which will produce the sound [music notation]

Consequently, if we want the B♭ clarinet to *sound* [music notation] , we must

Clarinet   Bass Clarinet

write  . On the A clarinet, the note A is the sound that results when written C is played. Therefore, if the sound [♭o] is wanted on an A clarinet, we must write [♭o] , a minor 3rd higher. In dealing with transposing instruments remember that the key of the instrument is the sound that results when written C is played.

Example 6 shows how a passage (given first at actual pitch) would be written for B♭ and A clarinets respectively.

Ex. 6

Notice the inclusion of key signatures. The chart below gives the key signature that would be used by each of the two instruments in each of the major keys. The term "concert key" means the actual or sounding key. The word "concert" is also applied to notes; for example, "concert G," means the actual sound G as opposed to the written G on a transposing instrument.

Ex. 7

In dealing with transposing instruments we encounter two types of transposition: (1) the "reading" type, the kind that is involved when we are reading a score and have the problem of converting *transposed* pitches to *actual* (or concert) pitches, and (2) the "writing" type, in which we must convert *actual* pitches to *transposed* pitches. (The difference between the two types is, of course, only one of direction.) If this distinction is understood at the outset and kept in mind, a good deal of confusion can be avoided.

Considering the complications which the transposition system involves for both orchestrator and score reader, a very natural question at this point is, "Why must it be used at all?" Although a complete answer to that question would entail excursions into technical points of acoustics and fingering, certain general reasons for the use of the system can be cited here. As far as resonance and good intonation are concerned, the B♭ and A clarinets are superior to the now obsolete C clarinet. Since they started out as transposing instruments and have been treated as such ever since, a change to another method of notation now would be all but impossible. (Certain composers make a practice of writing the parts for clarinets and other transposing instruments at actual pitch in the score; but even in such cases the individual parts for the players are written in transposed form.) An advantage of the transposition principle as applied to clarinets is this: it allows for a pattern of fingering common to clarinets of different sizes; the player need not learn a new fingering in order to perform on an alto or bass clarinet, for example. Instead it is the notation which changes in each case.

As a general rule, key signatures involving flats are easier for the instruments pitched in flat keys, while instruments such as the A clarinet find the sharp keys a bit more comfortable. However, the B♭ clarinet is frequently called on to play in keys up to three or four sharps, while the simpler flat keys are perfectly practical for the A clarinet. The advantage of having the two instruments available is that if a part would involve awkward fingering on one, it can nearly always be played with relative ease if assigned to the other. In general, the B♭ clarinet is first choice, the A clarinet being selected chiefly in cases where the B♭ instrument would have to play in a difficult key.

By way of illustration, let us suppose that we are to score a piece in the key of E♭ major, concert. If we use the B♭ clarinet, its part will be written in F major (an easy key for the instrument) while the A clarinet would be written in the more difficult key of G♭ major or, enharmonically, F♯ major. Obviously, the B♭ instrument is the better choice here. But suppose that the music to be scored is in A major, concert. The B♭ clarinet would call for a signature of five sharps, while the A clarinet would be written in C major. In such a case, the A clarinet would be the better choice. Of course, there are certain keys which are suitable to either instrument. For example, in music in G major, concert, the B♭ clarinet could play in A major about as easily as the A clarinet could play in B♭ major. However, the B♭ instrument would probably be chosen here, simply because it is the more commonly used and more generally available of the two.

Sometimes parts are best written enharmonically. For instance, if we are using B♭ clarinet and we come to a section in B major, a transposition of the part up a major 2nd would bring us out in the key of C♯ major (seven sharps) whereas the enharmonic equivalent, D♭ major (five flats), would be a great deal easier from the reading standpoint and should of course be chosen. Notice that such enharmonic respellings alter the interval used in the "transposition by interval" method.

Although changes from B♭ clarinet to A clarinet (or vice versa) in the midst of a work are possible and are occasionally called for, they are not recommended; the clarinet that has been lying unused will be cold and will consequently tend to be flat in pitch and sluggish in its general response until it has had time to warm up. There is, by the way, a slight difference in tone quality between the B♭ and the A instruments, but it is scarcely apparent to any but the most sensitive ear.

What has been said here about the use of the A clarinet does not apply in school orchestras. There the B♭ clarinet is used exclusively. The problem of difficult key signatures never arises because the concert keys are chosen with an eye to keeping the B♭ instruments in the easier keys.

The bottom octave or so of the clarinet is called the *chalumeau* register. It has a dark, strangely hollow quality. Notice that although the written range of both B♭ and A clarinets is the same, the A clarinet can go a half step lower in sound than the B♭ instrument, since the low written E sounds D on the B♭ clarinet and C♯ (or D♭) on the A clarinet. The middle register,

roughly from 🎼 to 🎼 , is rather neutral in quality and not too strong, while the octave above this (sometimes known as the *clarion*

register) is clear and bright. Above about 🎼 the tone is apt to be

shrill and the intonation doubtful. It is true that on paper the clarinet's "possible" range extends up to a high C above this. But these very high notes are not usable, for all practical purposes. Even in band work, where clarinets are often taken higher than in the orchestra, a written 🎼 is usually

considered the practical upward limit. Occasionally the very shrillness of this top register is used for humorous or grotesque effects, as in Stravinsky's

Petrouchka, where the high notes of the clarinet imitate the sounds of a peasant's reed pipe as he plays while his bear dances.

Of all the woodwinds, the clarinet is the most sensitive in the matter of dynamic range and control. It can reduce its warm, round tone to an incredibly soft whisper and can achieve the subtlest nuances of color and phrasing. These abilities make it an ideal solo instrument for *espressivo* melodies. In agility, it nearly equals the flute; it can perform rapid runs and arpeggios, skips, trills, and legato or staccato effects. However, because it is a single-reed instrument, it is somewhat limited in its ability to play rapid repeated notes.

In treatises on the clarinet, much has been made of the "break," a point on the instrument at which an awkward change of fingering is involved,[1] and of the register associated with it, which includes some notes of slightly inferior quality. From the standpoint of the fingering problem, the actual

break occurs between the written notes or

Passages which pass through this area in either direction cause no particular difficulty; it is only when a part involves a continuous use of these notes that the part becomes unduly awkward. As for tone quality, the three

written notes (particularly the B♭) are the weakest on the

instrument and are better not stressed in solo passages. Because of modern improvements in clarinet construction, the break is now much less of an obstacle than it once was. In fact, clarinet players today seem rather unconcerned about this difficulty that was apparently something of a thorn in the flesh for players of an earlier day.

Likewise, certain trills that were once listed as "awkward" or "better avoided" in clarinet writing are now quite usable. In fact, all trills are now practical on the instrument.

Although it is not the intention here to go into the historical background of instruments, it is worth noting that the clarinet did not begin to be accepted as a member of the symphony orchestra until Mozart's day; only two of the Mozart symphonies contain clarinet parts.

---

[1] In connection with this point at which the player begins to repeat his fingering pattern, it might be mentioned that the clarinet, being cylindrical, "overblows" at the 12th, whereas the oboe and bassoon, which are conical, overblow at the octave. (The flute, although cylindrical, behaves like an open pipe and consequently overblows at the octave.)

EXAMPLES

(All examples are given as written in the score. Those for B♭ clarinet will sound a major 2nd lower, those for A clarinet a minor 3rd lower.)

Ex. 8

(a) Sixth Symphony

(b) First Symphony

(c) Overture to *Tannhäuser*

(d) *Capriccio Espagnol*

THE BASSOON

Italian: Fagotto	*French:* Basson	*German:* Fagott
Fagotti	Bassons	Fagotte

Ex. 9

Although the bassoon is, like the oboe, a double-reed instrument, its tone is much less nasal and less highly colored than that of the oboe. In fact, its characteristic quality is a relatively neutral one, so that it is apt to be largely absorbed by any other orchestral color it is doubled with. For example, if bassoon is doubled with cellos (as it very frequently is), the cello tone will predominate but will have more body and focus than it would alone.

In the bottom octave or so of the bassoon, the tone is dark and full, even a little gruff in the bottommost notes, which are difficult to produce *pianissimo*. The next octave is middle ground, neither notably dark nor light in color, but probably the most used register of the instrument. The notes in the top octave become progressively thinner, until above about "A 440" they take on a pinched, complaining quality. Stravinsky, with his penchant for exploiting extreme registers, uses these top notes in a wonderfully effective bassoon solo at the beginning of *The Rite of Spring*. But such passages are extremely difficult, and it is better to let A or B♭ suffice as an upward limit.

Zintgraff, San Antonio, Texas

Bassoon   Contra Bassoon

When the part goes too high to be comfortably written in the bass clef, the tenor clef may be used.

The bassoon is sometimes spoken of as "the clown of the orchestra." Bassoonists resent the title, and with good reason. For while certain passages (especially *staccato* passages) have a way of sounding comical on the instrument, it can perform many other types of music effectively, including sustained melodies of a serious nature.

Technically, it is quite agile and is capable of making wide and sudden leaps. Because it does not have a great deal of power and because its color is so readily absorbed by that of other instruments, it is easily covered by the rest of the orchestra and should not be pitted against too heavy a background in solos. Probably its most frequent function is that of reinforcing other instruments in the bass or tenor registers.

There are a few trills to be avoided: those on D♭, E♭, or G♭ in all octaves,

on 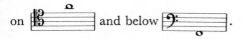 and below .

EXAMPLES

Ex. 10

(a) Fifth Symphony

(b) Fourth Symphony

(c) *The Sorcerer's Apprentice*

(d) Concerto for Orchestra

OTHER WOODWINDS

In addition to the woodwinds just discussed, there are others which are sometimes used: the piccolo, the English horn, the bass clarinet and the contra bassoon.[2] Except for the piccolo, which is generally found even in the medium-size orchestra, they are "extras" used chiefly in works scored for large orchestra. Occasionally, one or more of them may be included in smaller groups for the sake of a particular tone color or special effect.

The Piccolo

| *Italian:* | Flauto Piccolo (or) Ottavino | *French:* | Petite Flûte | *German:* | Kleine Flöte |

Ex. 11

---

[2] The E♭ clarinet might also be included in this list, but since it appears somewhat less frequently than the other instruments mentioned here, discussion of it is reserved for Chapter 18.

Just as the double bass is written an octave higher than it sounds in order to keep the part more nearly within the staff, the piccolo is written an octave lower than the sounds desired in order to avoid too many ledger lines above the staff. Even so, the player must often cope with three or four ledger lines; but he becomes accustomed to reading these and seems to prefer them to an "*8va*" sign over the notes written an octave lower. Although there is a D♭ piccolo that is sometimes used in bands, the instrument in C is the only one that figures in orchestral scores.

The piccolo is without doubt the most agile instrument of the orchestra, able to perform incredibly fast runs, skips, arpeggios, and elaborate figurations of all kinds. On the other hand, it is not often used for slow *cantabile* passages, though certain contemporary scores contain solos of a quiet, sustained nature that are surprisingly effective.

The bottom octave of the instrument is so weak and breathy as to be nearly useless in heavily scored passages. In fact, there is not much point in having the piccolo play at all in a *tutti* unless it is above a written

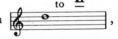 or so, for it will not have enough strength or brilliance to make

any difference. Notes below this are usable when the background is not too heavy. It should be noted that the written piccolo range does not include

the low C possible on the flute. The second octave, from 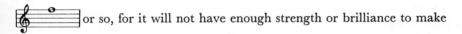 ,

is clear and bright, while notes above that are more piercing. From the high A upwards, the notes tend to be shrill, and the B♮ and C are extremely difficult to produce. They are better avoided except in cases where a phrase extends momentarily into this very high register.

Obviously the piccolo's most valuable talent is its ability to add a brilliant edge to a melodic line. It frequently doubles other woodwinds (or even strings) an octave higher. Now and then it is written so as to sound in unison with the flute to reinforce the flute's top tones. Like most brightly colored instruments, it cannot be used too continuously without losing in effectiveness; furthermore, if overused, it may give an unintentional "military band" feeling because of its long association with band music.

The fingering for piccolo is the same as that for flute, and the third flute player of an orchestra often doubles on piccolo. That is, he plays either a flute part or a piccolo part, as required; he may change from one instrument to the other several times in the course of a work, as directed by the composer or arranger. Of course such changes require at least two or three measures of rest, preferably more. This arrangement is often described at the beginning of scores by the expression "Flute III interchangeable with piccolo." If only two flutes are used, the second flute player may double on piccolo. Occasionally the piccolo part is listed below the flutes in the score in cases where the player is to change to flute III. But most often it is listed at the top of the page, and in many scores a player is assigned exclusively to the piccolo part. One hazard involved in changing from flute to piccolo (or vice versa) is that whichever instrument has been laid aside temporarily will be cold when it is picked up again; as a result, it will probably be flat in pitch and a bit sluggish in general responsiveness. Players like to have a few measures of rest in which to warm up the new instrument before actually playing.

EXAMPLES

(Sounding an octave higher)

Ex. 12

(a) Fourth Symphony

(b) *Háry János* Suite (*Viennese Musical Clock*)

Copyright assigned to Hawkes & Son (London) Ltd., 1939. By permission of the copyright owner, Boosey & Hawkes, Inc.

(c) *Petit Poucet* (*Hop o' My Thumb*) from *Mother Goose* Suite

(d) Seventh Symphony

The English Horn

Italian: Corno Inglese   *French:*   Cor Anglais   *German:*   Englisch Horn

Ex. 13

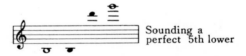

Sounding a
perfect 5th lower

Just how the English horn received its name and why it is not called "alto oboe" or some similar name are matters that have occupied writers on orchestration over the years. One theory that has been neither proved nor disproved is that because of the angle near the end of the instrument it was once called "*cor anglé*" in French, and that "*anglé*" became confused with "*anglais*" because of the similarity in pronunciation. That still leaves the term "horn" unexplained. Anyone who has ever read a program note on the English horn has been subjected to the inevitable comment that it is "neither English nor a horn."

The modern instrument, which is straight rather than "angled," differs from the oboe chiefly in being longer and having a bulbous distension at the end of the bell. The tone is akin to that of the oboe but more sonorous and melancholy. Possibly because of this serious quality, the English horn is seldom called on to play fast, technically complicated music, and it is not a particularly agile instrument by nature. The part for it is written a perfect 5th higher than the sounds desired.

Although the low B♭ is obtainable on the oboe, the lowest written note on the English horn is a B♮, sounding E below. Now and then one comes across an instrument that has the low B♭ (concert E♭) but not often enough to justify writing the note as a general practice. The bottom notes of the English horn are not only usable but highly effective; strangely enough, they do not seem to suffer from the coarseness that afflicts the lowest tones of the oboe. There is seldom any need to take the English horn above the written note [♪], even though notes up to a 5th higher are possible.

Moreover, the instrument loses some of its characteristic color in its topmost register and is consequently less effective there.

EXAMPLES

(Sounding a perfect 5th lower)

Ex. 14

(a) **Symphony in E minor** *(New World)*

(b) **Symphony in D minor**

(c) *La Mer*

Permission for reprint granted by copyright owner, Durant et Cie, Paris, France; Elkan-Vogel Co., Inc., agents for the U.S.A.

The Bass Clarinet

Italian: Clarinetto Basso   *French:*   Clarinette Basse   *German:*   Bassklarinette

Ex. 15

(or)

* Pitches down to the low written C (concert B♭)
are possible on some bass clarinets.

The bass clarinet differs from the clarinet not only in being larger but in having a curve near the mouthpiece and an upturned bell, the whole shape being a little like that of a saxophone. Although at one time there was a bass clarinet in A, it is now extinct. Therefore, the player must use the B♭ instrument and transpose when he plays a part written for bass clarinet in A.

In approaching the notation of the bass clarinet, we come across a rather confusing convention: when written in the treble clef, the instrument sounds a major 9th lower than written; but it may also be written in the bass clef, in which case it sounds a major 2nd lower than written. To give an example of the two methods of notation, the concert pitch ♭♭♭ would be written ♭♭♭ in the treble clef, whereas the same sound would be written ♭♭♭ in the bass clef.[3]

The first method is the one preferred today (perhaps because it has been used consistently in band works). But players and score readers must of course be able to read parts written either way; occasionally both systems are used at different places in the same score, as in Example 16(c).

[3] These two types of notation are sometimes known, respectively, as the "French system" (treble clef) and the "German system" (bass clef). However, these names must not be taken too literally, since there are instances of bass clef parts in French music and of treble clef parts in German music.

In its bottom octave the bass clarinet is extremely dark, almost sinister, in quality. The color becomes progressively less somber above that until, in the top octave, it is a bit strained and "white." There is little point in writing for the instrument in this top register, since other instruments can take these notes with better effect. But in its middle and lower registers the bass clarinet is valuable not only for doubling bass and tenor parts but in a solo capacity. Wagner is particularly fond of using it as a solo instrument to give a sense of gloom and impending tragedy. Other composers have exploited what Forsyth calls its "goblinesque" quality, a certain attactive grotesqueness. Although not quite so agile as the clarinet, it can move with considerable speed, and it shares the clarinet's phenomenal control of volume and dynamic nuance.

In some scores, the bass clarinet is interchangeable with the second or third clarinet; that is, the two parts are played by the same person. This is obviously a sensible arrangement where both instruments are not needed at once, and particularly where there is only a small part for the bass clarinet, or for the second or third clarinet.

Bass clarinets built to include the written D, D♭, and C below the low E♭ are available but not widely used. It is possible to add these notes to a bass clarinet not built with them initially by means of an extension attached to the bottom joint. Such an extension, which must be fitted at an instrument factory, can be made either so as to be removable or as a permanent part of the instrument. Khachaturian's Concerto for Piano and Orchestra, quoted in Example 16(a), is an instance of a work in which the bass clarinet part calls for notes down to the low written C at certain points.

EXAMPLES

(Sounding a major 9th lower when written in the treble clef, a major 2nd lower when written in the bass clef.)

Ex. 16

(a) Piano Concerto

(b) Symphony in D minor   Franck

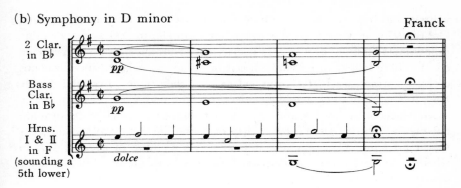

(c) *The Rite of Spring*   Stravinsky

The Contra Bassoon or Double Bassoon

Italian: Contrafagotto   *French:* Contre-basson   *German:* Kontrafagott

Ex. 17

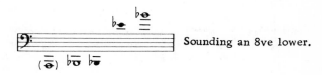

Sounding an 8ve lower.

As might be expected, the contra bassoon is one of the more ponderous instruments of the orchestra, in both appearance and sound. In fact, because of its great size it must rest on the floor in performance. Its tone is somewhat rough and thick; very soft effects are difficult to achieve, especially in the lower register. As a result, the instrument is valuable chiefly for adding volume and incisiveness to the bass parts in loud, heavily scored passages. Occasionally, it is used in other ways; for example, to add a somber tinge to low melodic lines, or as a solo instrument to produce a rather grotesque effect. There is seldom reason to use it in its upper register, since bassoons or bass clarinet are better equipped to play these notes. Like the double bass, it is written an octave higher than it is to sound.[4]

Most school orchestras and even many semi-professional orchestras do not own a contra bassoon, or, if they own one, do not have a competent player on hand. Consequently, it is always something of a gamble as to whether the part will really be played, unless one is sure of getting a major orchestra to perform the score.

Although Beethoven and Brahms wrote contra-bassoon parts that went as high as (written) ♭𝛺 , notes above ♭𝅉 are somewhat difficult. Heckel now makes a contra bassoon that is capable of playing the low A, one half step below the B♭ usually given as the bottom note. (Incidentally, this A is the lowest note on the piano.)

Rapid, intricate parts are not well suited to the technique of the contra bassoon. Its part should be fairly simple and should contain plenty of rests.

EXAMPLES

(Contra-bassoon parts sounding an octave lower)

Ex. 18

(a) *The Sorcerer's Apprentice*

Dukas

Permission for reprint granted by copyright owner, Durand et Cie, Paris, France; Elkan-Vogel Co., Inc., agents for the U.S.A.

---

[4] In a few scores (Wagner's *Parsifal* and Debussy's *Ibéria* and *La Mer*, for instance) the contra-bassoon part is written at actual pitch.

(b) *Beauty and the Beast* (from *Mother Goose* Suite)

Ravel

(c) *Through the Looking Glass* (*Jabberwocky*)

Taylor

WOODWIND REGISTERS

(Written notes)

Ex. 19

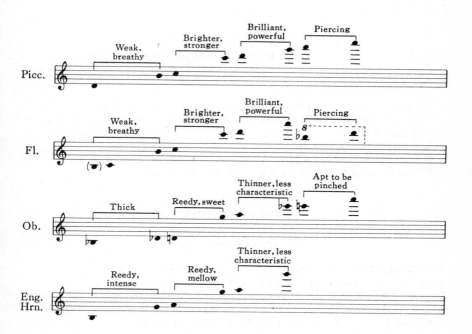

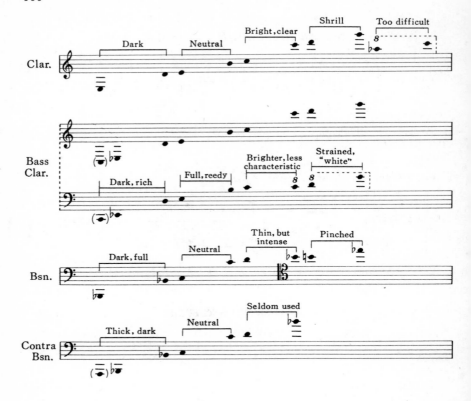

SUGGESTED ASSIGNMENTS

A. Know:

    1. ranges (possible and practical) of flute, oboe, clarinet, and bassoon.

    2. ranges (possible and practical) of piccolo, English horn, bass clarinet, and contra bassoon.

    3. transpositions where involved.

    4. colors and relative strengths of the various registers of each woodwind.

    5. particular abilities and limitations of each woodwind.

SUGGESTED LISTENING

Piccolo

Tchaikovsky, Fourth Symphony, 3rd movt., meas. 194.

Pierné, *Entrance of the Little Fauns* from *Cydalise.*

Debussy, *Ibéria,* Part I (*Par les rues et par les chemins*) many passages.

Ravel, *Mother Goose* Suite: II. *Petit Poucet,* figure 7; III. *Laideronette, Impératrice des Pagodes,* figure 1; *Daphnis and Chloe* Suite No. 2, figure 183.

Kodály, *Háry János* Suite, Part II (*Viennese Musical Clock*) and Part IV (*The Battle and Defeat of Napoleon*).
Shostakovitch, Seventh Symphony, 1st movt., figure 14.
Copland, Third Symphony, 3rd movt., 3 bars after figure 69; figure 71; 2 bars after figure 78; 3 bars after figure 83, etc.

Flute

Bach, Suite in B minor for flute and strings; Brandenburg Concertos Nos. 2, 4, 5.
Beethoven, Third Symphony, last movt., meas. 190, also meas. 292.
Mendelssohn, Fourth Symphony (*Italian*), last movt., meas. 6.
Brahms, First Symphony, last movt., meas. 38.
Tchaikovsky, Piano Concerto in B-flat minor, beginning of 2nd movt. (*Andantino*).
Dvořák, Fifth Symphony (*New World*), 1st movt., figures 5 and 12.
Bizet, *Carmen*, Entr'acte between Acts II and III.
Debussy, *Prelude to The Afternoon of a Faun*, beginning and many other passages.
Ravel, *Daphnis and Chloe* Suite No. 2, 3 bars after figure 176.
Kennan, *Night Soliloquy* for flute, strings, and piano.

Oboe

Bach, Brandenburg Concertos Nos. 1, 2.
Beethoven, Third Symphony, 2nd movt. (*Marcia Funebre*) meas. 8; Sixth Symphony, 3rd movt. (*Scherzo*) meas. 91; Seventh Symphony, 1st movt., meas. 300.
Schumann, Second Symphony, 3rd movt. (*Adagio espressivo*) meas. 8.
Brahms, Violin Concerto, beginning of 2nd movt.
Mahler, *Das Lied von der Erde*, beginning of 2nd movt.
Debussy, *Ibéria*, Part II (*Les parfums de la nuit*) beginning, also 4 bars before figure 40.
Ravel, *Le Tombeau de Couperin*, Trio of the *Rigaudon; La Valse*, figure 18.
Strauss, *Death and Transfiguration*, measure 30; *Don Quixote*, 8 bars before figure 3.
Shostakovitch, First Symphony, beginning of 3rd movt.

English Horn

Berlioz, *Fantastic Symphony*, beginning of 3rd movt. (*Scène aux champs*).
Wagner, *Tristan und Isolde*, beginning of Act III.
Franck, Symphony in D minor, 2nd movt., near beginning.
Dvořák, Fifth Symphony (*New World*), 2nd movt., near beginning.
Debussy, *Nocturnes:* I. *Nuages*, meas. 5; *La Mer*, figure 16.
Sibelius, *The Swan of Tuonela*.
Stravinsky, *The Rite of Spring*, section entitled *Ritual of the Ancestors*, figure 129; *Petrouchka*, 9 bars after figure 72.

Clarinet

Beethoven, Fourth Symphony, 2nd movt., meas. 26; Sixth Symphony, 2nd movt., letter D.
Weber, Overture to *Oberon*, meas. 64.
Schubert, Symphony in B minor (*Unfinished*), 2nd movt., meas. 66.
Tchaikovsky, Fifth Symphony, beginning; 2nd movt., meas. 66; 3rd movt., measure 28; Sixth Symphony, 1st movt., meas. 163, also meas. 326.

Debussy, *Ibéria*, meas. 8.
Rachmanioff, Second Piano Concerto, 2nd movt., near beginning.
Stravinsky, *Petrouchka*, figure 100.
Prokofieff, *Peter and the Wolf*, figure 11 ("The Cat").
Britten, *Four Sea Interludes* from *Peter Grimes*, I. *Dawn*.

Bass Clarinet

Wagner, *Tristan und Isolde*, Act. II, "King Mark's Song."
Tchaikovsky, *Nutcracker* Suite: *Dance of the Sugar Plum Fairy*.
Strauss, *Don Quixote*, Variation III.
Stravinsky, *Petrouchka*, figure 65 (The Moor dances).
Khachaturian, Piano Concerto, 1st movt., meas. 390; 2nd movt., beginning and meas. 220.

Bassoon

Beethoven, Fifth Symphony, 2nd movt., meas. 205.
Tchaikovsky, Fourth Symphony, 2nd movt., meas. 77; Sixth Symphony, beginning; last movt., meas. 30.
Rimsky-Korsakoff, *Scheherazade*, 2nd movt., meas. 5.
Mussorgsky-Ravel, *Pictures from an Exhibition*, beginning of Part II (*The Old Castle*).
Dukas, *The Sorcerer's Apprentice*, figure 7.
Stravinsky, *The Rite of Spring*, beginning; *Petrouchka*, 4 bars after figure 68 (end of Moor scene).
Bartók, Concerto for Orchestra, beginning of Part II (*Giuoco delle Coppie*).

Contra Bassoon

Mahler, Ninth Symphony, last movt., meas. 28.
Ravel, *Mother Goose* Suite: IV. *Les Entretiens de la Belle et de la Bête*, figure 2.
Dukas, *The Sorcerer's Apprentice*, figure 42.
Taylor, *Through the Looking Glass*, Part II (*Jabberwocky*) figure 13.
Stravinsky, *Petrouchka*, 9 bars after figure 72.
Bloch, *Schelomo*, last 5 bars.

Chapter 6

THE WOODWIND SECTION

The proportions of woodwind sections of various sizes were listed in Chapter 1, and it might be well to look over that material once again before going on with this chapter. The average woodwind section consists of two flutes, two oboes, two clarinets, and two bassoons ("woodwinds in pairs"), plus piccolo if desired. Although major orchestras also include English horn, bass clarinet, and contra bassoon, most school orchestras and some nonprofessional orchestras do not. Consequently, unless one is sure of getting a performance by an orchestra that does have these "extra" woodwinds, it is safer to write for woodwinds in pairs. In scoring for groups of limited size, it is a good idea to remember the possibility of letting the second flute player double on piccolo, the second oboist on English horn, and so on.

As has been mentioned earlier, the orchestra of the classical period did not regularly include clarinets. For example, the woodwind section used in the early Haydn symphonies consists of one or two flutes, usually two oboes, and one or two bassoons. But by Beethoven's time, woodwinds in pairs (including clarinets) had become the accepted arrangement.

The table on page 3 shows the standard order in which instruments are listed on the page. This consistency of arrangement is obviously a great help to the eye of the conductor or the score reader. The only possible variation in order is the placing of the piccolo part below that of flutes I and II in cases where the piccolo is interchangeable with flute III.

As a rule, each pair of woodwinds is written on the same staff. When the two instruments are playing different parts, the upper notes are normally taken by the first of the pair, the lower notes by the second. As with *divisi* string parts on one staff, a single stem for both notes may be used as long

103

104

as the time values in both parts are the same, but separate stems must be used if the time values are different:

Ex. 1

(Notice the proper notation of the interval of a 2nd—with the two stems lined up.) If the parts cross briefly, both can still be written on the same staff, the abnormal arrangement of the parts being shown by the direction of the stems. But if they involve continuous crossing or are so independent as to be awkward on one staff, it is better to use separate staves.

We now come to a point that should be noted very carefully, for it seems to be one that students have a hard time remembering. Whenever two wind instruments are written on the same staff and a single melodic line is involved, indications must be included to show whether the passage is to be played by the first instrument of the pair, by the second, or by both. Otherwise the part is simply ambiguous. If the first is to play, either of the following systems may be used:

Ex. 2

(The first arrangement here is the easier and more commonly used of the two.) Similarly, if the second instrument[1] is to play, the part could be written in either of these ways:

Ex. 3

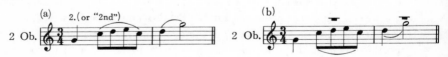

In case the passage is a solo, the word "solo" should be written in at the beginning of it. Solos are usually, but not necessarily always, given to the first of each pair. Sometimes the solo indication is used even when the passage in question is not the chief melodic idea but must be played in such a way

---

[1] Sometimes "1°" and "2°" are used to designate the first and second of each pair. These are abbreviations of the Italian words "primo" and "secondo," corresponding to our "1st" and "2nd."

as to give it a certain prominent or important quality. If both instruments of a pair are to take a melodic line in unison, the passage can be written in either of the following ways:

Ex. 4

(Literally, "a 2" means "to two" in Italian.) Here, again, the first way is the usual one; the double-stem system used in the second version is normally reserved for passages where both instruments play in unison for just a few notes, as in the following:

Ex. 5

If a melodic line to be played by both instruments in unison is of solo quality, the word "soli" may be written in at the beginning of it. The direction "a 2," by the way, is never used for passages in which the two instruments play *different* parts; in such cases no indication is needed, since it is quite obvious that both instruments are playing.

For the benefit of students who have played in bands, it might be well to point out that although the expressions *divisi* and *unisono* are appropriate in band music where a whole section of clarinets is to divide or unite, these terms are used only for strings, never for winds, in an orchestra.

When one instrument of a pair is already playing and the other enters, it is customary to label the entering voice as being 1. or 2. and to show at what dynamic level it should enter. All dynamic markings must be shown beneath each staff, of course, just as with strings.

TONGUING AND SLURRING

In performing on a wind instrument it is possible to articulate each note with a separate "*tu*"[2]—in which case the note is said to be "tongued"—or to slur it with the note that precedes or follows. Where no slur mark is pre-

---

[2] Or variations of this syllable, such as *du, ta,* and *da,* depending on the instrument, the register, and the effect involved.

sent, the note is to be tongued. For instance, in the following passage the first two notes are slurred together, the next two are slurred, the next four are slurred, the next note is tongued separately, and so on.

Ex. 6

Third Symphony   Brahms

But there is no break in sound between the last note of each slurred group and the note that follows; the general effect is *legato*. For an even smoother, more *legato* effect, the whole passage could have been slurred together. Or, if a sharply *marcato* effect had been wanted, the passage might have been written entirely without slurs (each note tongued separately). And there are possibilities other than the one shown that involve alternate slurring and tonguing. When repeated notes occur, they must be tongued (though not necessarily sharply) in order to sound with a fresh attack. For example:

Ex. 7

However, slurs plus dots or slurs plus a line next to each note are sometimes used to indicate a "soft tonguing," even with repeated notes:

Ex. 8

The second type of notation here would imply a kind of pressure on each note, with less separation between notes than in the case of the dots.

In some scores, phrasing rather than slurring is shown in the woodwind parts. But since phrasing and slurring are indicated in exactly the same way, players are frequently in doubt as to which is which, and the whole question becomes hopelessly confused. One possible solution is the use of dotted lines for phrasing, solid lines for slurring (or vice versa, as long as one way is used consistently). There has been some successful experimentation with this plan already. But until some such system comes into general use, it seems

best to indicate slurring rather than phrasing in woodwind parts. If necessary, breathing points between phrases may be indicated by the same symbol
used in vocal music: ' .

A question that often arises is this: when strings and woodwinds play
the same melodic line, what is the relationship between bowing in the
strings and slurring in the winds? There is no hard and fast rule to follow
here. In some cases the slur marks in the woodwinds will correspond with
the bowing slurs in the strings, and certain composers use this approach
more or less consistently. Certainly a general unity of effect is desirable; for
example, a sharply *marcato* passage would undoubtedly call for separate
bows in the strings along with separate tonguings in the woodwinds. But
there are many cases in which the actual slurrings in the two sections will
not necessarily be the same. Sometimes, for instance, several measures of
a wind part will be slurred together, whereas the strings will need to change
bow a good many times within the course of these measures.

In double-tonguing the player rapidly alternates *tu* and *ku:*

Ex. 9

tu ku tu ku tu ku tu ku

In triple-tonguing the pattern is *tu tu ku* (or *tu ku tu*), which is suited to
music involving triplet figures. Both types of tonguing are useful in articu-
lating passages which are so fast that single-tonguing would be impractical.
Both are easy and effective on the flute but impractical on the clarinet and
bassoon. Although most orchestration books speak of them as being out of
the question for the oboe as well, some skilled oboists are able to achieve
them.

Flutter-tonguing (German: *Flatterzunge*) comes under the heading of
special effects. To produce it the player executes a rapid roll with his tongue.
The result is a kind of eerie whir which may be applied either to sustained
tones or to melodic lines. Strauss and Stravinsky, in particular, are fond of
using it for very rapid scale passages. The indication is usually the same as
that for unmeasured tremolos in the strings (three lines through the stem)
plus the word "flutter-tongue" written in. Sometimes, especially in very
fast passages, the indication "flutter-tongue" alone suffices. The effect is
well suited to the flute and piccolo, possible (though less easily produced
and rarely used) on the clarinet, and extremely difficult on the oboe.

There are two matters involving attack and release in wind instruments
that need to be mentioned. The first is the *fp* or *sf p* effect, in which the
tone is started with a strong attack and then reduced in volume immediately.

After that, it may be sustained at a constant dynamic level or allowed to diminish even more (*fp*, *diminuendo*) or made to increase in volume (*fp*, *crescendo*). In any case, the *fp* marking indicates an effect rather than a particular degree of volume and may be used at any dynamic level, from very soft to very loud. This device is of course not the exclusive property of the woodwind and brass sections, for the strings and the percussion make frequent use of it.

The other matter is a point of notation which arises constantly in orchestral scoring. In piano and vocal music sustained tones followed by a rest are usually written 𝅝 ⸺ or 𝅗𝅥. 𝄾 or 𝅝 | 𝄼 , etc. A more usual plan in the orchestra is to write 𝅗𝅥 ♪ 𝄿 𝄾 or 𝅗𝅥. ♪ 𝄿 or 𝅝 | ♪ 𝄿 𝄾 ⸺ , the sustained tone being tied into the beginning of the next beat. The reason is that if the first notation is used, players tend to differ as to the exact point at which they release the note (since it is difficult to cut off the sound on the last fraction of a beat), and a "ragged" effect is likely to result when a group is involved. The second notation gives an easier and more definite cut-off point and consequently leads to a cleaner, more unified release. Of course, there are cases where, for harmonic or other reasons, it would be inappropriate to tie the notes into the next beat; but for the most part this system is preferable, not only in woodwind writing but in the strings, brass, and percussion as well.

Muting possibilities in the woodwinds are few and seldom used. Because of the flute's construction, muting is not possible. The clarinet can reduce its tone to the merest whisper anyway and consequently has no need for a mute. With the oboe it is possible to achieve a muted effect (chiefly on the notes) by inserting a chamois or cloth into the bell.

However, this system has a tendency to throw certain notes out of tune. An example of muted oboes can be found in the closing measures of Stravinsky's *Petrouchka*. Muting of the bassoon can be accomplished in the same fashion or with an actual mute, and although this effect is seldom called for specifically in scores, some bassoonists employ a mute in very soft passages to reduce the volume of tone in the lower register of the instrument, especially between and . One disadvantage of this arrangement is that it makes the bottom B♭ unplayable.

SCORING FOR WOODWINDS IN PAIRS

The same chorale excerpt used earlier for examples of string scoring has been selected for purposes of illustration here:

Ex. 10

Jesu, meine Freude

Bach

We are going to confine ourselves, at first, to a woodwind section consisting of two flutes, two oboes, two clarinets, and two bassoons. First of all, let us examine the ranges of the voices and see what instruments could take them (ruling out for the moment the possibility of transposing the excerpt). The bass could be taken only by the bassoon, since that voice goes too low for any of the other instruments. The tenor could be taken by the bassoon or the clarinet (the latter in its dark *chalumeau* register). The alto, with its B at the end, is too low for most flutes, and even if we were sure of having a flute with the low B on it, that register of the instrument is so weak that good balance would be very hard to achieve. Although the alto is within the range of the oboe, the oboe's low B tends to be a bit coarse in quality; consequently, the clarinet would be a better choice for that voice. The soprano could be taken by flute, oboe, or clarinet, though it would be relatively weak on the flute. Here are some possible scorings, then:

Ex. 11

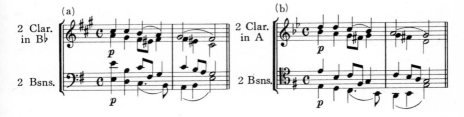

(a)

2 Clar. in B♭

2 Bsns.

(b)

2 Clar. in A

2 Bsns.

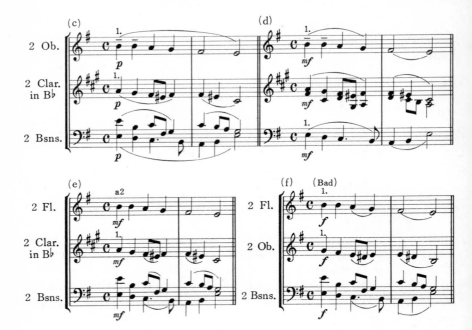

Versions (a) and (b) would sound alike. In (b) clarinets in A have been used instead of B♭ clarinets, and the bassoons have been written in the tenor clef.

Versions (c) and (d) differ from the preceding ones in that the top voice, in the oboe, will stand out sharply from the other voices below. Any separate color on a part will tend to produce that result, but the distinctive oboe tone has a particular way of asserting itself.

In version (e) two flutes are used on the melody to give more body in the weak lower register of the instrument and to bring about better balance.

Version (f) has been included as an example of what *not* to do. The oboe would outweigh the flute in that register and would be too prominent in character for an inner voice. The doubtful quality of the low B has already been mentioned.

Various slurrings have been used here for purposes of illustration.

Assuming that there is no reason why we must retain the original key, transposition will give us a good many new possibilities. By placing certain of the instruments higher in their range, we can arrive at better resonance and blend:

One undesirable feature of (a) and some of the other versions in Example 12 is the fact that the oboes play the interval of a 4th in a sustained chord

Ex. 12

(at the end). This is not a good plan, as a rule, because the incisive oboe color accentuates the "bareness" of the 4th. Sixths or 3rds sound much better. But if we are to give the two top voices to the oboes here, there seems to be no way of avoiding the 4th except by changing the original voice-leading in the cadence and (in [a], for example) having the second oboe go from F♯ up to G (instead of down to D), thus omitting the 5th of the chord.

The objections that applied to version (f) in Example 11 do not apply to (c) in Example 12 because the oboe is in a sweeter, thinner register and because the flute is better able to assert itself in this higher version. Even so, the flute has been marked one degree louder than the other instruments to make doubly sure that it comes out clearly on the melody.

Version (d) in Example 12 involves the use of mixed colors (flute plus oboe) on the two top parts, whereas we have used mostly pure colors previously. Notice that two clarinets and two bassoons are indicated here, for the sake of proper balance. It would have been possible to mix clarinet and bassoon colors on the tenor and bass parts, also.

So far we have used only the original four-voice structure, with no octave doublings. Doublings of the soprano, or of all three upper voices, an octave higher will allow the flutes and clarinets to play in a much brighter, more telling register:

Ex. 13

In Example 13 (a) the melody is doubled an octave higher in the flutes, while the first oboe doubles the melody in unison with the first clarinet. In (b) the alto and tenor are both doubled an octave higher (in the clarinets); the melody is doubled an octave higher in the flutes. In (c) the melody, alto, and tenor are all doubled an octave higher, and the melody is doubled an octave lower in the bassoon. Remember that not all pieces of music lend themselves to a doubling of the melody an octave below the original pitch. In some cases the result would be too thick.

Notice that the clarinets frequently play above the oboes, in terms of pitch, even though they are listed below them on the page. Actually, the strongest register of the oboe is roughly [musical notation], while the clarinet's

brightest and most solid octave is [musical notation].

Therefore, when brilliance and power are called for, it is often better to place the clarinets higher than the oboes.

SCORING FOR A LARGE WOODWIND SECTION

Following are three possible ways of scoring the same chorale excerpt for a woodwind section that includes piccolo, English horn, bass clarinet, and contra bassoon in addition to woodwinds in pairs. Three different gradations of coloring have been aimed at: brilliant, medium, and dark. In Chapter 10, more will be said about color possibilities, woodwind doublings, and various ways of arranging the wind instruments in chords.

Ex. 14

Notice that in Example 14 (b) clarinets in A have been chosen in order to avoid a key signature of six sharps (or six flats) for the B♭ clarinet. Inasmuch as the only bass clarinet in current use is pitched in B♭, we are forced to write its part in either six sharps or the enharmonic equivalent of six flats. The latter key has been chosen here as being preferable for a B♭ instrument.

In the dark version (c) the piccolo has been given rests. Obviously the brilliance of its upper register is not wanted here, and it is so weak and breathy in its bottom octave that in this case there is no point in writing for it there.

Having learned in harmony courses that parallel 5ths are generally unacceptable in Bach style, students may wonder about the 5ths that occur in Ex. 14(c) on the second and third beats of the clarinet part. (They also occur in certain preceding versions but are not as easily seen there.) Actually, these are not parallel 5ths of the *verboten* variety at all; they are merely an inversion of the parallel 4ths in the original, brought about by the doubling of the melody an octave below the original pitch. Since they are not a part of the basic four-voice harmonization, there is not the slightest objection to them.

SUGGESTED ASSIGNMENTS

A. Know:

1. instruments involved in the "average" woodwind section and in the "large" woodwind section.
2. arrangement of the woodwinds on the page—order and grouping.
3. indications for showing whether the first or second of each pair is to play or whether both are to play.
4. indications for slurring, tonguing, and phrasing.
5. principles of balance in the woodwind section.
6. ways of achieving brilliant or darker coloring in woodwind scoring.

B. The following are suitable as exercises in scoring for woodwinds:

1. Bach, any of the chorales. Select a short phrase from one of these and score it:
   (a) in three different ways for woodwinds in pairs, using no octave doublings;
   (b) in two different ways for large woodwind section, using octave doublings.
2. Beethoven, Sonata, Op. 2, No. 1, 3rd movt. Omit trio.
3. Beethoven, Sonata, Op. 2, No. 3, 3rd movt., meas. 1–36.
4. Beethoven, Sonata, Op. 7, 3rd movt., meas. 1–24.
5. Beethoven, Sonata, Op. 53, 1st movt., meas. 196–211.
6. Beethoven, Sonata, Op. 106, 2nd movt., meas. 1–46.
7. Schubert, Sonata, Op. 122, 1st movt., meas. 1–28.
8. Chopin, Prelude in A major, Op. 28, No. 7.
9. Mendelssohn, Song Without Words No. 41 (A major). Score for large woodwind section.
10. Schumann, "Burlesque" from *Album Leaves*.
11. Tchaikovsky, "A Winter Morning" from *Album for the Young*.
12. Mussorgsky, "Tuileries—Children Quarreling at Play" from *Pictures from an Exhibition*.
13. Debussy, "The Little Shepherd" from *The Children's Corner*.
14. MacDowell, "From Uncle Remus" from *Woodland Sketches*.
15. Hindemith, "Fuga Secunda in G" from *Ludus Tonalis*.

SUGGESTED LISTENING

Woodwinds

Mozart, Divertimenti and Serenades for woodwinds.

Beethoven, Violin Concerto, 1st 9 meas.

Mendelssohn, *Scherzo* from *Midsummer Night's Dream* music, beginning and other portions.

Tchaikovsky, Fourth Symphony, 3rd movt., *Meno mosso* section (middle).

Rimsky-Korsakoff, *Russian Easter*, beginning (rare unison doubling of all woodwinds).

Wagner, Overture to *Die Meistersinger*, meas. 122–134 (E♭ major, *Im mässigen Hauptzeitmass*).

Strauss, *Don Quixote*, Variation I (imitation of rural band).

Mussorgsky-Ravel, *Pictures from an Exhibition*, *Promenade* preceding Part II (*The Old Castle*); Part III (*Tuileries*); *Promenade* preceding Part V; Part V (*Ballet of the Chickens in their Shells*).

Stravinsky, *Symphony of Psalms*, Fugue, beginning; *The Rite of Spring*, beginning; *Petrouchka*, number 13 (page 22 in Kalmus edition) and following.

Bartók, Concerto for Orchestra, Part V (*Finale*) meas. 148–175 (*fughetta* beginning with bassoon solo).

Copland, Third Symphony, 3rd movt., end; 4th movt., beginning.

Chapter 7

THE HORN

Italian: Corno	*French:* Cor	*German:* Horn
Corni	Cors	Hörner

The name "French horn" is seldom used by musicians. The instrument is referred to simply as "the horn," and that name is sufficient even in scores. Actually, it is difficult to understand why the adjective "French" was ever introduced into the name, since the development of the modern horn centers chiefly around Germany.

In order to understand the workings of the horn, we must know something about the basic principles on which brass instruments operate. Whereas most of the woodwinds make use of a reed, brass instruments do not, but instead involve a mouthpiece and an air column vibrating sympathetically with the player's lips. Fractional vibrations of the air column produce overtones, and a certain number of these may be made to sound by proper use of the breath and lips. The fundamental or generating tone itself is either very difficult or unobtainable on most brass instruments. If the length of tubing is altered by means of valves (or a slide, in the case of the trombone), a new set of overtones results. For purposes of initial tuning, each brass instrument is equipped with a "tuning slide" which enables the player to vary the basic tube-length of the instrument somewhat.

Although in construction and technique of performance the horn is clearly a brass instrument, its tone is capable of blending almost equally well with either woodwind or brass, and it is very often used as if it were a member of the woodwind family. Its bore is predominantly conical in shape, with the result that its sound is less sharp-edged and incisive than those of the trumpet and trombone.

117

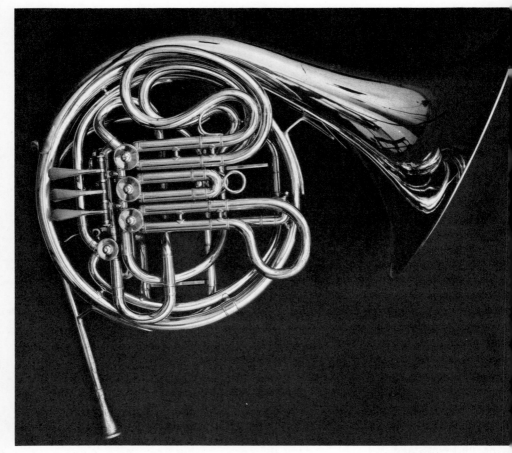

Studio Gilmore, Austin, Tex

French Horn

THE NATURAL HORN

Being essentially hunting horns and valveless, the horns of Haydn's and Mozart's day could play only the notes of one harmonic series at a time, plus a few rather uncertain intermediary tones made possible by the insertion of the hand in the bell of the horn and/or by "lipping." Parts for the instrument were therefore extremely limited from a melodic standpoint; stepwise passages could be written only within a relatively small pitch area in the upper portion of the harmonic series, and chromatic passages were out of the question altogether. To cope with the problem of music in different keys, a system of "crooks" was in use, a crook being a piece of tubing which could be inserted into the tubing of the horn to alter the pitch of its fundamental tone and thus create a new harmonic series. The crook to be chosen was indicated by a direction at the beginning of the work or movement: "Horn in E♭" or "Horn in A," etc., as the case might be, and the part was invariably written in the key of C. The written notes of the harmonic series usable on the horn were as follows (numbered on the basis of partials):

Ex. 1

The fundamental, or first partial, was normally unplayable. "Out of tune" notes (according to our system of tuning) are shown in black. The eleventh partial for example, was really something between an F and an F♯ and could be humored so as to produce either note. Of course the actual sound of the horn's notes depended on the crook being used. Following is a table to show how the instrument sounded when crooked in various keys (and notated in treble clef):

Horn in	Sounding
B♭-alto	a major 2nd lower than written
A	a minor 3rd lower than written
A♭	a major 3rd lower than written
G	a perfect 4th lower than written
F	a perfect 5th lower than written
E	a minor 6th lower than written
E♭	a major 6th lower than written
D	a minor 7th lower than written
C	an octave lower than written
B♭-basso	a major 9th lower than written

("Alto" and "basso" are used here to mean "high" and "low" respectively.)

Horns in other keys (B-alto, F♯, D♭, B-basso and A-basso) were called for only rarely. Horn in F♯ appears in Haydn's *Farewell* Symphony, and horns in G♭ and D♭ (among numerous others) in *Carmen*.

Normally, parts for the natural horn were written in the treble clef. But in the rare cases where the bass clef was employed, a curious and illogical custom applied: the pitches were notated an octave lower than they would have been notated in the treble clef. That meant that they were *lower* than the concert pitches by the inversion of the interval that figured in the normal treble-clef transposition. For instance, in the bass clef horn in D was notated a major 2nd lower than the sounds instead of a minor 7th higher, horn in F a perfect 4th lower instead of a perfect 5th higher, and so on. Example 2 shows the notation of a specific pitch for these instruments, in treble and bass clefs, respectively:

Ex. 2

Here is an excerpt from a horn part of the Classical period:

Ex. 3

Sixth Symphony

which will sound:

Another characteristic passage for natural horn is shown next:

Ex. 4

Overture to *Der Freischütz*

During the Classical period the usual practice was to employ one pair of horns, pitched in the home key. However, if the music was in minor, a second pair, pitched in the key of the relative major, was occasionally added to supply certain important notes that were not available as members of the harmonic series in the home key. Later on, the device of using two pairs of horns pitched in different keys was sometimes employed even in major keys to provide richer possibilities in writing for the horns and to allow for modulations.

We are told that in the day of the natural horn the player kept an assortment of crooks hanging on his arm in order to be prepared for necessary changes! Fortunately for player, composer, and audience, the introduction of valves revolutionized the technique of horn playing and the type of part that could be written for the instrument. Instead of having only one harmonic series at a time to work with, the horn now boasted seven different series (the results of various combinations of the three valves), and a complete chromatic scale was available for the first time. As a result, the horn achieved the status of a real melodic instrument. Although the invention of valves occurred in 1813, the valve horn did not come into general use until about the middle of the nineteenth century, and even then the natural horn continued to be used with it for many years.

THE MODERN VALVE HORN IN F

Ex. 5

 Sounding a perfect 5th lower

Out of the many horns once employed, the horn in F seems to have proven the most satisfactory, and it has survived, with valves added, as the one horn in general use today. When parts written originally for the natural horn are played on it, the player must transpose as he goes—unless, of course, the original part happened to be for horn crooked in F.

Most players now use the so-called "double horn" (pictured on page 118). That instrument has two sets of tubing, one in F and one in (high) B♭; a lever enables the player to switch instantaneously from one to the other. Because of its shorter tubing, the B♭ horn (that is, the B♭ part of the double horn) allows for greater facility. But its use is entirely optional with the player, and the transposition problems involved in switching to B♭ horn are his concern; the part is always written as if for F horn—a perfect 5th higher than the sounds desired. Although the B♭ horn is capable of producing certain very low pedal tones not available on the F horn, these have little practical value.

Traditionally, the horns are written without key signature, sharps and flats being written in wherever necessary. But it is possible nowadays to use a key signature, and that plan would seem to be a sensible one in scoring music of a diatonic nature. Enharmonic notation (for example, B♭ instead of A♯) is not uncommon in horn parts, especially in non-diatonic music.

Concerning notation in bass clef, the old custom of writing the F horn a 4th lower than the concert pitches persisted until relatively recently, but the current practice is to write the part a 5th higher in bass clef as well as in treble. Examples of the two systems of notation follow:

Ex. 6

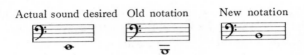

Actual sound desired   Old notation   New notation

Because players have become used to the old system, it is wise to include a note in scores and parts, whenever the new system is employed, to the effect that notes in bass clef are intended to sound a 5th lower. However, the bass clef is little used, since it is needed only for extremely low tones. Horn parts should be written in treble clef wherever possible, even if several ledger lines below the staff are involved.

In its bottom register, up to about the written note ![notation], the horn is inclined to be a bit unsolid in quality, somewhat lacking in focus, and often doubtful in intonation. This register is useful chiefly for sustained tones; melodic passages at this level are generally awkward and ineffective. From ![notation] up to about ![notation] (written), the tone is considerably brighter. This is the middle and most characteristic register, in which the horn does the greatest part of its playing. From ![notation] to the top ![notation], the notes become progressively more brilliant. Just as the high notes of a tenor voice sound much higher than they would if sung at the same pitch by a soprano, the top notes of the horn give the impression of being extremely high because the player must strain somewhat to get them.

Notes above written ![notation] are difficult to produce, and they should be led up to; that is, the player should not be asked to attack them without preparation. Because they are almost impossible to play softly, it is better not to write for the horn in this register unless it is meant to be heard prominently.

There is a certain "division of labor" among the four horns which are commonly used in the orchestra today. In order to understand this point we must first become acquainted with the traditional arrangement of the horns in harmonic passages. Horns I and II are normally written on one staff, horns III and IV on the staff below, and one might naturally suppose that in writing a four-note chord for horns, the two highest notes would be given to horns I and II and the two bottom notes to horns III and IV. But this is where tradition steps in and dicates a different procedure: the horns are written so as to interlock on paper; that is, horns I and III take the high notes, horns II and IV the low notes. For example, if we were to score

an F major triad  for four F horns, it would look like this:

Ex. 7

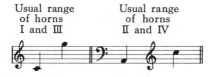

Even when only the first three horns are playing, horn III is generally placed between horns I and II (in a chord).

Because the first-horn and third-horn players are accustomed to taking the higher notes, they have become specialists in this upper register; likewise, the second-horn and fourth-horn players are especially adept at taking lower pitches. Consequently, we might divide the general range given earlier in this chapter into two "usual" ranges, one for each pair of horns:

Ex. 8

A tight, tense "lip" is required for high pitches, while lower notes call for a much looser embouchure; there is therefore a definite advantage in being able to concentrate on one general type of embouchure instead of having to switch constantly from one kind to another. Of course there is

a middle ground (roughly from written $\quad$ *to* $\quad$) in which all

the horns can play equally comfortably. And it must not be inferred from this talk of specialization that each pair of horns is never asked to exceed its own "usual" range. Particularly in passages where all four horns play in unison, the second and fourth are often taken quite high along with the first and third, and it is possible, though rare, for the first or third horn to play in the very low register.

The horn is not by nature a particularly agile instrument. Very fast running passages and quick leaps are simply not in its province except, with limitations, in virtuoso solo work. And because the player must "hear" each note in his mind's ear before playing it, the melodic lines written for the instrument should be as smooth as possible and should avoid awkward leaps. There should be sufficient rests. Since the horn is undoubtedly one of the most difficult of all orchestral instruments to play, scoring for it must be approached with special care and understanding.

Horns may be employed in various ways in the orchestra. The most important of these are:

1. *On harmony parts.* In its middle register, the horn tone is ideal for background, because it can be made unobtrusive without losing in warmth or body. Usually these harmony parts are sustained, although sometimes they consist of repeated notes or repeated short figures. Incidentally, repeated notes on the horn do not sound as sharply articulated as do repeated notes on some other instruments. The effect is more that of a pulsation on the pitch involved. Example 8 shows the horns in a typical harmonic role. (The melodic line in the violins has been included in order to show how the harmony parts fit into the general musical scheme; there are many other instruments playing.)

Ex. 9

Symphony in D minor

Simply because the horns can handle this sort of part so successfully, there is a temptation to use them constantly in this way, with a resulting monotony of color and general effect. It is largely this constant use of the horns on middle register harmony parts that gives orchestral music of the romantic period its characteristic plushy richness.

2. *In a solo capacity.* The horn is excellent as a solo instrument. It can be tender or heroic, as the music demands, and it possesses a wonderful nobility and breadth of tone all its own.

Ex. 10

(a) Third Symphony

(b) Fifth Symphony

(c) *Siegfried*

(d) *Till Eulenspiegel*

3. *Two or more horns in unison on a melodic line.* Horns are frequently doubled on a part, sometimes for purposes of volume or balance, occasionally to give a greater degree of security in difficult passages. All four horns playing in unison, *f* or *ff*, give an especially robust, heroic sound.

Ex. 11

(a) Symphony in E minor *(New World)*

Copyright, 1929, by Howard Hanson.

In cases where horns I and III play one melodic line and horns II and IV another for a considerable length of time, it may be easier to write I and III on the upper staff and II and IV on the lower, with an "a 2" indication on each staff. That way, only two melodic lines instead of four need be written for the horns.

The chamber orchestra usually includes one horn; the small orchestra, one or two. While four is the standard number employed today, it is possible, of course, to use only three if that number seems best fitted to the demands of the music in question. In most symphony orchestras one can see five horn players on the stage. This does not mean that there are five separate horn parts. The extra performer is an "assistant first horn" player; that is, he sits beside the first horn player and doubles that part at times, for added security or volume; or he may play some of the part by himself, allowing the first-horn player to save himself for important solo passages to follow.

Certain works are actually scored for more than the standard four horns. For example, Stravinsky writes for eight horns in *The Rite of Spring*, where the proportions of all sections are unusually large; and the orchestra used by Wagner in the *Ring* includes eight (four of them alternating with Wagner tubas).

It might be well to include a word about Wagner's horn notation, for it is likely to be confusing—and understandably so. The horn parts are intended to be played on valve horns, yet they are written as if for a succession of natural horns pitched in different keys. For example, we may have a passage for horn in E♭, then a few measures for horn in G, then a passage marked "Horn in F," and so on. It is difficult to follow the logic of this strange system.

In most of the examples quoted above, the horn took the chief musical idea. But it can be equally effective on subordinate countermelodies. Several horns in unison may even be allotted to such a part if considerable volume and a broad, virile effect are in order.

SPECIAL EFFECTS

The tone quality of the horn is controlled chiefly by the position of the player's hand in the bell of the instrument. Normally, the hand is inserted only part way into the bell and cupped. But there are special effects which demand a slightly different technique. Muting, for example, may be achieved by inserting the hand a little farther into the bell. Or an actual mute made of metal, wood, or cardboard may be used. Players seem to differ in their preference for one or the other of these methods; some employ both at different times: the hand method for short muted passages, a mute for longer passages. The choice depends partly on the instrument being used. In any case, this question need not be settled by the orchestrator. All he needs to do is to include the direction *con sordino* or "mute" at the appropriate spot, and the player will produce the muted effect in whichever way he prefers. As with the strings, at least a measure or two in moderate time should be allowed for putting on or taking off mutes. (With the hand-muting method the change from open to muted sound or vice versa can be made instantaneously.) The muted effect is indicated in French by *sourdine* and in German by *mit Dämpfer* or *gedämpft*. When a return to the unmuted tone is wanted, the direction is *senza sordino* or "open" (*ouvert* in French, *offen* in German). An "O" above the note is sometimes used as a symbol for "open."

Even if it were possible to describe tone color accurately in words, it would be difficult to give a description of the muted horn sound that would apply to all players and all instruments. The basic tone quality of the individual instrument, the style and technique of playing used, and the player's conception of how a muted tone should sound all enter in. But as a general comment it can be said that muting cuts down the volume of sound and

veils the tone slightly. Below about a written , muted notes are difficult, although a skilled player can mute as low as .

An excellent example of muted horns can be found in the closing measures of Debussy's *Prelude to The Afternoon of a Faun*.

"Stopped" notes on the horn are produced by inserting the hand (or a mute) so far into the bell that the opening in it is almost completely blocked, the tones being forced out. The resulting sound is curiously nasal and metallic, with a sharp edge to it. It is especially effective for single notes, played *fp*. In both muting and stopping, the volume is reduced and, unless a non-transposing mute is used, the pitch is altered to such an extent that the player must employ fingerings that differ from those used for the corresponding open tones. But he will make this adjustment automatically, and it need not concern the arranger; stopped tones are notated in the same way as open tones, as far as pitch is concerned. There are two methods for indicating the stopped effect, either or both of which may be used: (1) The French word *bouché* (or simply "stopped" in English) is written in. The German equivalent is *gestopft*, the Italian, *chiuso*. (2) A small cross is placed above each note to be played stopped. In the following example, both indications are present.

Ex. 12

Capriccio Espagnol

Another much-used direction in horn writing is the French word *cuivré*, meaning "brassy." The brassy quality is attained chiefly by increased tension of the lips and is possible in connection with open, muted, or stopped notes. *Bouché-cuivré*, a composite term often encountered, calls for a tone that is both stopped and brassy. Where only a suggestion of brassiness is wanted, Debussy marks the passage *cuivrez légèrement* (literally translated, "brass lightly".)

"Bells in the air" (*pavillons en l'air* in French, *Schalltrichter auf* in German) is a rarely used effect for which the horn is turned with the bell pointing upward, so that the sound is projected outward toward the audience more directly than in the normal playing position. Inasmuch as the hand cannot be used in the bell here, the tone is completely open and lacking in any subtlety of coloring. "Bells in the air" is therefore appropriate only for loud, hearty passages in which refinement of tone is not called for.

The horn has an uncanny ability to sound as if it were being played a great distance away. When that effect is wanted, the part should be marked *pp* or even *ppp*, and the word *lontano* ("distant" in Italian) may be added. To achieve this effect, some players employ a partly muted tone; others mute completely; still others play "open" but extremely softly.

One of the most successful sounds available on the horn is the *fp* effect mentioned earlier. Used with a stopped tone it has a biting, almost snarling quality, while in open horn it is dramatic and arresting.

Ex. 13

(a) Fifth Symphony

(b) Symphony in B minor (*Unfinished*)

Glissandos, which produce a loud upward rush of sound, are sometimes seen in contemporary scores. They may be written so as to involve any portion of any harmonic series, provided they do not start lower than

or end higher than   . One example may help to

give an idea of the usual notation:

Ex. 14

The Rite of Spring   Stravinsky

SUGGESTED ASSIGNMENTS

A. Know:

    1. the extreme possible range of the horn and the usual ranges of horns I and III and horns II and IV.

    2. transposition (including the old system of notation in the bass clef).

3. differences between the old "natural horn" and the modern valve horn, both as to their operation and the type of part written.
4. the color and weight of the horn in various registers.
5. the particular abilities and limitations of the horn.
6. special effects on the horn and foreign names for them.

B. Find five examples of parts for horns in keys other than F and rewrite them for F horn (a few measures will suffice for each example). Write the original version above and the rewritten version on a staff below it.

SUGGESTED LISTENING

Horns[1]

Mozart, Symphony No. 40 (K. 550), 3rd movt., Trio.
Beethoven, Third Symphony, 3rd movt. (*Scherzo*), Trio.
Mendelssohn, Nocturne from *Midsummer Night's Dream* music, beginning.
Brahms, B♭ major Piano Concerto, beginning; First Symphony, last movt., beginning of *Più Andante* section; Third Symphony, 3rd movt., meas. 40–52 and 98–110; Fourth Symphony, 2nd movt., beginning and many other passages.
Tchaikovsky, Fifth Symphony, 2nd movt., beginning.
Rimsky-Korsakoff, *Capriccio Espagnol*, section II (*Variazioni*), beginning.
Dvořák, Fifth Symphony (*New World*), 1st movt,. beginning of *Allegro molto* following introduction; last movt., 11 bars after figure 6, also numerous other passages.
Strauss, *Don Juan*, measure 311; *Till Eulenspiegel*, meas. 6; Waltzes from *Der Rosenkavalier*, especially beginning.
Ravel, *Pavane pour une Infante Défunte*, beginning.
Shostakovitch, Fifth Symphony, 2nd movt., at figures 54, 56, 70, and 72.
Hanson, First Symphony, 2nd and 3rd movts. in particular.
Britten, *Serenade for Tenor, Horn and Strings*, Op. 31.

---

[1] Examples of the horns in conjunction with the rest of the brass section are included in the *Suggested Listening* at the end of Chapter 9.

Chapter 8

THE TRUMPET,
TROMBONE, AND TUBA

THE TRUMPET

Italian: Tromba   *French:* Trompette   *German:* Trompete
Trombe   Trompettes   Trompeten

THE TRUMPET IN THE EIGHTEENTH CENTURY

In order to understand the trumpet parts in certain works of Bach and
his contemporaries, it is necessary to know that at that time there existed
the art of "clarino playing," which involved producing the very high partials of the instrument. The trumpet most often used was a (large) trumpet
in D. In the last half of the eighteenth century this special technique fell
into disuse and disappeared entirely. Today such high trumpet parts are
generally performed on a trumpet that is even smaller than the B♭ and C
instruments now standard, and on which the high notes called for are relatively lower in the harmonic series and therefore easier to produce. The
trumpet in D or E♭ and the trumpet in F are the two most frequent choices
for such parts. (Information on these trumpets is given on page 310.)

THE NATURAL TRUMPET

Much of what was said in the preceding chapter about the natural horn
applies to the natural trumpet as well. The latter's repertoire of written notes
was also limited to certain members of the harmonic series on C, and crooks

131

of different lengths were used to produce the desired pitches in various keys. As with the horn, the fundamental was unplayable on most trumpets; but, in addition, the second partial was too doubtful in intonation to be usable, and the notes above the twelfth partial were seldom called for. Thus the written notes normally available on the trumpet during the classical period were the following, numbered here on the basis of partials:

Ex. 1

Unlike the natural horn, the natural trumpet could not fill in certain intermediate tones by the use of the hand in the bell, nor could it adjust the intonation of the seventh and eleventh partials by that method. Nevertheless, the latter notes were sometimes called for, and in such cases whatever correction of intonation was possible had to be accomplished with the lips. As a result of all these considerations, the natural trumpet was even more limited than the natural horn in the type of part it could play.

In the eighteenth century, crooks were used with trumpets of various sizes; by the early nineteenth century the trumpet in F had become more or less standard as the one to which crooks were added. In its uncrooked state it sounded a perfect 4th higher than written. That possibility and those involving the crookings then available are shown next:

	Trumpet in	*Sounding*
Sounding higher than written	F	a perfect 4th higher than written
	E	a major 3rd higher than written
	E♭	a minor 3rd higher than written
	D	a major 2nd higher than written
	C	as written
Sounding lower than written	B	a minor 2nd lower than written
	B♭	a major 2nd lower than written
	A	a minor 3rd lower than written

Since there were not crooks for all keys, it was sometimes necessary to use a trumpet pitched in a key other than that of the music. For example, in the case of a composition in G, a trumpet in some other key (most often C) had to be employed, if trumpets were to be included. Of course it was possible to omit them altogether if the key presented too many problems. Occasionally a composer elected to use a trumpet in a key other than that of the composition even when a trumpet in the proper key was available. For instance, Beethoven's Seventh Symphony in A major uses trumpets in D, presumably to avoid a combined crooking necessary for trumpets pitched in keys lower than C.

Example 2 shows a typical trumpet part of the classical period:

Ex. 2

Symphony No. 101 in D major

It can be seen that such parts necessarily tend to be repetitious and uninteresting melodically because of the limited number of notes available. Occasionally the natural trumpet was able to take portions of themes that happened to fit the harmonic series, as in the excerpt from the *Eroica* shown in Example 3.

Ex. 3

Third Symphony

But the limitations of the instrument are all too apparent here. Beethoven apparently preferred not to risk taking the part up to a high written G in the third measure and has it descend to the lower octave of the theme instead. From the fifth measure on, the notes of the melody are not all available in the trumpet's harmonic series, so that if the instrument is to continue playing, it must take other pitches that fit in. The most serious problem, however, is illustrated in the third measure from the end. There the second trumpet should logically go down a whole step from the E to the D and then to C, in octaves with the first trumpet. But it is unable to do so because the D just above middle C is not present in the harmonic series. Instead, it jumps up a 7th to a D that *is* playable and then down a 9th, an arrangement that is far from ideal in terms of voice-leading and balance. The alternative in such cases was of course to let the trumpet simply drop out for a beat or two at the points where it had trouble supplying an appropriate note, and that was sometimes done. But such an approach was likely to lead to a fragmentary and unsatisfactory part.

THE EARLY VALVE TRUMPET IN F

Ex. 4

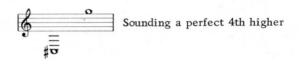

Sounding a perfect 4th higher

It was the F trumpet commonly used in Beethoven's day to which valves were added to produce the first valve trumpet that gained acceptance. This was apparently the only one of the "old family" (that is, the large type) to survive in valve form. Parts for it are found in many late nineteenth century scores by such composers as Franck, d'Indy, Bruckner, Mahler, and Strauss.

At the same time, parts for trumpets in other keys of the crooks continued to appear. Presumably these parts were transposed and played on the valve trumpet in F, although there is uncertainty on this point (just as there is uncertainty as to whether all the parts labeled F trumpet were actually played on *that* instrument).

In any case, the much smaller trumpets in B♭ and C succeeded the valve trumpet in F and are standard today.

THE MODERN VALVE TRUMPET

Ex. 5

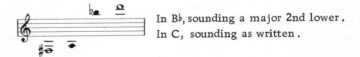

In B♭, sounding a major 2nd lower.
In C, sounding as written.

The modern trumpet is far more flexible than its ancestor, and the tone is lighter. As Forsyth says, "It is not merely that the instrument has become chromatic. It has also become, except in name, a different instrument."

The modern trumpet, in its open form, has a written harmonic series an octave higher than that of the natural trumpet. The other series available by means of valve combinations have as their bottom notes the six semitones below middle C, respectively. In each series the seventh partial (not

shown in Ex. 6) is flat and is normally avoided. The notes playable in the
seven valve positions are, then:

Ex. 6

For many years the B♭ trumpet was made with a small slide which could
be adjusted to pitch the instrument in A. But since the A slide brought on
serious intonation problems, it was not of great value and is not included
on most B♭ trumpets made today.

Although not so widely used as the B♭ instrument, the C trumpet seems
to find favor with contemporary composers, many of whom write for it
entirely. It is a bit more brilliant but its tone is generally not quite so rich.
One disadvantage to writing for it is that many players own only a B♭
trumpet and must transpose to play C parts. In school orchestras the B♭
instrument is invariably used.

From about [musical notation: to] is the trumpet's most-used register.

Notes below the C tend to be a little less penetrating, while those above the
F are more difficult to produce softly and are best led up to. Although high
D is given as the top note possible, symphonic trumpet parts do go as high
as E♭ or E on rare occasions, but the part never stays that high. Even so,
such passages are apt to be a bit uncomfortable for everyone concerned.

At this point, readers who have had some experience with trumpet playing
in the dance orchestra are sure to object that the upper limit given here for
the trumpet is much too conservative. It is perfectly true that some dance

band trumpeters go up to [musical notation] or even higher. But they usually

achieve these very high notes only at the expense of tone quality; the shrillness
that goes with this pitch level would normally be inappropriate in the
symphony orchestra.

Obviously the trumpet is a much more agile and quick-speaking instrument than the horn. It can manage runs and arpeggios and skips as long as
they are not extremely fast, but such passages should not be too extended
or too frequent. Its use in fanfares is such a familiar and natural one as
scarely to require comment. (See the Beethoven and Strauss excerpts in
Ex. 7.) Rapid repeated notes and double-tonguing and triple-tonguing

Studio Gilmore, Austin, Texas

Cornet
Trumpet

are particularly well suited to the character of the instrument; even flutter-tonguing is possible. Along with the trombone, the trumpet is capable of tremendous volume and has extraordinary powers of crescendo.

The trumpet lacks the noble warmth of the horn but has, instead, a bright, incisive quality that is especially effective in crisply assertive passages. While it can also play more lyrical melodies, there is a certain danger involved: if the melody is strongly romantic in feeling, the trumpet may sound overly sentimental, a little too reminiscent of the old-style "cornet solo."

Incidentally, the trumpet and the cornet must not be thought of as being one and the same instrument. The cornet, which is seldom employed in symphonic music today, is shorter and of slightly different shape (roughly two-thirds conical and one-third cylindrical, whereas these proportions are approximately reversed on the trumpet). The cornet tone is a bit mellower and more romantically colored than the trumpet tone, though it can be made to sound very much like the latter. Some French scores contain parts for cornets, but these parts are often played on trumpets. Cornets, like trumpets, may be pitched in B♭ or (rarely) C; the B♭ instrument is standard in band work. Everything possible on the trumpet is possible on the cornet, and the two instruments have the same range.

Muting is a frequent and effective device in orchestral trumpet writing—effective as long as it is not used too often or for too long at a time. All that was said about muting in connection with the horn applies here, except, of course, that the trumpet cannot be muted with the hand as the horn can, but must use an actual mute. It has no real equivalents of the horn's *bouché* and *cuivré* effects. To the symphony player, "mute" means the straight mute unless another kind is indicated. The straight mute, made of wood, fiber, plastic, or metal, produces a cutting, nasal quality and reduces the volume of tone somewhat. So far, the many other types of mute used in the dance orchestra have been little exploited in serious symphonic music. Some of these are the Harmon, the cup, the bucket, the solotone, and the whisper mutes. There is also the possibility, usable with either open or muted trumpet, of pointing the bell of the instrument into a hat or a music stand to achieve a more subdued tone. The direction is simply "hat" or "in stand." Still another device is the use of a "plunger," which greatly reduces the volume.

EXAMPLES

Ex. 7

(a) *Leonore* Overture No. 3

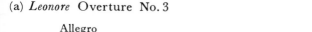

(b) *Scheherazade*

138

(c) *Ein Heldenleben*

Strauss

(d) Fifth Symphony

Sibelius

(e) *Schelomo*

Bloch

THE TENOR TROMBONE

Italian: Trombone   *French:* Trombone   *German:* Posaune
           Tromboni   Trombones   Posaunen

Ex. 8

* Pitches down to the low C are possible with an F attachment.

As a rule, instruments pitched in keys other than C are transposing instruments. Not so with the tenor trombone; although built basically around the harmonic series of B♭, it sounds as written. It may be notated in either bass or tenor clef, the latter being commonly chosen for higher passages in order to avoid the use of too many ledger lines. (In music for school orchestras, however, trombones rarely use the tenor clef.) The alto clef, found in some older scores, is almost never employed for the trombone nowadays. It is a hangover from the period when the alto trombone was in common use.

The mechanism of the instrument differs radically from those of the horn and the trumpet in that it includes no valves.[1] Instead, the length of tubing is varied by means of the slide. Seven different positions of the slide are possible, each one producing a different harmonic series. The seven fundamentals or generating tones of these series are shown in Example 9.

Ex. 9

The first of these "pedal tones," the B♭, is easily playable and is seen frequently in commercial scoring, much less often in symphonic music. Below that, the notes become increasingly difficult to produce and insecure in quality; A♭ or G is the bottom limit for most trombonists. In any case, pedal tones below the B♭ are called for only very rarely.

The notes available in the series on E, known as seventh position, are as follows:

---

[1] Valve trombones have had a considerable vogue abroad, notably in Italy. Although they are sometimes used by jazz musicians in the United States, they have never had any wide acceptance in our symphony orchestras.

Ex. 10

In sixth position the notes playable are:

Ex. 11

And so on, up to first position, where additional overtones may be used to stretch the upper range a bit higher:

Ex. 12

By adding a B♮ and C♯ at the top of the second position, we get a complete chromatic scale up to the second F above middle C as a possible range.

But notes above ![notation] are more difficult and are rarely used in orchestral parts.

Many tenor trombones today are equipped with an "F attachment," a device which, by adding extra tubing, extends the range downward a major 3rd (to a C) and also simplifies the technical problem by eliminating certain awkward changes of position.

In music for the trombone, it is not so much distance between notes as distance between positions that determines the technical difficulty of the part. A little reflection will make it clear that certain notes can be taken in one of two or more different positions. For example, ![notation] can be taken

---

* The seventh partial (sixth overtone) in each position is slightly flat. However, it can be brought into tune by an adjustment of the slide, in all positions except the first. The slide is already drawn up as far as it will go, and a raising of the flat pitch is therefore impossible.

in the first position (series on B♭) or the fourth position (series on G) or the seventh position (series on E), and the player can choose whichever position is easiest. With three choices, one of them is bound to be close to the position he is already playing in, and such cases should cause no difficulty. But certain notes, such as those in Example 13, can be taken in only one position.

Ex. 13

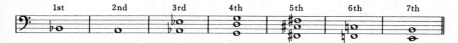

For the seventh position the slide is extended its full length; for first position it is drawn up as far as possible in the other direction. Therefore, very rapid or repeated changes from first position to seventh position (or vice versa) are awkward and are better avoided. Occasional changes of this sort, when not too fast, are acceptable. Less difficult are changes involving such other distant positions as the second and sixth, but frequent use of them in a rapid tempo naturally does not make for grateful trombone writing.

In order to illustrate what *not* to write for the trombone, we have devised the diabolically awkward passage shown in Example 14. (The numbers above the notes refer to the positions involved.) An actual performance of this by a trombonist will show, very graphically, why such changes as these are best avoided. The passage is somewhat easier on a trombone with an F attachment, however.

Ex. 14

It should be remembered that because the notes of the harmonic series lie closer together in the trombone's upper register, the whole problem of position becomes less acute there and the instrument therefore has a greater degree of agility in that register than it does in the lower portions of its compass.

The trombone's lowest register is dark and full. The low E tends to be slightly inferior in quality and is perhaps better avoided in any prominent passage. Other than that, the entire range up to the B♭ above middle C is solid and effective, the notes becoming progressively more brilliant toward the top.

A basic problem in trombone playing is the difficulty of achieving a completely legato effect when a change of slide is involved. If the player

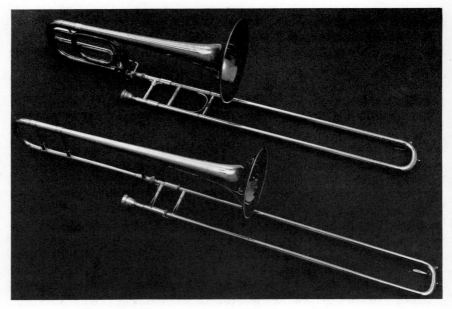

Bass Trombone
Tenor Trombone

were to keep the air column vibrating continuously, he would produce not only the actual notes intended but a glissando between each two of them as the slide moved from one position to another. Consequently, he must stop the air column momentarily between notes. To give the effect of a legato connection under these circumstances would seem to be impossible, yet experienced trombonists succeed in doing it surprisingly well, especially at softer dynamic levels. The gap between notes is so slight as to be scarcely apparent to the ear. (Of course two notes in the same harmonic series, such

as ⟨notation⟩ and ⟨notation⟩ , require no change in the position of the

slide and can therefore be played *legatissimo* by means of a "lip slur".)

In its most familiar role, the trombone is an instrument that excels at loud, heroic passages. But it can also play softly, either on the chief musical idea or as background; this side of its nature is too often forgotten. Rapid running passages and light, fanciful parts that skip around a great deal are obviously not well suited either to trombone technique or to trombone quality. However, the instrument can play rapid repeated notes, including double- or triple-tonguing, and *short* figures that move quickly.

Muting on the trombone works just as it does on the trumpet, and the effect is relatively the same. Even though the mute cuts down the volume somewhat (in addition to altering the quality), the muted trombone can still hold its own in a *tutti*.

The glissando effect mentioned earlier is normally avoided; but there are times when it is used purposely for comic or bizarre passages. The usual indication in the part is a line between the notes to be connected and the abbreviation *gliss*. This is a device which has long since lost its novelty; when used in serious music today, it has a tendency to sound merely vulgar and dated.

As a point of historical interest, it might be mentioned that although the trombone was employed as early as 1600 or so by Gabrieli and was later used by Mozart, Gluck, and others in opera, its first appearance in an actual symphony occurred in Beethoven's Fifth Symphony.

THE BASS TROMBONE

Italian: Trombone basso   *French:* Trombone basse   *German:* Bassposaune

Ex. 15

* Possible with an E attachment.

At one time there was a complete family of trombones: alto, tenor, bass, and double-bass. The alto and double-bass instruments have long since fallen into disuse, and the bass trombone in F (or G) has recently followed suit, at least in the United States. For their third trombone, most orchestras in this country now use a B♭ trombone equipped with an F attachment— and often with an E attachment as well, so that the low B♮ can be played. The instrument is usually made with a large bore and bell, and in this form it goes by the name of bass trombone. Sometimes it plays the bass, either alone or in unison or octaves with the tuba; at other times it plays the tenor voice, leaving the bass to the tuba. While its upper range is, theoretically, the same as that of the tenor trombone, bass trombone parts involve a lower tessitura and almost never go above the F shown as the top practical note. Traditionally, they use only the bass clef. Pedal tones are possible, as on the tenor trombone, and the bass trombone is, in fact, more often called upon to play them.

EXAMPLES

Ex. 16

(a) First Symphony

(b) Overture to *Tannhäuser*

(c) *Petrouchka*

(d) Symphony: *Mathis der Maler*

Reproduced by permission of Schott & Co., Ltd., London.

(In [a] the complete scoring [except for timpani] is included to show how the bassoons, contra bassoons, and horns are combined with the trombones to complete the harmony.)

THE TUBA

Italian: Tuba   *French:* Tuba   *German:* Basstuba

Ex. 17

Tubas in various keys are employed in the orchestra, those in C and BB♭ being the ones most favored today. The choice of instrument rests with the player and is determined by the range of the part, fingering problems, and personal preference, among other things. All the tubas are nontransposing (that is, sound as written) and all are four-valve instruments. While they differ slightly as to range, it seems unnecessary to catalog the individual ranges here, since in writing a tuba part we can be governed by the composite range just given, and since all tubas are capable of playing within the practical range shown.

The tuba seldom has occasion to go very high inasmuch as the notes in the upper part of its register are as a rule better given to trombone or horn.[2] The extremely low notes, those below the low F, tend to be weaker and less solid in quality and are better avoided. The instrument seems to be most effective when used neither very low nor very high but in its middle register.

[2] An exception is the amusing passage from Stravinsky's *Petrouchka,* quoted at the end of this section, where the tuba in its extreme upper register gives exactly the right "lumbering" effect for a dance by a trained bear. But this sort of thing comes under the heading of special effects and is not recommended for everyday use. The passage is frequently played by a euphonium or baritone (see page 312).

Zintgraff, San Antonio, Texas

Tuba

For such a large instrument it is perhaps more agile than might be expected, though there are definite limits to the speed and complexity of the parts it can play. Since it calls for the expenditure of a great deal of breath in performance, parts for it should not be too continuous and should include sufficient rests.

The tone quality of the instrument has been alternately praised and maligned in orchestration books. The writer's experience indicates that with a good instrument and a good player the tuba tone can be unusually velvety and pleasant in soft passages, robust and exciting in a *forte* or a *fortissimo*. It differs from those of the trumpet and trombone in being "rounder" and less cutting. This difference results partly from the fact that the tuba is, like the horn, essentially conical in bore, whereas the trumpet and trombone are predominantly cylindrical. Also, the tuba bore is relatively larger than that of the other brass instruments (the horn included).

Muting of the tuba is a device which is employed only rarely. An example may be seen in the introduction of Strauss's *Don Quixote*.

The most frequent use of the tuba in the orchestra is as a bass for the brass section; but it may also be used to strengthen the double basses or lower woodwinds. On rare ocasions, it may take the bass alone or play a solo part.

Because it is so often combined in unison with the double bass and the contra bassoon, both of which sound an octave lower than written, students have a way of insisting that the tuba should use the same transposition. At the risk of sounding repetitious, we might include a reminder to write the tuba part at its actual pitch.

EXAMPLES

Ex. 18

(a) Prelude to *Die Meistersinger*

(b) *Siegfried*

(The tuba is used here to personify Fafner, the dragon.)

(c) *Don Juan*

(d) *Petrouchka*

THE OPHICLEIDE

Certain nineteenth-century scores, including some by Wagner, Berlioz, Mendelssohn, Verdi, and Schumann, contain parts for the bass ophicleide. This was "the bass of the Keyed-Bugle," as Forsyth puts it, a metal instrument with a broadly conical upright bell, and of "coarse, powerful tone." It customarily played bass parts in the orchestra until about the middle of the nineteenth century, when the tuba began to supplant it. Since it is now obsolete, parts written for it are played by the tuba.

SUGGESTED ASSIGNMENT

Know:

1. ranges of the trumpet, trombone, and tuba.
2. transpositions where involved.
3. principles involved in the positions on the trombone and in the various harmonic series available on the other brass instruments by means of different valve combinations.
4. colors and relative weights in different registers.
5. abilities and limitations.
6. possibilities for muting and special effects.

SUGGESTED LISTENING

Trumpet

Beethoven, *Leonore* Overture No. 3, meas. 272.
Wagner, Prelude to *Parsifal*, meas. 9; *Siegfried*, scenes of Mime; *Die Meistersinger*, scenes of Beckmesser (latter two are examples of *muted* trumpet).
Scriabin, *The Poem of Ecstasy*, 4 bars after figure 32; many other passages.
Mussorgsky-Ravel, *Pictures from an Exhibition*, opening *Promenade;* also Part 6 (*Samuel Goldenberg and Schmuyle*), figure 58 (muted trumpet).
Strauss, *Ein Heldenleben*, fanfare section, figure 42; *Don Quixote*, figure 3 (muted trumpets).
Debussy, *Nocturnes:* II. *Fêtes*, 9 bars after figure 10 (3 muted trumpets).
Ravel, *Daphnis and Chloe* Suite No. 2, 2 bars before figure 204.
Stravinsky, *The Rite of Spring*, 4 bars before figure 84 (muted).
Bloch, *Schelomo*, figure 5.
Copland, Third Symphony, fanfare section near beginning of 4th movt. (figure 85).

Trombone

Mozart, Requiem, *Tuba Mirum.*
Berlioz, *Roman Carnival* Overture.
Wagner, Overture to *Tannhäuser*, letter A; *The Ride of the Valkyries.*
Rimsky-Korsakoff, *Russian Easter* Overture, letter M.

Tchaikovsky, Fourth Symphony, last movt., meas. 84; Sixth Symphony, last movt., letter L.
Strauss, *Salome*, closing scene (muted trombone).
Mahler, Third Symphony, 1st movt., figure 33.
Sibelius, Seventh Symphony, 1st movt., letter L.
Stravinsky, *Pulcinella*, Minuet movt.; *Petrouchka*, figure 112.

Tuba

Wagner, *Siegfried*, beginning of Act II.
Mussorgsky-Ravel, *Pictures from an Exhibition*, beginning of Part 4 (*Bydlo*).
Strauss, *Don Quixote*, figure 3 (muted tubas), figure 9, etc. (This work illustrates the use of both tenor and bass tubas.)
Stravinsky, *Petrouchka*, 2 bars after figure 100.
Shostakovitch, First Symphony, 3rd movt., before figures 7 and 20.

Chapter 9

THE BRASS SECTION

The brass section to be used here for purposes of illustration is the average one: four horns, two or three trumpets, three trombones, and tuba.

An accepted axiom in scoring for brass is this: if the dynamic marking is *mf* or louder, two horns are needed to balance one trumpet or one trombone; below that dynamic level, one horn will give satisfactory balance. Consequently, we must know just how loud a passage is to be before we can score it properly for brass. In the examples that follow, various dynamic markings have been assumed.

The horns have been written in some cases without key signature (the traditional way) and in others with key signature (which seems the more sensible way here). As in the examples for woodwinds, different possibilities in slurring have been shown.

Once again we have elected to use the chorale excerpt that has served for illustration in earlier chapters:

Ex. 1

Jesu, meine Freude

Bach

Example 2 illustrates some of the many ways in which the passage could be scored for brass instruments.

Ex. 2

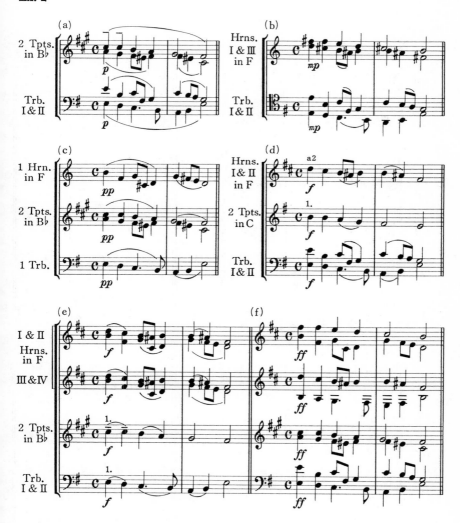

Version (c) shows how the instruments would normally be arranged in scoring for a brass quartet.

Although the arrangement of the horns in (f) may appear to be a natural and workable one, it is actually not too satisfactory. The range in most four-voice music is such that the first horn is apt to be taken uncomfortably high, while the fourth horn is so low that it may become weaker and unsolid.

With good players, this sort of arrangement is possible in certain pieces; with school groups or less experienced performers, it had better be avoided.

Unlike the versions in Example 2, those in Example 3 use keys other than the original, and all but (a) include octave doublings.

Ex. 3

In Example 3 (c) the upper octave of the chorale melody has been given to two trumpets in order to bring it out more strongly than the other voices, while in (d) the bottom octave of the melody has been weighted a great deal more heavily than normal balance would require (four horns in unison plus a trombone).

In (d) and (e) three trumpets rather than two are included. Since third trumpet parts are apt to get down into the lower, less penetrating register, it is often a wise idea to reinforce them with a trombone or a horn (or even two horns). That has been done in (d) with a trombone, in (e) with a horn. Of course if the third trumpet part lies fairly high, no such reinforcement is necessary.

In general, trumpets and horns sound better in close spacing (close position) than they do in open. Trombones may also be arranged in close spacing in their middle and upper registers. (If placed quite high, they give an effect of great brilliance.) But since they must often play the lower notes of the harmony, where close spacing would be too muddy, they are seen about

as frequently in open spacing. Such arrangements as  in three

trombones give a fine solid resonance.

Beginning orchestrators often make the mistake of expecting the brass instruments to enter on an extremely high note. Such entrances are risky. Even when successful, they are apt to sound unpleasantly strained and tense. The following written pitches might be set as safe upward limits for entrances, in trumpet, horn, and trombone, respectively:

Ex. 4

Horn	Trumpet	Trombone

Of course, higher pitches are practical when the player has a chance to lead up to them instead of having to hit them without preparation.

The excerpt in Example 5 is a good example of effective scoring for brass choir alone. The complete scoring is shown except for two chords for full orchestra which occur at the two holds. The second of these chords (the one in the last measure) is given, in condensed form at concert pitch, on page 169.

154

Ex. 5

Symphony: *Mathis der Maler*

Hindemith

Reproduced by permission of Schott & Co., Ltd., London.

SUGGESTED ASSIGNMENTS

A. Know:

1. make-up of the average brass section.
2. arrangement of instruments on page—order and grouping.
3. principles of balance as applied to the brass section.
4. commonly used "voicings" (in brass scoring).

B. The following are suitable as exercises in scoring for brass:

1. Bach, a short excerpt from any of the chorales, to be scored for: (a) two B♭ trumpets and two trombones; (b) two C trumpets, one F horn, and one

trombone; (c) full brass section, including three trumpets if desired. In this last version use octave doublings.
2. Bach, *Wachet Auf* (chorale).
3. Bach, Fugue in G minor, from *Eight Little Preludes and Fugues for the Organ.*
4. Bach, *The Art of Fugue*, Fugue I, Contrapunctus IX, many other portions.
5. Schumann, "Norse Song" from *Album for the Young.*
6. Schumann, "War Song" from *Album for the Young.*
7. Grieg, *Sailor's Song.*
8. Chopin, Prelude in C minor.
9. Franck, Prelude from *Prelude, Aria and Finale*, meas. 1–12, transposed to E♭ major or F major.
10. Mussorgsky, "Promenade," beginning of *Pictures from an Exhibition.*
11. Bartók, Folk Song No. 8, from *Ten Easy Pieces for Piano.*
12. Kabalevsky, Prelude 24 from *24 Preludes*, meas. 46–55 (suggests inclusion of piano and percussion as well).

SUGGESTED LISTENING

Brass

Dvořák, Fifth Symphony (*New World*), last movt.
Brahms, First Symphony, last movt., "chorale" section.
Franck, Symphony in D minor, last movt., "chorale" section.
Wagner, Prelude to *Parsifal;* Funeral Music from *Götterdämmerung;* Overture to *Tannhäuser.*
Tchaikovsky, Fourth Symphony, 3rd movt., Tempo I following the *Meno mosso* section; last movt., many passages.
Rimsky-Korsakoff, *Capriccio Espagnol*, beginning of section IV (*Scena e Canto Gitano*).
Mussorksgy-Ravel, *Pictures from an Exhibition*, opening *Promenade;* Part 8 (*Catacombs*); Part 10 (*The Great Gate of Kiev*).
Kodály, *Háry János* Suite, Part IV (*The Battle and Defeat of Napoleon*).
Bartók, Concerto for Orchestra, Part I (*Introduzione*), meas. 342 (about the middle); Part II (*Giuoco delle Coppie*), meas. 123 (middle portion); Part V (*Finale*), meas. 556.
Hindemith, Symphony: *Mathis der Maler*, "Alleluia" at end (brass parts shown on page 154); also many other portions, especially 1st movt.
Stravinsky, *Fire Bird* Suite, *Finale.*
Respighi, *Pines of Rome*, last section (*Pines of the Appian Way*); *Roman Festivals.*
Copland, Third Symphony, 2nd movt., beginning; 4th movt., figure 85 to figure 88, figure 126.

Chapter 10

SCORING OF CHORDS FOR EACH SECTION AND FOR ORCHESTRA

WOODWIND CHORDS

There are four ways in which instruments of different kinds may be combined in a chord. These are demonstrated here, using woodwinds in pairs. (All notes shown are actual sounds.)

Ex. 1

Juxtaposition[1] Interlocking[1] Enclosure Overlapping

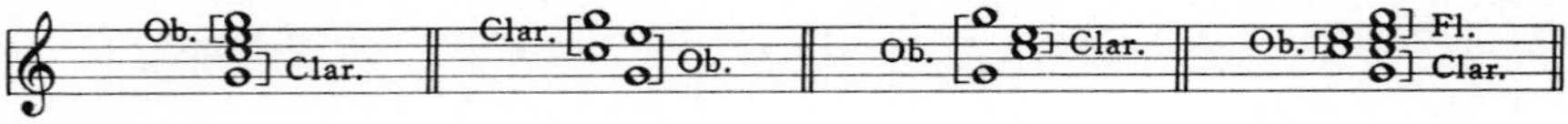

Juxtaposition is used very frequently. Pairs of instruments are simply put side by side, usually in the normal order of register.

Interlocking has the slight advantage of mixing the colors in such a way that a more homogeneous blend results. However, there are cases in which interlocking does not work well. For instance, in the following chord the second flute would be relatively weak:

* In Rimsky-Korsakoff's *Principles of Orchestration* the translator has used the term "overlaying" rather than "juxtaposition" and "crossing" rather than "interlocking." Certain other orchestration books refer to interlocking as "dovetailing." The terms chosen here are those which seem to offer the least chance for ambiguity or confusion.

Ex. 2

A similar lack of balance would result if interlocking forced the oboe, for example, to play in an abnormally high register where it would be too thin.

Enclosure is likely to be less successful than the first two methods in arranging woodwinds, at least when one *pair* encloses another. The difficulty is that when two instruments of a kind are spread an octave or more apart, they are likely to be playing in different registers and therefore to differ considerably from each other in strength and color; consequently, balance and blend may suffer. Consider the difference in sound between the first and second flutes in Example 3.

Ex. 3

(The second flute is obviously too weak here.) On the other hand, if a pair is enclosed by two *different* instruments, the effect may be perfectly good. (See Ex. 4.)

Ex. 4

The overlapping method, though much in vogue during the Classical period, is seen less often today. Its weakness is the fact that the outer notes (especially the bottom one) are not as strong as the others.

Whereas overlapping involves only a partial duplication of notes, there is another more complete and balanced form of duplication that is much used, as in Example 5.

Ex. 5

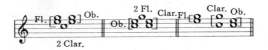

The obvious question at this point is: how does the arranger decide on the best method to use? There is no general answer that can be given to that question; range, voice-leading, instruments involved, the coloring desired, and other factors will all enter into the choice. Juxtaposition and interlocking are chosen much more frequently than the other methods, however. Two or more methods are often used in the same chord—when the chord consists of more than four notes. In any case, the difference in sound between a chord that uses juxtaposition, let us say, and one that uses interlocking is not really a very startling one. The important thing is to plan for proper balance and blend, whichever system is chosen.

It should be understood that this material on voicing is illustrated by isolated chords only for the sake of convenience and that it applies to the part-writing of harmonic successions as well.

Except in small orchestras which include only one of each woodwind, chords are rarely arranged with a different color on each note (Ex. 6).

Ex. 6

Because of the several different timbres involved in such an arrangement, a good blend is difficult to achieve. If the chord were a widely spaced one in a higher register, the resulting sound would be somewhat better (Ex. 7).

Ex. 7

However, this sort of spacing is almost never used today in writing for wind instruments in the orchestra. Although at one time woodwind chords were often arranged with gaps between the upper chord members, the current practice (which is certainly preferable) is to write the upper woodwinds in close spacing. The occasional gaps that occur as a result of special voice-leading or doubling are not objectionable (Ex. 8 [a] and [b]) nor is the octave gap that is caused by a doubling of the top voice an octave higher (8[c]).

Ex. 8

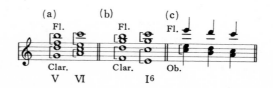

Before going on to the examples of chords scored for woodwinds, the reader would do well to review the hints on spacing and doubling given near the end of Chapter 3. One small point might be added here, even though it does not figure in the scoring of isolated chords: when a progression involves both stationary and moving voices, it is better to give the stationary voices to one color, the moving voices to another:

Ex. 9

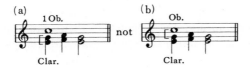

In the examples that follow, some of the chords are scored for woodwinds in pairs plus two horns (the latter included because they are so often combined with woodwinds). Another section of the illustrations makes use of a large woodwind section: piccolo, two flutes, two oboes, English horn, two clarinets, bass clarinet, two bassoons, and contra bassoon. And there are a few examples for woodwinds in threes, a less frequently used combination. With both the large woodwind section and woodwinds in threes, juxtaposition works far better than any of the other systems. Interlocking is especially unsuccessful in the case of woodwinds in threes because it pushes instruments of a kind too far apart.

Ex. 10

Complete duplication, with three of each woodwind, allows for a uniformly mixed color in three-note chords. (See Ex. 11.)

Ex. 11

In scoring for a large woodwind section, the piccolo may double the flute an octave higher or may take the top chord tone immediately above the flutes. The English horn may be placed just below the oboes to form a three-note chord in close spacing or it may play lower down, with other instruments between it and the oboes. The bass clarinet, on the other hand, is much less often placed immediately below the clarinets to form a three-note chord; it is far more apt to take the bass, since it is most effective in its lower and middle registers. It is, in fact, better than the bassoon for the bass of a woodwind chord; it has enough body to give a solid foundation to the chord, whereas two bassoons would often be required to achieve the equivalent sense of solidity. The role of the contra bassoon as the bottom of the chord is an obvious one. It normally doubles the bass an octave lower.

Most of the chords in the following examples are scored in such a way as to be fairly brilliant in coloring, but in two of them, (g) and (m), the instruments have been placed relatively low in their respective registers to produce a darker coloring. The clarinets in their bottom octave are particularly good at adding a somber tinge. Obviously, there is no point in including the piccolo in such cases, and even the flutes have been omitted in (m). In fact, any instrument may be omitted at any time for the sake of color or volume, or possibly to keep it fresh for an entrance that is to follow.

Ex. 12

(For woodwinds in pairs and two horns)

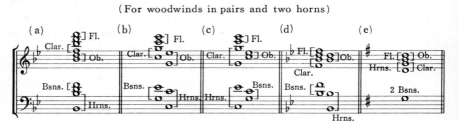

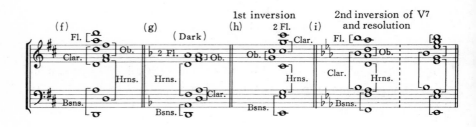

(For large woodwind section)

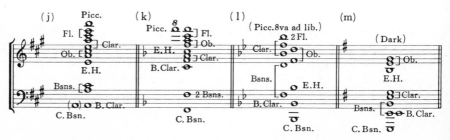

(For woodwinds in threes)

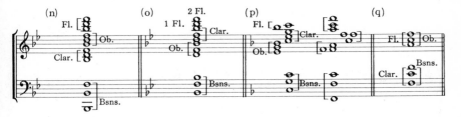

In general, the same dynamic marking can be given to all the instruments in each one of the arrangements just shown. One possible exception concerns the horns. Since they are capable of a more robust *forte* than any of the woodwinds, it would be safer to mark them *mf* when the woodwinds are marked *f*, and *f* when the woodwinds are marked *ff*.

BRASS CHORDS

Juxtaposition, interlocking, and enclosure are all used frequently in scoring chords for brass. Overlapping as a method is rarely seen, though a low trumpet note is sometimes overlapped by the top trombone or by a horn for the sake of better balance.

If our brass section consists of four horns, two trumpets, three trombones, and tuba, we have ten instruments. As long as the dynamic marking is softer than *mf*, these instruments can actually play ten notes. But in a *mezzo-forte* or louder, the horns will normally be used two to a note, and the section can then cover only eight notes at the most. When chords of more than eight notes are to be scored *forte* or louder for the brass section we have just described, the two-horns-to-a-note principle must obviously be abandoned; the horns are given four different pitches and (when possible) marked one degree louder than the rest of the brass. This type of arrangement is shown in Example 13 (i). Of course if the chord to be scored has fewer than eight notes, instruments may simply be omitted, or certain ones may be doubled on a pitch so as to bring out a particular voice if that is appropriate.

Some of the following examples have been scored for two trumpets, some for three, since brass sections vary in that respect. Three would seem to be the more satisfactory number, because it allows for a complete three-note harmony in the trumpet color.

As before, the chords have merely been sketched on two staves at concert pitch. It should perhaps be stressed that the examples here and elsewhere in this chapter make no pretense of exhausting all the possibilities; they simply show some of the more usual arrangements.

CHORDS FOR BRASS

Ex. 13

(With two trumpets)

(With three trumpets)

STRING CHORDS

Having wended his way through the maze of possibilities in scoring woodwind and brass chords, the reader may be relieved to be told that the problem of scoring chords for strings is a bit less involved. In the first place, the difference in color between one string group and another is not nearly so decided as the difference in color between, say, a flute and an oboe. Consequently, the strings present fewer problems of blend. And they do not vary in strength from register to register as much as the woodwinds do. This means that balance is more easily calculated.

On the other hand, strings involve two possibilities that wind instruments do not: (1) double, triple, and quadruple stops; (2) the use of an entire section that can be divided into any number of parts. As pointed out earlier, double stops may be used even in sustained chords, whereas triple and quadruple stops are valuable principally for short, sharply punctuated chords. In this latter type of chord, the main objectives are usually maximum resonance, fullness, and volume, and it is unnecessary to worry much about exact balance or correct voice-leading because the chord is not heard long enough for these features to be very apparent to the ear. The open strings so often involved in chords of this sort not only give added resonance but simplify the technical problem of the player.

As for *divisi* writing, remember that the fewer the players the riskier it is to divide a section. This is particularly true of division into more than two parts. Ideally, of course, we are scoring for an orchestra of full professional proportions, in which case a division of the violas into four separate parts is quite practical. But the sad reality of the matter is that we are much more likely to be working with a college orchestra that is able to muster perhaps only three viola players. Under such circumstances, division into four or more parts is obviously an impossibility; division into three parts, though possible, is hardly advisable if the parts involve any technical difficulties, for each player is left alone and unsupported on a part. Furthermore, when such small string groups are divided, the result is a solo quality rather than a group quality on each voice. (It takes at least three violins or violas on a part to give the effect of a group of strings.) While the other string groups tend to be somewhat better staffed than the viola section, they can still suffer from overdivision if the orchestra is not full-sized or if the players are inexperienced.

Juxtaposition (illustrated in the first three of the chords in Example 14) is the method used most often in arranging strings. On rare occasions, interlocking is employed to achieve a more complete blend (d). Overlapping of one string group with another (also rare) produces a richer, composite quality (e). Enclosure seldom figures in string scoring. As mentioned earlier, open harmony is more successful in strings than in woodwinds or brass. Examples (f) through (j), which are shown in actual score form, are string chords taken from orchestral literature. Each illustrates a particular effect or device. Notice the interlocking of the notes in the triple stops in (f), a frequent arrangement in multiple-stop chords. Interlocking also figures in (g) and (h).

Ex. 14

(Condensed at actual pitch)

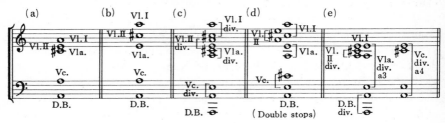

(In score form)

(f) Beethoven, Seventh Symphony (last movt. , letter A)
(g) Hindemith, Symphony : *Mathis der Maler* (second measure)
(h) Strauss, *Don Juan* (eight measures after G)
(i) Bartók, Concerto for Orchestra (fifth measure of Finale)
(j) Wagner, *Lohengrin*, Prelude to Act I (beginning)

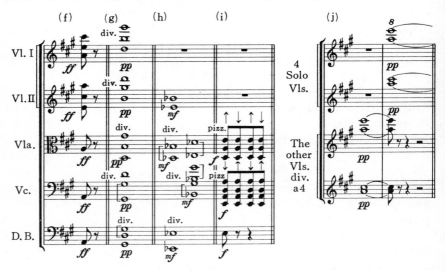

Example 14 (g) reproduced by permission of Schott & Co., Ltd., London; Example 14 (i) copyright, 1946, by Hawkes & Son (London) Ltd. By permission of the copyright owner, Boosey & Hawkes, Inc.

CHORDS FOR ORCHESTRA

In considering the scoring of chords for orchestra, we must remember, first of all, that there is a vast difference in the weight of the three sections (woodwind, brass, and strings). That is, if each section is marked *ff*, the brass will be louder than the woodwinds or strings. Though still present in a *forte* marking, this imbalance in terms of decibels diminishes as the dynamic level gets softer. Example 16a in Chapter 8 illustrates the successful use of woodwinds to fill in certain notes not taken by the brass, in a passage marked *p, dolce*. But at higher dynamic levels that approach will seldom work; there the brass must generally be balanced as a unit.

If we carry this process over into the woodwinds and strings and arrange the chord in such a way that each section would sound complete and balanced if played by itself, the composite sound of the three sections playing at the same time is bound to be good. This is, in fact, a fool-proof method and one that is often used. It is demonstrated in Example 15 (a), (e), and others that follow. But it is not the only way, nor is it necessarily the most effective, because it sometimes involves putting the upper woodwinds in the same register as the trumpets, in which case the woodwinds are all but drowned out and actually add little. If the flutes and clarinets, especially, are placed well above the trumpets, they are better able to make themselves heard, first because they are not covered by the trumpets in the same octave, and second because they are much more powerful and brilliant in the higher register. (We are assuming here that a loud, brilliant effect is wanted.) With this sort of arrangement, there is often a gap in the middle of the woodwind chord, but that is not objectionable. Although the woodwind section would not sound entirely satisfactory if played by itself, it will be effective when combined with the brass and strings.

The same general principle applies to the role of the strings in a chord for orchestra. That is, they may either play the complete chord or merely reinforce certain notes of it. But, unlike the woodwind section, they are frequently arranged in open spacing; sometimes, in fact, they are spread out even more widely, with gaps of an octave or more between certain notes. At other times they are simply arranged in straightforward four-part fashion, using close spacing. Octave doublings may be added or not, depending on whether a full, rich effect is wanted. Some of the more likely possibilities can be seen in the examples that follow, all of which are condensed at actual pitch.

Chords (a), (b), (c), and (d) in Example 15 use woodwinds in pairs, (e) and (f) a large woodwind section. In (d) a dark coloring has been aimed at. In (e) and (f) are shown two different scorings of the same chord, the first very brilliant, the second about "medium" color. Chords taken from well-known scores are given in (g) to (o). The last chord (o) differs from the others in being a bitingly dissonant one.

CHORDS FOR ORCHESTRA

Ex. 15

(Condensed at actual pitch)

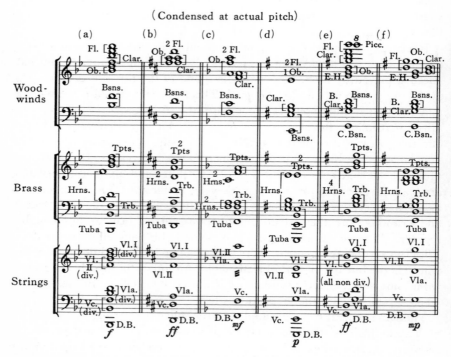

(The dynamic marking below each chord applies to all the instruments.)

(g) Beethoven, Fifth Symphony (measure 316)
(h) Franck, Symphony in D minor (last chord)
(i) Strauss, *Till Eulenspiegel* (five measures before 37)
(j) Wagner, *Götterdämmerung*   (*Trauermusik* , measure 16)
(k) Wagner, *Tristan und Isolde* (last chord)

(l) Prokofieff, Fifth Symphony (last chord in first movt.)

(m) Strauss, *Sinfonia Domestica* (last chord)

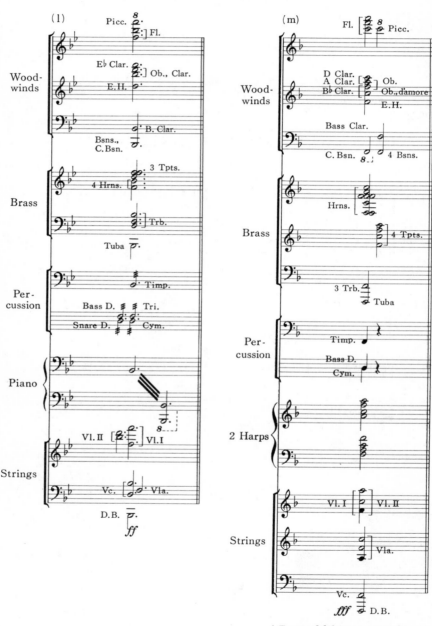

(Four ad libitum saxophone
parts are not shown here.)

(n) Symphony:

Mathis der Maler (last chord)   (o) Third Symphony (figure 117)

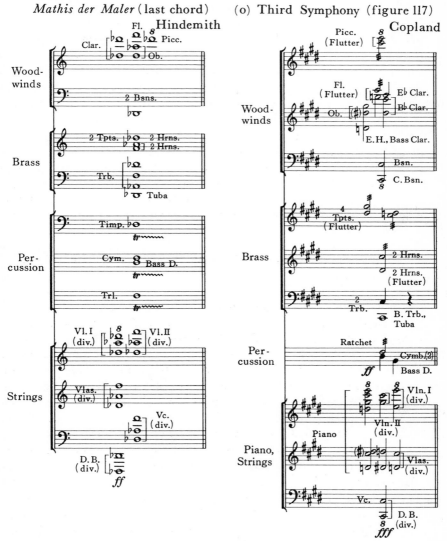

It should not be inferred from the comments and examples given here that in a chord for orchestra all the sections must have the same dynamic marking. There is no law, for instance, against marking the strings and woodwinds *ff*, the brass *f* or *mp* or even *pp*, if that will produce the particular sound that is wanted.[1] (It is important, by the way, to remember that the brass, particularly the trombones and horns, can provide an extremely quiet but rich background for the other instruments if need be.) Similarly, it would be possible to mark the strings louder than the woodwinds or vice versa, in order to bring out a certain timbre or register. However, there would seldom be any point in marking the brass much *louder* than the strings or woodwinds, since the latter tend to be overshadowed by the brass even when the dynamic markings are equal. It should perhaps be mentioned that certain scores, particularly pre-twentieth-century scores, use "block" dynamics—all the instruments invariably marked the same in a *tutti;* but in such cases the conductor is obviously expected to adjust the dynamic proportions wherever that becomes necessary.

Dissonances are more prominent and acute when given to instruments of the same kind, milder when allotted to different instruments. For instance,

 accentuates the dissonance much more than

This principle has been used in intensifying the dissonance in chord 15 (o).

It would be impractical to attempt to catalog all the doublings possible between woodwinds, brass, and strings. Some of the possibilities in woodwind and string doubling are discussed in Chapter 12, and a few of the combinations involving woodwinds and brass will now be mentioned here. In general, the doubling of woodwinds in unison with brass makes the brass tone somewhat less transparent and brilliant in timbre; clarinets and flutes "soften the edges" of the trumpet tone, while oboes tend to accentuate the nasal quality of it. Clarinets in their *chalumeau* register add a rich, dark touch to the brass. Bassoons doubled in unison with horns or trombones make those instruments a little grayer and more opaque in quality; the bassoon color is largely absorbed by the brass color.

Leaving the matter of actual doublings, it might be helpful to pass on a small point which Rimsky-Korsakoff and others have mentioned: there is a certain resemblance between the tone of the oboe (or English horn) and that of stopped horn or muted trumpet; consequently, these instruments can be combined in a chord (on different notes) with surprisingly good results. Even the unmuted trumpet tone is close enough to the oboe tone for the two instruments to give a fairly unified sound when placed side by side. One hears chiefly the trumpet quality; in fact, such combinations may even give the illusion of being played entirely by trumpets. A similar affinity

[1] See pages 295–97 for a more detailed commentary on this point and for an example that illustrates it.

of tone quality exists (rather surprisingly) between the low notes of the flute and soft trumpet tones in that register.

SUGGESTED ASSIGNMENTS

Score the following chords as directed. The chords are to have the root in the bass unless an inversion is indicated. Either they may be written with a key signature (assuming that each is the tonic chord) or the key signature may be omitted and accidentals inserted where necessary. Include dynamics in every case. (Supply your own where none are given.) Use the principles discussed in the text to produce the type of coloring called for. You will achieve better results and save time in the long run if you sketch the layout of each chord at actual pitch before writing out the scored version.

A. For two flutes, two oboes, two clarinets, two bassoons, and two horns:
    1. F major, F in the soprano, brilliant.
    2. C major, G in the soprano, medium color.
    3. E♭ major, 1st inversion, E♭ in the soprano, brilliant.

B. For piccolo, two flutes, two oboes, English horn, two clarinets, bass clarinet, two bassoons, and contra bassoon:
    1. E major, G♯ in the soprano, very brilliant.
    2. B major, B in the soprano, medium color.
    3. D minor, A in the soprano, dark (omit piccolo).

C. For four horns, two or three trumpets (B♭ or C), three trombones, and tuba:
    1. D♭ major, F in the soprano, brilliant, *forte*.
    2. F minor, C in the soprano, medium color, *mezzo-piano*.
    3. F major, F in the soprano, rather dark, *pianissimo*.

D. For string orchestra:
The chord of G major, G in the soprano, arranged in four different ways to illustrate: (1) close spacing; (2) open spacing; (3) octave doublings (use either *divisi* writing or double stops or both here); (4) triple and quadruple stops (this chord is to be the short, vigorous type).

E. For orchestra consisting of two flutes, two oboes, two clarinets, two bassoons, four horns, two trumpets, three trombones, tuba, and strings:
    1. B minor, F♯ in the soprano, brilliant, *fortissimo*.
    2. F major, A in the soprano, medium color, *pianissimo*.

F. For orchestra consisting of piccolo, two flutes, two oboes, English horn, two clarinets, bass clarinet, two bassoons, contra bassoon, four horns, three trumpets, three trombones, tuba and strings:
    1. A♭ major, 2nd inversion, A♭ in the soprano, very brilliant, *fortissimo*.
    2. C minor, G in the soprano, medium color, *piano*.
    3. E minor, G in the soprano, very dark, *mezzo-forte*.

Chapter 11

PROBLEMS IN
TRANSCRIBING PIANO MUSIC

In scoring piano music for orchestra, the arranger often comes across certain features that are essentially pianistic rather than orchestral. In such cases, a literal transcription of the notes is likely to be awkward technically or ineffective or both; a better solution is to translate the effect wanted into orchestral terms.

In order to save space and to illustrate the points in question as simply as possible, the problem has been limited, in the body of this chapter, to arrangements for string orchestra. However, except for devices and patterns peculiar to string writing, the material can be applied just as well to scoring for other instruments. At the close of the chapter are some excerpts from transcriptions of piano pieces for an orchestra that includes woodwinds and horns in addition to strings.

First of all, if the original music is in a remote key—say, for example, more than four sharps or flats—it is sometimes a wise idea to choose a more comfortable and resonant key for the orchestral version (probably a half step higher if the piece is brilliant, a half step lower if it is not). This is particularly true in the case of school orchestras. Readers who possess pitch recognition are especially likely to protest at this point, for they will be painfully aware of a transposition from the original key in music they know. And one does not have to have absolute pitch to object that altering the key of a work can destroy its characteristic color and flavor. Admittedly, the business of tampering with the composer's choice of key is questionable from an esthetic standpoint. But the advantages to be gained from playing in a more grateful key are often impressive enough to justify transposition.

172

In choosing a key, it is well to remember that sharp keys are better than flat keys for the strings. Because of the tuning of stringed instruments the resonance is much greater in sharp keys, and the fingering is easier. This is only a general principle and does not mean that in string writing flat keys must be avoided like the plague.

Then there is the matter of the damper pedal, which figures almost constantly in piano music (this is the pedal on the right, which, when depressed, allows the tones to ring). Obviously, it must be changed (raised and lowered again) at each new harmony if a blur is not to result. In some piano music these changes are indicated by a small "Ped." beneath the staff, with an asterisk for a release. But in a great deal of music, no directions for pedaling are shown; in such cases, the arranger must ask himself whether pedal would be used, and if so, what the effect would be. (Usually when no pedal is to be used in a given passage, *senza pedale* is written in.)

Here is the beginning of a Chopin *Nocturne*:

Ex. 1

Nocturne, Op. 9, No. 1

Because of the sustaining effect of the pedal, the music will actually sound more or less like this:

Ex. 2

Therefore, certain notes must be written with longer values in the orchestral arrangement than in the original piano version. Not all notes sustained in the piano version need be sustained in the arrangement; it is simply a matter of aiming at the general effect of the original. Very often it is possible to divide up the figuration among the various string groups. That has been done in Example 3 (which has been transposed to a better key for the strings).

Ex. 3

Or it may be possible to have some instruments taking the harmony in block-chord fashion while others take the figuration:

Ex. 4

In both versions, the background has been marked a degree softer than the melody so that the latter will be sure to stand out.

It is impossible to transfer music from one medium to another intelligently without understanding its harmonic structure. For instance, unless we are aware that the second harmony in this Chopin excerpt involves a tonic pedal-point beneath the dominant 7th, we may very well make the mistake of using the tonic note among the upper harmonies as if it were an actual chord tone (with very bad results) or of putting some other note in the bass, thereby destroying the pedal-point effect. If the harmonic skeleton of the original piece is not perfectly clear at the outset, be sure to analyze before going further.

In transcribing, it is sometimes best to change the pattern of the pianistic figuration altogether (not the harmony, of course, and usually not the *rhythm* of the figuration). Let us suppose that this excerpt from the last movement of the Beethoven *Moonlight* Sonata is to be scored for strings:

Ex. 5

Sonata, Op. 27, No. 2

Beethoven

Although the "Alberti bass" figure in the left hand is *possible* for the cellos, it is not well suited to string technique, and the effect would be thin and a little ludicrous that way. Also, the spacing is poor for orchestral purposes; the third of the chord is too low, the small intervals are at the bottom, and there is a wide gap between the left-hand part and the melody in the right. It would be better to rearrange the chord and distribute the notes among the string groups, possibly like this:

Ex. 6

Example 7 shows another pianistic figure that is better rearranged.

Ex. 7

Here, again, the solution is to lift and respace. Of course there are other patterns of figuration that might profit from the same treatment.

Widely spread out arpeggio passages, such as the left-hand part in the next example, offer several problems in scoring.

Ex. 8

The White Peacock   Griffes

Piano   *ff*

Copyright renewal assigned, 1945, to G. Schirmer, Inc.

In the first place, they cover so much ground that they can seldom be handled comfortably by any one orchestral instrument except the harp. Because of this fact and because the harp is so eminently suited to arpeggios, it is often the best choice for such passages (usually with sustained harmony elsewhere in the orchestra). But not all orchestras include a harp, and the instrument would not be appropriate in all types of music. Nor does it have enough volume to supply the requisite sense of motion on its own in some heavily scored passages. Therefore, we had better be prepared to provide another solution if need be. In some cases it is possible to reduce the spread of the arpeggios to a point where they can be taken by one instrument (by one group in the case of the strings). Actual rearrangement of the figures will also be necessary as a rule. Sometimes it is best to divide the figuration between two or more instruments, again with whatever rearrangement will make for grateful parts and effective sonorities. Example 9 shows one way in which the left-hand part of Example 8 could be transcribed for strings. (We are assuming here that the violins are engaged in playing the upper parts of the original version and therefore cannot be called on to help out with the figured background.)

Ex. 9

Occasionally, passages of the sort we have just been discussing can be carried over almost literally into the orchestral version by simply dividing them among the strings. In such cases it is wise to let each string group end its figure *on* a beat instead of just before a beat and to overlap the last note played by each group with the first note of the group that follows it. These points are illustrated in Example 10, which shows first the left-hand part of a piano piece and then a possible arrangement of it for strings.

Ex. 10

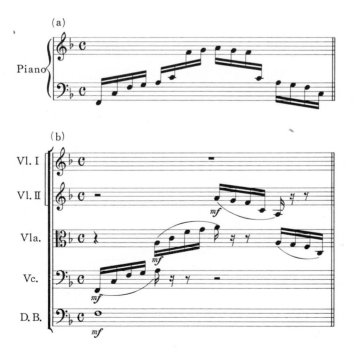

Sustained harmony in other instruments usually accompanies this sort of arrangement.

In piano music, melody and accompaniment are often assigned to the same hand, and it is important to distinguish one from the other in scoring. Example 11 illustrates this point.

Ex. 11

Here it is obvious that the right-hand part actually includes two distinct musical ideas: a melody on top (the first, third, and fifth eighth-notes in each measure) and a repeated-note figure below. This in spite of the fact that the notation gives the appearance of a single melodic line. In scoring the example, then, we would break up this line into its component parts and allot these to separate instruments. One possible version is given here:

Ex. 12

Chords like the one in Example 13 can be dramatic and effective on the piano.

Ex. 13

The same thing in the orchestra would sound poor; the bottom notes are much too thickly spaced for that low register, and the gap in the middle needs to be filled in. Something like Example 14 might be a satisfactory solution in the strings.

Ex. 14

Triple and quadruple stops are used here for greater fullness and volume. Notice the use of open strings and of the interlocking principle.

It sometimes happens that piano music contains three-note chords which must be divided, in the orchestral arrangement, between second violins and violas. The best solution in that case is to give two notes to the second violins and one to the violas (which are fewer in number). The two notes in the second violins can be taken *divisi* or, if convenient, as a double stop; but this latter method should not be called for with inexperienced players or in a quick succession of chords where double stops would be awkward. Four-note chords can be taken by double stops in both second violins and violas or by *divisi* parts in each.

Broken octaves are especially characteristic of piano music of the Beethoven period. (See Ex. 15.)

Ex. 15

Sonata, Op. 22

180

These are best rendered, in the strings, by the sort of arrangement found in Example 16.

Ex. 16

The same applies to broken 6ths and other intervals (although broken 3rds are practical on most orchestral instruments).

In piano music of the Romantic period (especially in song accompaniments) this sort of tremolo sometimes appears:

Ex. 17

The obvious solution in the orchestra is a string tremolo. (See Ex. 18).

Ex. 18

Although a bowed tremolo has been used here and is ordinarily preferable for such passages, a fingered tremolo might be employed if a softer, more placid effect were called for.

In piano music, chords are sometimes written with a wavy line at the left to indicate that they are to be arpeggiated or broken slightly, or the arpeggiation may be written out in small notes. At other times, the chord is broken into two parts, the lower part being played as a "grace note" to the upper. Such devices may be introduced for the sake of artistic effect or out of sheer pianistic necessity, if the chords involve stretches that are too wide to be played at once. In any case, the arpeggiated or broken effect is often omitted altogether in transcribing such passages for orchestra. In case it is felt to be such an integral part of the music that it should not be changed, it may be given to the harp if that is stylistically appropriate, or to strings playing either bowed broken chords (for a vigorous passage) or pizzicato chords in arpeggiated fashion. (Much use is made of the latter effect in Examples 19 and 20 [a]).

Staccato notes in the piano version may be given to strings playing *pizzicato* or *spiccato* or *group staccato*, depending on the degree of shortness required and on the dynamics and tempo. Remember, however, that *pizzicato* is not practical in very fast passages.

Una corda, meaning literally "one string" in Italian, is the standard direction, in piano music, for using the soft pedal (the one on the left). In the orchestra, muted strings are often an effective parallel for the *una corda* sound on the piano. But there are other times when the muted effect would seem out of place, and in such cases very soft dynamic markings in the orchestral parts must suffice.

The author does not want to convey the impression that every piece of piano music can be successfully transcribed for strings—or for orchestra. A good many works are so purely pianistic in conception that it would be absurd to attempt an orchestral version of them. Nevertheless, the problems discussed here are likely to come up from time to time, if only because at least part of the work in orchestration courses normally consists in arranging piano music.

In order to demonstrate the application of some of the principles just discussed to scoring that involves other instruments in addition to strings, some excerpts from music written originally for the piano and later transcribed for orchestra by the composer are shown next. Points to observe include the following: ways of rendering rolled chords; ways of rendering left-hand arpeggios; the treatment of staccato notes; the use of sustained notes (where none are included in the original) to approximate the effect of the pedal; the introduction of octave doublings; the addition of voices for greater fullness. The excerpts from the Ravel *Pavane* consist of three different versions of the same theme that occur in the course of the piece. The *cors simples en sol* are two natural horns in G, sounding a 4th lower than written. Ravel presumably wanted their quality as opposed to the "modern" sound of the valve horn. The principle behind the enharmonic notion in the harp part (C♭ for B♮) will be explained in Chapter 15. The original piano versions are included here only for purposes of comparison and are not meant to be played in the orchestral versions. These last examples give a preview of some possibilities in scoring for woodwinds, horns and strings—the subject of the next chapter.

Ex. 19

Pavane pour une infante défunte

Ravel

184

Ex. 20

Le Tombeau de Couperin
(a) *Forlane*

(b) *Menuet*

SUGGESTED ASSIGNMENTS

The following are suitable as exercises in transcribing pianistic music for strings (or for other combinations). Bowing should be included in all cases. Respacing, filling of gaps, rearrangement of figuration, etc., are to be introduced where necessary.

1. Beethoven, Sonata, Op. 2, No. 3, 1st movt., meas. 1–16.
2. Beethoven, Sonata, Op. 10, No. 3, 1st movt., meas. 1–30.
3. Beethoven, Sonata, Op. 22, 1st movt., meas. 1–20.
4. Mozart, Sonata in B♭ major, K. 333 (excerpts).
5. Chopin, Nocturne, Op 9, No. 2 (E♭ major), meas. 1–4.
6. Chopin, Nocturne, Op. 27, No. 2 (D♭ major), meas. 1–5.
7. Grieg, Sonata in E minor (excerpts).
8. Brahms, Intermezzo, Op. 117, No. 2, beginning.
9. Liszt, Etude in D♭ major (*Un Sospiro*), beginning.
10. Any of the works in the "Suggested Listening" list that follows. Much can be learned by making an orchestral arrangement of one of these from the piano score and comparing it with the published orchestral arrangement. In that case, the student should of course not listen to a recording of the published arrangement until he has completed his own scoring. Since most of these works suggest the use of the complete orchestra, projects in scoring them should ordinarily be delayed until Chapters 12 through 16 have been covered.

SUGGESTED LISTENING

The following are works which were written originally for piano and which have been arranged for orchestra, either by their composers or by other skilled orchestrators:

Bach, many works transcribed by Sir Edward Elgar, Sir Henry Wood, Leopold Stokowski, Alexandre Tansman, Schönberg, etc.
Brahms, *Variations on a Theme by Haydn* (issued first in a version for two pianos).
Grieg, *Aus Holbergs Zeit.*
Dvořák, *Slavonic Dances.*
Mussorgsky, *Pictures from an Exhibition* (orchestrated by Ravel and Sir Henry Wood among others).
Debussy, *Petite Suite.*
Ravel, *Pavane pour une Infante Défunte; Alborado del Gracioso; Mother Goose* Suite; *Le Tombeau de Couperin.*
Albéniz, *Iberia; Catalonia.*
Griffes, *The White Peacock.*
Bartók, *Fifteen Hungarian Peasant Songs.*

Chapter 12

SCORING FOR WOODWINDS, HORNS, AND STRINGS

In an earlier chapter we took up the arranging of chords for the various sections and for orchestra. There we made a practice of using all the instruments of a section in each chord, in order to learn how to calculate balance and blend in a complete group. In this chapter, a different problem is involved, one requiring much more taste and imagination and one that represents the usual situation in practical orchestration: we are given some music to score for an orchestra of a particular size, and we must choose the instruments that seem appropriate to the musical ideas. When an instrument is not actually needed in the scoring, it will simply be given a rest; even whole sections will rest from time to time. (In the full orchestra the brass section is apt to rest a good deal of the time; woodwinds, both individually and as a section, normally rest a bit more than strings.)

As we look over the music to be scored with an eye to the possible ways in which it could be orchestrated, there are certain questions that naturally suggest themselves:

What is the character of the passage in question—lyric and *espressivo*, or airy and fanciful, or sharply rhythmic, or dirgelike, or any one of the many other possibilities?

Does the passage suggest a relatively light or heavy scoring? Does it call for a simple texture or should it be expanded by means of octave doublings?

What coloring seems appropriate—brilliant or somber, warm or cool?

How does the passage relate to what has gone before and what is to come after it? (In other words, we must consider the form of the piece as a whole.)

What instruments are best fitted to play the respective parts from the standpoint of (1) range and (2) technical abilities?

What *style* of scoring is appropriate, considering the period and composer involved?

Is the music chordal, or homophonic, or polyphonic, or a combination?

As for the last question, we have already had some experience in scoring a chordal texture, and the arranging of polyphonic music for full orchestra is discussed in Chapter 16. But this is a good point at which to consider the orchestration of homophonic music; that is, music that consists of a prominent melodic line against a subordinate harmonic background.

Suppose, for instance, that we wished to transcribe this excerpt from a Brahms piano piece for strings, woodwinds in pairs, and four horns:

Ex. 1

Intermezzo, Op. 119, No. 2 (middle section)

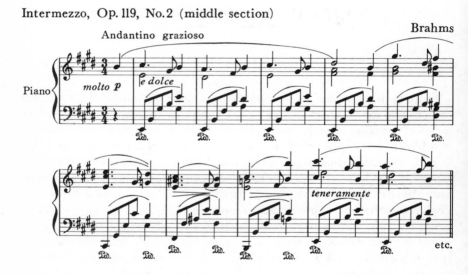

Inasmuch as we cannot score this or any other music well without understanding its structure, we had better take time for harmonic analysis before going on to the orchestration. The harmony in the first measure proves to be tonic (E major) with a nonharmonic C♯ on the first beat in the right hand. (The important thing here is that the C♯ must not be included in the harmony parts; the "added 6th" effect would hardly be appropriate in Brahms!) Because of the sustaining effect of the pedal, the notes in the left hand which are written as eighths actually sound through the measure. The second measure involves a V⁷ sound above a tonic pedal point. (The E in the bass has the effect of a pedal point since it is held through the bar by the pedal.) We are not going to pursue the harmonic analysis any further here, since the examples that follow involve only the first two bars and bars 9 and 10, which have the same harmonic pattern as the first two. Looking at the music from the standpoint of form, we discover that the eight-measure melody is repeated in octaves beginning with the up-beat to the ninth bar. (Not all of this repetition is shown here.)

To make use of some of these observations in planning our scoring, we must, first of all, find some way of approximating the sustained effect of the piano version in the orchestra. A good solution is to add a B and G♯ on the first beat of the first measure (below the E in the treble staff) which will hold through the measure and then continue on harmony notes in the measures that follow. This has the added advantage of filling in the large gap that occurs at the beginning of each measure. Also, we shall want to hold the E in the bass, and it would even be possible to hold the B above it as well. The eighth-note arpeggios could be given entirely to cellos or divided between cellos and violas as in Example 2(b), or even given to bassoons as in Example 3(d), although that plan seems a little less desirable. If a harp were included, it might take these arpeggio figures.

In music of this sort it seems appropriate to let the melody stand out clearly from the background, and we can best achieve that effect by giving the melody to one color, the background to another. In this case, the simplicity and delicacy of the first eight bars suggest a relatively light scoring, possibly a solo woodwind against soft strings. Flute, though weak in this register, would come through if the background were kept light, and it would have a certain quiet charm. Oboe (in its most characteristic register) would be more pungent and penetrating. Clarinet would also be possible—a bit more warm and romantic in quality than the other woodwinds. Incidentally, clarinet in A is preferable to B♭ clarinet here, since the latter would have to be written with a key signature of six sharps (or, enharmonically, six flats) while clarinet in A involves a signature of one sharp. Violins on the melody would be expressive and effective; the harmonic background in that case might be given to horns rather than strings, in order to let the melody stand out more sharply, or it could still be allotted to strings. (Muting of the string background would produce a slightly different color from the melody.) By taking the melody down an octave we could give it to the cellos or to one solo cello in a particularly expressive register of the instrument. If that is done, some rearrangement of the harmony parts is necessary. This last scoring is used in version 2(d).

The second eight measures seem to demand a fresh color on the melody as well as a little more weight. If a solo woodwind has been used in the first version, the melody might well be given to strings in octaves here, or to strings and woodwinds doubled in octaves. If strings took the melody in the first eight bars, an octave doubling of woodwinds would give the greatest contrast in the second eight, or the combination of strings and woodwinds in octaves would be effective. Even two-octave doublings could be used, as in versions (b), (c), and (d) of Example 3. There are additional harmony parts in the second eight bars.

Examples 2 and 3 show some of the possibilities in scoring the first eight bars and the second eight bars, respectively. For reasons of space, only the first measure or two of each version is given here.

SOME POSSIBILITIES IN SCORING THE FIRST EIGHT MEASURES OF THE BRAHMS EXAMPLE

Ex. 2

SOME POSSIBILITIES IN SCORING THE SECOND EIGHT MEASURES OF THE BRAHMS EXAMPLE

Ex. 3

* Horn in bass clef to sound a 5th lower.

DOUBLINGS IN THE WOODWINDS

It is very common, in arranging, to give a melodic line to two or more different woodwinds in unison. We did not happen to make use of that device in the first eight measures of the Brahms example, but some woodwind doublings (both unison and octave) were involved in the scorings of the second eight measures. The list that follows shows some of the more usual combinations.

Unison Doublings in the Woodwinds	*Comments*
Flute and Oboe	Oboe predominates but is "softened" (in quality) by flute
Flute and Clarinet	Warm, round tone; not strong in the octave above middle C
Oboe and Clarinet	Mixes oboe's tang with clarinet's mellowness
Clarinet and Bassoon	Rich; somber if clarinet is low
Flute, Oboe, Clarinet	Thoroughly mixed color

Octave Doublings in the Woodwinds	*Comments*
{ Flute (upper 8ve) Oboe (lower 8ve)	Good; frequent
{ Flute Clarinet	Good; frequent
{ Oboe Clarinet	Good; frequent
{ Clarinet Oboe (or English Horn)	Infrequent with oboe; English horn usually better because its range extends lower
{ Clarinet Bassoon	Very dark if instruments are in their lower register
{ Flute and Oboe Clarinet and Bassoon	May take bassoon uncomfortably high; English horn may substitute for bassoon
{ 2 Fl., 2 Ob., 1 Clar. 1 Clar., 2 Bns. (and/or Eng. Horn)	Strong; good composite color; better balance with English horn included

Two-Octave Doublings in the Woodwinds	*Comments*
{ Flute Oboe Clarinet	Effective
{ Flute Oboe Bassoon	Fairly frequent in scores of the Classical period (also with violins in the middle)
{ Flute Clarinet Bassoon	Effective
{ Flute .... (2 8ves Bassoon apart)	Good. Omission of the middle octave makes for a particular effect
{ Flute .... (2 8ves Clarinet apart)	Rare; unusual coloring; uses bright register of flute with dark register of clarinet

Three-octave doublings are possible with the addition of piccolo at the top, or bass clarinet or contra bassoon at the bottom; even four-octave doublings are occasionally seen.

There is not room here for detailed comment on the more rarely used doublings, such as flute and bassoon in unison, flutes an octave below oboes, low flutes with piccolo two octaves higher, clarinets two octaves apart, and so on. These combinations produce unusual and intriguing colors, but one must have a very intimate knowledge of the orchestra to use them successfully.

DOUBLINGS BETWEEN WOODWINDS AND STRINGS

In unison doublings of woodwinds and strings, the woodwind tone tends to be overshadowed by that of the strings. Flute chiefly adds body, although not much. Oboe makes the string tone a bit more nasal and may even give it a pinched quality if the number of strings is small. English horn, on the other hand, can be combined with violas to produce an unusually poignant and attractive tone. (Remember, for example, the "love theme" in Tchaikovsky's *Romeo and Juliet*.) Clarinet lends a certain warmth and "roundness" to string timbre, plus a dark richness in its lower register. Bassoons are constantly associated with cellos or violas for the sake of added body. The unison combination of horn and cello in the tenor register gives an expressive, noble sound that is well suited to slower, *cantabile* melodies.

Certain doublings in which a woodwind (or pair of woodwinds) plays one octave and strings another are effective and allow the woodwind tone to be heard more clearly than it is in unison doublings. Flute above violins is good; clarinet or oboe above violins less satisfactory. But clarinets or bassoons can play an octave *below* violins with good effect. The combination of woodwinds in octaves plus strings in octaves is a powerful and useful one.

In closing these remarks on doubling, it might be well to issue a small word of warning: remember that too constant use of mixed or composite colors becomes uninteresting and tends to make a score sound opaque and nondescript. Pure colors are needed for sparkle and transparency.

THE USE OF CONTRASTING SECTIONS

In order to deal with another aspect of scoring, let us turn to a small excerpt from the second movement of Beethoven's "Moonlight" Sonata (Ex. 4).

Ex. 4

Sonata, Op. 27, No. 2 (second movement)

Beethoven

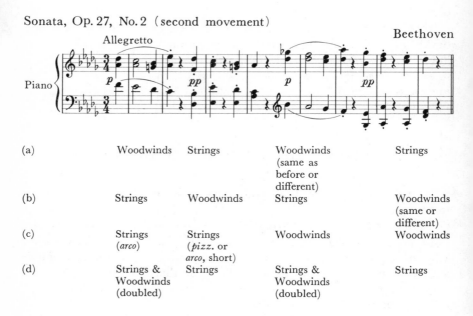

(a)		Woodwinds	Strings	Woodwinds (same as before or different)		Strings
(b)		Strings	Woodwinds	Strings		Woodwinds (same or different)
(c)		Strings (*arco*)	Strings (*pizz.* or *arco*, short)	Woodwinds		Woodwinds
(d)		Strings & Woodwinds (doubled)	Strings	Strings & Woodwinds (doubled)		Strings

Beneath the music are four possible layouts, the sections being listed below the measures they would play. This passage involves two four-measure phrases, each one consisting of two segments. We can accentuate the strong antiphonal feeling between the segments of each phrase by using contrasting colors every two measures, as in (a), (b), and (d); or we can use one color on the first four measures, another on the second four, stressing the antiphonal feeling between the two phrases, as in (c). Of course this excerpt is an extreme case; few pieces of music would lend themselves to so many contrasts of color within a few measures. It is quite possible to overuse the device of contrasted sections, with a resulting "patchy" quality in the scoring. In fact, one of the most common failings of beginning orchestrators is that they tend to think in terms of separate sections and to avoid the possibilities for combining instruments of different sections.

In the light of what was said earlier about avoiding remote keys, transposition to D major or C major might seem to be in order in the Beethoven excerpt. However, the original key has been retained here, for several reasons: the music demands no great resonance and presents no technical problems; most important of all, transposition to another key would completely destroy the striking parallel relationship between the somber C♯ minor of the famous first movement and the bright D♭ major of the second (it is assumed that both movements are being scored and that the original key is being retained in the first).

Of course the layouts shown beneath the excerpt do not exhaust the ways in which it could be scored. They are merely a few possibilities that demonstrate the technique of contrasted sections.

This is the way version 4(a) might look, written out in actual score:

Ex. 5

The examples that follow illustrate scoring for woodwinds, horns and strings in music of several different periods, styles and textures. (The instrumentation of the works quoted in Examples 6, 8, and 9 includes two trumpets as well, but these do not play during the passages shown here.) The examples should be studied for doublings, balance, the distribution of the various musical ideas, the use of pure color versus composite color, and stylistic characteristics, among other things. Of course they represent only a few of the endless possibilities in scoring for this combination of instruments. Clarinets are among the woodwinds used in the works quoted in Examples 6 and 8, although they do not happen to figure in the excerpts shown. They are not included in the instrumentation of Example 7, however.

Ex. 6

Overture to *The Marriage of Figaro*

Mozart

Ex. 7

Fifth Symphony (B♭ major, D. 485)

Menuetto   Allegro molto

Schubert

Ex. 8

Variations on a Theme of Haydn. Var. III

Con moto

Brahms

Note: This score departs from the usual practice in using slurs to indicate phrasing rather than bowing, in the string parts.

Ex. 9

(a) *Prelude to the Afternoon of a Faun*

200

Permission for reprint granted by Editions Jean-Jobert of Paris, France, Copyright Owners; Elkan-Vogel Co., Inc. of Philadelphia, Pa., Sole Agents in the United States.

Ex. 10

Classical Symphony, III. Gavotta

Prokofieff

* The clarinets are written here at actual pitch.

Ex. 11

Sinfonietta, III. Tarantella

SUGGESTED ASSIGNMENTS

A. Be able to comment on:

1. considerations in scoring music that involves a prominent melodic line against a subordinate background.
2. possibilities in contrasting one section of the orchestra with another.
3. the effect of doubling various woodwinds with each other or with strings, either in unison or at the octave.

B. The following are suitable as exercises in scoring for woodwinds, horns and strings:

1. Beethoven, Sonata, Op. 10, No. 2, 1st movt.
2. Beethoven, Sonata, Op 10, No. 3, 2nd movt.
3. Beethoven, Sonata, Op. 14, No. 1, 2nd movt., meas. 1–32.
4. Beethoven, Sonata, Op. 90, 1st movt., meas. 1–24.
5. Schumann, "Little Romance" from *Album for the Young.*
6. Schumann, "Echoes from the Theater" from *Album for the Young.*
7. Schubert, Sonata, Op. 143, 1st. movt.
8. Schubert, Sonata, Op. 147, 3rd movt.
9. Chopin, Prelude in A major, Op. 28, No. 7.
10. Chopin, Nocturne in F minor, Op. 55, No. 1. Score the first two measures in five different ways. Make some use of octave doublings.
11. Tchaikovsky, "Polka" from *Album for the Young.* Score for one flute. one oboe, one clarinet, one bassoon, one horn if desired, and strings.
12. Tchaikovsky, "At Church" from *Album for the Young.*
13. Tchaikovsky, "Morning Prayer" from *Album for the Young.*
14. Brahms, "Es ist ein Ros' Entsprungen" from *Eleven Chorale Preludes for the Organ,* Op. 122.
15. Grieg, Nocturne in C major.
16. Scriabin, Etude in C♯ minor, Op. 2, No. 1.
17. Wolf, "Verborgenheit" (song).
18. Debussy, *The Girl with the Flaxen Hair* (No. 8 in first book of Preludes).
19. MacDowell, "A Deserted Farm" from *Woodland Sketches.*
20. Bartók, No. 12 from *Fifteen Hungarian Peasant Songs.*
21. Kabalevsky, Sonatina, Op. 13, No. 1, 1st movt.
22. Kennan, Prelude I from Three Preludes.
23. Rochberg, Bagatelle VIII from *Twelve Bagatelles.*

C. The following suggest the use of a harp in addition to woodwinds, horns and strings. It is therefore suggested that they not be assigned until after Chapter 14 has been studied.

1. Fauré, *Pavane.*
2. Debussy, "Clair de Lune" from *Suite Bergamasque.*
3. Palmgren, *May Night.*
4. Ravel, Minuet from Sonatine.
5. Ravel, *Pavane pour une Infante Défunte* (the completed scoring may be compared with Ravel's).
6. Ravel, *Le Tombeau de Couperin* (the completed scoring may be compared with Ravel's).

SUGGESTED LISTENING

Scoring for Woodwinds, Horns and Strings

Haydn, Symphonies.[1]

Mozart Symphonies[1]; Divertimenti; Overture to *The Marriage of Figaro*.[1]

Beethoven, Symphonies[1] (the Fifth, Sixth, and Ninth also include trombones).

Mendelssohn, *Midsummer Night's Dream* music (particularly the *Intermezzo* and *Nocturne*); Symphonies No. 3 and 4[1]; *Fingal's Cave* Overture.[1]

Schumann, Second Symphony, 3rd movt.[1] (good example of different scorings of the same theme).

Brahms, Serenades; *Variations on a Theme of Haydn*.[1]

Schubert, Fifth Symphony.

Wagner, *Siegfried Idyll*.[1]

Debussy, *Prelude to The Afternoon of a Faun*; *Nocturnes*: I. *Nuages*; *Rondes de Printemps*.

Ravel, *Mother Goose* Suite; *Pavane pour une Infante Défunte*; *Le Tombeau de Couperin*.[1]

Prokofieff, *Classical Symphony*.[1]

Delius, *On Hearing the First Cuckoo in Spring*; *Summer Night on the River*.

Britten, Sinfonietta.

---

[1] These scores (or some of them, in the case of the Haydn and Mozart Symphonies) also include parts for trumpets. However, since in these cases the trumpets play only a small portion of the time, the works serve for the most part as examples of scoring for strings, woodwinds, and horns. The same is true, to a lesser extent, even of works scored for a larger instrumentation. That is, even when a full brass section is included, it will not play constantly by any means, and there will therefore be abundant instances of scoring that involves only woodwinds, horns, and strings.

Chapter 13

THE PERCUSSION:
INSTRUMENTS OF
DEFINITE PITCH

THE TIMPANI (OR KETTLEDRUMS)

Italian: Timpani   *French:* Timbales   *German:* Pauken

Ex. 1

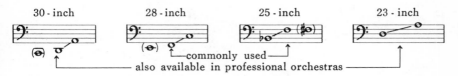

The spelling "tympani" (the plural of the Latin *tympanum*) is also widely used, but "timpani" (the plural of the Italian *timpano*) is preferred inasmuch as Italian rather than Latin forms are used for most of the other instruments.

Until relatively recently, timpani were of the hand-tuned variety; changes in pitch were made by tightening or relaxing screws around the edge of the "head," the piece of calfskin stretched across the top of the drum. Considerable time (a minimum of about eight measures in a moderate 4/4) was required for each change. During the Classical period the two timpani normally used were tuned in advance to the tonic and dominant notes of the home key and not altered in the course of the work or movement, although changes between movements of symphonies were sometimes called for. Later on, composers began to require changes in the midst of a composition or movement and to use three timpani instead of two.

Today, pedal timpani have completely replaced the hand-tuned kind. Changes in pitch are made by means of a foot pedal that controls the degree of tension in the head, which is now often made of plastic rather than calf-skin. The motion of the foot can be made quickly, and many players are able to arrive at the new pitch with considerable accuracy simply by estimating the proper angle of the pedal. Nevertheless, it is safer to allow a few measures (at least four in a moderate 4/4) for each change, in order that there will be time to test the new pitch softly.

Tuning gauges, which are included on some timpani, give the player a mechanical means of arriving at pitches quickly with a high degree of accuracy. They are of particular value in such passages as the one shown in Example 13 (g). It should be pointed out, though, that that passage is an exceptional one in its demands for rapid changes; such parts are rare and should be written only with professional timpanists in mind.

As indicated in Example 1, professional orchestras today have all four sizes of the timpani shown there. School orchestras normally have at least two timpani (the 28-inch and the 25-inch sizes) and may have one or both of the other sizes as well. However, in writing for such groups it is obviously safest to plan the timpani part in such a way that it will be playable on two

Studio Gilmore, Austin, Texas

Pedal Timpani

drums and will not go below $\begin{array}{c}\text{𝄢}\\\text{𝅝}\end{array}$ or above $\begin{array}{c}\text{𝄢 ♯𝅝}\end{array}$. In scores

designed for professional or semi-professional orchestras, three timpani are frequently called for. These are most often the two basic sizes plus either the 23-inch or the 30-inch drum, though a second 25-inch or a second 28-inch drum may be used to make up the three if that happens to be convenient and appropriate to the pitches required.

Normally there is one player for all the timpani, no matter what their number. If, as happens very infrequently, the part is designed to be performed by more than one player, that must be specially indicated. (See, for example, the *Fantastic Symphony* of Berlioz or Stravinsky's *The Rite of Spring*.)

Timpani are notated in bass clef at actual pitch. The tuning is shown at the beginning of the composition in either of the ways illustrated in Example 2.

Ex. 2

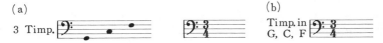

(a)   (b)

3 Timp.   Timp. in
G, C, F

Ordinarily, the part is written without key signature, accidentals being added wherever necessary. In older scores even the accidentals are sometimes omitted, once the tuning of each drum has been shown. Another obsolete custom occasionally found in older scores is that of using the notes C and G to indicate the tonic and dominant notes, respectively, in keys other than C. In that case the actual tuning of the drums was shown at the beginning of the part.

As a general rule, timpani should be used only on notes that fit in as members of the harmony. The chord member most frequently allotted to them is the bass, but they may also take any other harmony note with good effect. For example, let us suppose that we have started a piece with three timpani tuned to G, C, and F as in the illustration above. At a certain point in the music we have a C major triad and want to include a timpani note or roll. C would be the most natural choice; but G would also fit in. In an F major triad either F or C could be used, with the tuning at hand, whereas in a G major triad G would be the only possibility. If a diminished 7th sound on G♯ (G♯, B, D, F) were involved, we would probably use the F already "set" on the top drum rather than tune the bottom drum up to G♯.

Let us imagine, now, that we have come to a G♭ major triad at a point where timpani are needed. With the present tunings, no one of the three drums is able to supply a tone that fits into the harmony. Assuming that there is time for a change before this passage, any one of five different retunings would give us a chord tone: (1) G down to G♭; (2) C up to D♭; (3) C down to B♭; (4) F down to D♭; or (5) F up to G♭. Any such change must be indicated in the part, preferably at the first rest where the player could make the change, so that he will have as much time as possible for the retuning operation. If the first of the five possible changes were chosen, we would write in the part "Change G to G♭." Scores using Italian terms throughout would say "G muta in G♭," the French version would be "Changez Sol en Sol♭," and in German the same direction would be "G nach Ges umstimmen." More than one change may be called for, provided there is sufficient time. It should now be obvious that in writing for timpani one cannot simply put down any notes desired and let the player worry about how to get them. It is necessary to score with a specific number of timpani in mind and to plan each note for a particular timpano; problems of retuning must be kept in mind constantly.

Occasionally it is possible to "get by" with timpani notes foreign to the harmony. These cases usually involve a chord of such short duration that the ear scarcely has time to be aware of the foreign timpani note before the next chord is heard. In a passage where the harmony is sustained, any deviation from a chord tone would be apparent. In cases where it is impossible to prepare the required note on the timpani in time and a foreign note is unacceptable, one solution is to use the bass drum instead, since its pitch is indeterminate. The effect, of course, is not the same.

Single notes, rhythmic figures, and rolls are all effective on timpani. The roll may be written in either of these ways:

Ex. 3

(As with bowed tremolos in string writing, three lines through a stem ordinarily signify an unmeasured roll, whereas two mean measured sixteenths and one means eighths.) However, the trill sign is preferable for an unmeasured roll, because the other type of notation may be confused with an actual measured thirty-second note roll (particularly in slow tempos). Where several measures of roll are involved, it is safest to connect the notes with a tie to avoid any possibility that the player may think a fresh attack is wanted on each note:

Ex. 4

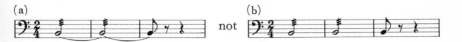

Or, if the trill sign is used, write as in Example 5(a).

Ex. 5

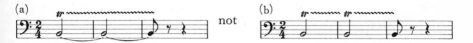

With the last notation shown, the player would almost certainly make a new attack on each note. Notice that in these illustrations the roll is carried over so as to end on the beat. This is a frequent practice in percussion writing, the reason being that it is difficult to end a roll neatly on the last fraction of a beat. However, there are cases in which it would be inappropriate to carry the roll over into the next beat, and skilled players are able to cope with such spots. If a separately articulated stroke is wanted at the end of a roll, then the tie into the last note is omitted and the wavy line is stopped short of the last note:

Ex. 6

Rolls (measured or unmeasured) on two different timpani are also a possibility:

Ex. 7

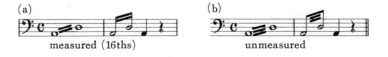

The importance of careful and detailed dynamic markings in percussion writing cannot be overstressed. It is not enough to write:

Ex. 8

The height of the crescendo here might be anything from *p* to *fff*, as far as the player can tell from the part. To give complete directions we would have to write:

Ex. 9

In long rolls it is not too much to indicate dynamics along the way:

Ex. 10

Probably the most frequent and obvious use of the timpani is that of backing up the rest of the orchestra in rhythmic figures. (It was conventional, in the Classical period, to give the timpani and the trumpets the same rhythmic figure.) At other times they may play a separate rhythm of their own. They are also excellent for reinforcing crescendos and for providing excitement or support in climaxes by means of rolls. Extended solos are seldom given to them, though isolated notes and groups of two or three notes played solo are frequent and highly effective. (See certain of the excerpts in Ex. 13. See also Ex. 4 [k] in Chapter 14.) Other works containing notable timpani solos are: Hanson, Third Symphony; Harris, Third Symphony (in the fugue); Strauss, *Burleska* for piano and orchestra; Shostakovitch, First Symphony (last movement). It is a mistake to think of the timpani as being valuable only for loud passages. Although they can supply a tremendous volume of sound, they are equally telling and dramatic in soft passages; in fact, their tone can be reduced to a barely audible pulsation.

One word of warning might be added: because their tone quality is very different from that of other instruments, they must not be expected to fill in a chord tone by themselves—except that they can effectively play pedal points which are not doubled elsewhere in the orchestra.

Several special effects are possible on the timpani. One involves the use of wooden sticks, in place of the usual soft felt-headed sticks (Italian: *bacchette di legno;* French: *baguettes en bois;* German: *mit Holzschlägeln*). Usually, the object is to produce a harder, more sharply percussive quality, though soft effects are also possible, as, for example, the soft roll with snare drum sticks in Elgar's *Enigma Variations*. The indication for soft sticks is not normally included unless the player has previously been using hard sticks (Italian: *bacchette di spugna;* French: *baguettes d'éponge* or *baguettes molles;* German: *mit Schwammschlägeln*). Still different types of tone result from using sticks with Spanish felt heads or sticks with large or small heads. Another device calls for the use of both sticks at once on a drum; it is indicated by double stems. The result is thicker and weightier than the normal sound.

Ex. 11

Revised edition copyright 1943. By permission of the copyright owner, Boosey & Hawkes, Inc.

It is also possible to play on two different timpani at the same time, as in this example:

Ex. 12

Berlioz even wrote three-note and four-note chords for timpani in the *Fantastic Symphony*, but of course these require two players. A particular tone quality can be achieved by striking the drum in the center instead of near the edge. (See Gershwin's *An American in Paris*.) Timpani may be muffled (or "muted") by placing a cloth about two inches square on the head of the drum near the edge. The Italian direction is *timpani coperti*. A special effect, achieved by changing the pedal while the drum is sounding, is the glissando. As in string writing, the indication is a line between the notes (both of which must be within the range of one timpano, of course). Example 13(f) involves repeated use of the glissando device.

EXAMPLES

Ex. 13

(a) Ninth Symphony

(b) Symphony in E minor *(New World)*

(c) *Don Juan*

(d) First Symphony

(e) Third Symphony

Harris

(f) *Music for String Instruments, Percussion and Celesta*

Bartók

(g) Concerto for Orchestra

Bartók

THE ROTO TOM[1]

Ex. 14

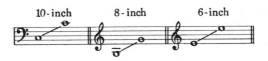

This instrument, introduced in 1968, is a small tom-tom that can be tuned to specific pitches by rotating the drum on a base to which it is attached, thereby tightening or relaxing the tension of the drumhead. It is made in three sizes, which produce the respective ranges shown above.

[1] Made by Remo, Inc., Los Angeles, California.

Normally, a mechanical device prevents each drum from rotating beyond the point at which the top note shown for each range will be produced. If that device is removed, each drum is capable of extending its upward range by an octave or more, but these higher tones are of a different quality —extremely dry and lacking in resonance. The Roto Tom may be played with wooden snare drum sticks, with soft marimba mallets, with yarn-covered xylophone mallets, with felt mallets, with the hands, or with wire brushes.

THE XYLOPHONE

Italian: Silofono (or Xilofono)   *French:* Xylophone   *German:* Xylophon (Old name: Strohfiedel)

Ex. 15

Sounding an 8ve higher.

The xylophone consists of a set of wooden bars of varying lengths, arranged in the same pattern as the notes on the piano, sometimes with a tuned resonator beneath each bar. It is played with hard mallets, normally two, although three or four may be used to play chords. Forsyth gives a good idea of the tone of the instrument when he speaks of its "hard dry clatter." The notes are necessarily short and crisp, there being no way of sustaining them except by means of a roll. The xylophone is therefore generally unsuited to music of a lyric or *espressivo* nature, but it can perform rapid scales, arpeggios, repeated notes, glissandos, and many other figures with surprising ease. (Incidentally, passages entirely on the "white" keys are more difficult than those involving both black and white keys.) In certain music it manages to give a saucy, mocking quality; at other times it may simply add a brittle edge to a melodic line or point up certain notes. (See Debussy's *Ibéria*, the section entitled *Les parfums de la nuit*, for an example of this last use. An excerpt from that section is given in Ex. 22 of Chapter 16.)

Xylophones are built in various sizes; consequently it is impossible to give one range that will apply to all of them. Some do not include the notes shown in parentheses, and still others have an even shorter compass at the bottom. Notation is on a single staff, in treble clef, one octave lower than the sounds desired. Many books on orchestration recommend writing the xylophone part at actual pitch, and that system has been much used. But it was based on the belief that the instrument's range extended only up to

whereas the top sound on all xylophones is actually c⁵, an octave higher than the pitch just shown. In view of this fact, the system of notation recommended here is a much more sensible one, since it avoids the use of an unreasonable number of ledger lines in high passages.

Xylophone parts should be written with a key signature, just as other parts are.

Mallets of different degrees of hardness will produce correspondingly different gradations of intensity in attack; the range of materials is from medium-hard rubber to hard rubber to plastic.

EXAMPLES

Ex. 16

(a) *Petrouchka*

(b) *Song of the Nightingale (Chinese Court Festival)*

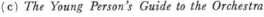

Permission for reprint granted by Elkan-Vogel Co., Inc., Philadelphia, Penna., copyright owners.

(c) *The Young Person's Guide to the Orchestra*

Copyright, 1947, in the U.S.A. by Hawkes & Son (London) Ltd. By permission of the copyright owner, Boosey & Hawkes, Inc.

THE MARIMBA

Ex. 17

The marimba resembles the xylophone in appearance, but its tone is more mellow and lacks the xylophone's spicy brittleness. Rarely used in the orchestra, it must be given a somewhat exposed part if it is to come through, for it is played with relatively soft sticks—softer than those normally employed for the xylophone.

THE GLOCKENSPIEL OR ORCHESTRA BELLS[2]

Italian: Campanelli   *French:* Jeu de Timbres   *German:* Glockenspiel
(or Carillon)

Ex. 18

Sounding two 8ves higher.

The glockenspiel generally used in orchestras today consists of a set of metal bars attached to a portable case which is opened up and placed on a table in performance. Another type, now rarely seen, includes a supporting frame and resonators beneath the bars.

The bright, ringing tone of the glockenspiel is normally produced by striking the metal bars with hard mallets or with metal hammers. A somewhat more subdued quality can be achieved by using soft mallets, but these should be called for specifically in the part when desired. (The same directions, in foreign languages, as those given for "soft sticks" in the section on timpani are used.) Although it is possible for the player to hold two mallets in each hand and therefore to play three-note and four-note chords, parts for the instrument usually consist of a single melodic line. Their most frequent function is to add a bright tang to melodies taken by other instruments, but solos are practical and effective. (A very early example is the extended glockenspiel solo in Mozart's *The Magic Flute.*) The part is normally written two octaves lower than it is intended to sound. However, in Wagner scores and in certain others it is notated only *one* octave below the concert sounds.

---

[2] Not to be confused with tubular bells, or chimes, which will be discussed later.

Glockenspiels, like xylophones, are built in various sizes; not all of them have the complete range shown here.

To compound the confusion, there is a third instrument that sometimes goes by the name of glockenspiel. This is the "bell lyre," which has come into the public eye as a member of most marching bands. It is a vertical and abbreviated version of the true glockenspiel, generally inferior in intonation and too loud and harsh for use in the concert hall.

There is also a keyed glockenspiel which is commonly used in Europe but is rarely seen in this country. This is the instrument for which the formidable-looking glockenspiel part in Dukas' *The Sorcerer's Apprentice* was designed, by the way.

EXAMPLES

Ex. 19

(a)   Symphony: *Mathis der Maler*

Hindemith

(b) *Die Meistersinger*

Wagner

Reproduced by permission of Schott & Co., Ltd., London.

THE VIBRAPHONE

Ex. 20

A child of the electrical age, the vibraphone is a relative newcomer to the instrumental scene. Although for a time it was associated chiefly with dance orchestras and commercial music, it has since found great favor with many serious composers, including some who have used it in combination with electronically-produced sounds. It resembles the xylophone in general pattern. Metal bars arranged in "keyboard" fashion on a stand are resonated by tuned tubes below. But the instrument is distinguished by an ingenious feature: small metal discs, one at the top of each resonating tube, are made to revolve by means of an electric motor, producing a kind of pulse or "vibrato" in the tone (a quantitative rather than a pitch vibrato, however). The speed with which the discs revolve can be regulated, with a corresponding variation in the speed of the vibrato. It is possible to cut out the vibrato effect entirely by turning off the motor (direction: "fan off"). There is a damper pedal which may be used to sustain or damp the sound ("damper off" for the sustained effect).

Parts for the vibraphone may be either melodic or harmonic in character. Isolated chords (up to four notes) that are allowed to ring seem to show off the peculiar floating, undulating tone to best advantage in the orchestra. Either hard or soft sticks may be used (most often the latter). The part is written on a single staff, in the treble clef, at actual pitch.

Ex. 21

Third Symphony

Harris

Vibra- phone

THE TUBULAR BELLS (OR CHIMES)

Italian: Campane   *French:* Cloches   *German:* Glocken
(or Tiefe Glocken)

Ex. 22

 Sounding an 8ve higher.

Of the various kinds of bells that have been tried in the orchestra over the years, the tubular bells are the only type now in standard use. They are hung from a rack and, when used as a complete set, are arranged like the white and black keys of the piano; that is, the bells that correspond to the black keys are hung behind the others and slightly higher so that there will be space to strike them. But since bell parts often consist of only a few notes, it is usually easier to hang up only those bells actually needed for a given work. Some sets of bells include a pedal by means of which the sound may be damped or allowed to ring. Because of the varying sizes of different makes of bells, the range given here is not an invariable one but may be considered more or less standard, at least in the United States.

The indication "sounding an octave higher" which appears next to the range of the bells needs a note of explanation, for it does not correspond with traditional practice. Heretofore, bell parts have usually been written as if they were sounding at actual pitch, the reason apparently being that bell tones give the illusion of being lower than they actually are. Percussionists now recommend a more accurate system of notation in order that the exact octave in which the passage is to sound will be clear to the player.

Ex. 23

(a) *Ibéria*

Debussy

Permission for reprint granted by copyright owner, Durand et Cie, Paris, France; Elkan-Vogel Co., Inc., agents for the U.S.A.

(b) *Háry János* Suite (*Viennese Musical Clock*)

Kodály

Copyright assigned to Hawkes & Son, Ltd., 1939. By permission of the copyright owner, Boosey & Hawkes, Inc.

THE ANTIQUE CYMBALS

Italian:	Crotali	*French:*	Cymbales Antiques (or Crotales)	*German:*	Antiken Zimbeln

Ex. 24

 Sounding an 8ve higher.

These very small cymbals, modeled after ancient Greek instruments, are made so that each pair sounds a definite pitch. They are held with one in each hand and struck lightly at the rims, the small bell-like sound being allowed to ring. Among the composers who have used them are Berlioz (*Romeo and Juliet*), Debussy (*Prelude to the Afternoon of a Faun*), Stravinsky (*Les Noces, The Rite of Spring*), and Ravel (*Daphnis and Chloe* Suite No. 1). The first three works call for two pairs, the last for six pairs.

The antique cymbals have been written both at actual pitch and an octave below the sounds desired. Therefore, parts for them should specify which method of notation is being used.

Needless to say, many orchestras do not own antique cymbals and must play parts written for them on some other instrument, most often the glockenspiel.

THE FLEXATONE

Italian: Flexatone   *French:* Flexatone   *German:* Flexaton

This unusual and rarely used instrument consists of a band of metal bent somewhat in the shape of an inverted U, to one side of which are attached two small pieces of metal topped by wooden knobs, which strike the metal band when the instrument is shaken. The player holds it by a cylindrical handle at the bottom and uses his thumb to control the angle (and therefore the pitch) of the metal portion that is vibrating. The resulting sound is a bit like that of a musical saw, although more percussive. In the Khachaturian Piano Concerto, a footnote to the flexatone part at measure 49 of the second movement says, "Whistling sound required." Another instance of the instrument's use can be seen in the Schönberg *Variations for Orchestra,* Op. 31 (Variation 3). The composite range of the parts in these works is

Ex. 25

SUGGESTED ASSIGNMENTS[3]

A. Know:

1. ranges of timpani of various sizes.
2. which timpani are in common use.
3. how tuning operation works.
4. special effects possible on timpani.
5. ranges, transpositions, and special abilities of other instruments discussed in this chapter.

B. Write a part for two timpani (28-inch and 25-inch) for "The Star-Spangled Banner." The timpani need not play continuously.

C. Write a part for three timpani (one 28-inch, one 25-inch, and either a 23-inch or a 30-inch) for "America" or for another short, vigorous composition.

D. Write a timpani part (the number of timpani to be specified by the instructor) for "Important Event" (from *Scenes from Childhood*) by Schumann.

[3] Material for suggested listening is given at the end of Chapter 14.

Chapter 14

THE PERCUSSION:
INSTRUMENTS OF
INDEFINITE PITCH

THE SNARE DRUM (OR SIDE DRUM)

Italian: Tamburo   *French:* Tambour (Militaire)   *German:* Kleine Trommel
(Militare)   (or Caisse Claire)[1]

Along with other instruments of indeterminate pitch, the snare drum may be notated, in the score, either on a staff or on a single line:

Ex. 1

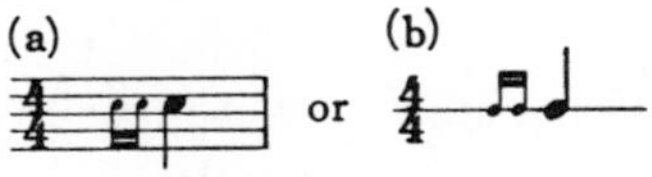

For a long time it was common, in scores using the staff notation, to include a treble clef sign to distinguish the snare drum part from the bass drum and cymbal part, which often used bass clef. That system is no longer recommended.

The snare drum part may be written in the third space or anywhere else on the staff that is convenient. (More will be said about this later.) When two percussion parts are written on the same staff in order to save space, separate stems—one up, one down—are used.

---

[1] Strictly speaking, the *caisse claire* is a very small drum; but the name is often used in contemporary French scores to mean snare drum.

The snare drum is at its best in crisp, sharply rhythmic passages. It is played with wooden sticks and involves a technique that differs somewhat from that of any of the other percussion instruments.

Some strokes which it uses frequently are the following:

The *flam* ♪♩ . In the "closed flam," which is the usual form, the first note is played before the beat, unaccented, and joined quickly with the second. This stroke is used to strengthen or lengthen a note. The "open flam," in which the first note is articulated separately with more of an accent is extremely rare in orchestral playing.

The *drag*, usually ♫♩ , in which two very rapid notes precede an accented note. These preparatory notes are generally not heard separately but merge into a brief roll effect that is performed so quickly as to seem almost like a part of the note it precedes.

The *four-stroke ruff* ♫♩ , in which three notes precede an accented note. This stroke is played "open" (with the preparatory notes articulated).

The *roll* 𝅗𝅥 or 𝅗𝅥 .

Comments on the notation of the roll made in connection with the timpani apply here as well. This is one of the snare drum's most effective devices. As anyone who has ever seen a tight-rope act will remember, an extended roll on the snare drum has an uncanny way of creating a sense of tension and expectancy. Shorter rolls are used constantly in march rhythms and in other orchestral parts played by the snare drum.

A special effect which originated in the dance band and occasionally finds its way into the concert hall is the "rim shot." In the symphonic version of this stroke, one stick is placed with the tip on the drumhead and the butt on the rim and is then struck with the other stick. The result is a sharp, dry sound. Another possibility, which figures constantly in the dance band but only rarely in symphonic music, is the use of wire brushes on the snare drum.

Rhythmic patterns of all kinds and complexities are possible on the snare drum. But it must not be kept going steadily, for if overused it becomes either ineffective or downright tiresome. Forsyth comments, "Like almost all the other Percussion Instruments, its principal effect is its entry." Apropos of this point, an axiom to keep in mind is that instruments of highly individual color are generally effective in inverse proportion to the amount they are used.

Zintgraff, San Antonio, Texas

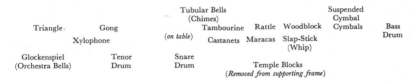

		Tubular Bells (Chimes)				Suspended Cymbal	
Triangle	Gong		Tambourine	Rattle	Woodblock	Cymbals	Bass Drum
	Xylophone	(*on table*)	Castanets	Maracas	Slap-Stick (Whip)		
Glockenspiel (Orchestra Bells)	Tenor Drum		Snare Drum				
				Temple Blocks (*Removed from supporting frame*)			

Percussionists feel that it is desirable for composers to specify whether the sound of wire snares or gut snares is wanted ("Concert snare drum with wire snares," or "Field drum with gut snares.") The snares may be loosened, in which case the instrument loses its characteristically brittle quality and sounds rather like a tom-tom. The clearest direction for this effect is "snares off." Another special effect can be achieved by covering the drumhead with a handkerchief (direction: "cover head"). This is, by the way, the crispest sound obtainable on the snare drum. The term "muffled snare drum" has unfortunately been used to describe both these effects; consequently, it has become ambiguous and is better avoided altogether.

Certain modern composers, Bartók among them, occasionally specify whether the snare drum is to be played at the edge or at the middle of the head.

(Examples of passages for snare drum and for other instruments discussed here are given in Ex. 4.)

THE FIELD DRUM

Italian: Tamburo (Militare)   *French:* Tambour   *German:* Rührtrommel

As can be seen, there is a good deal of ambiguity in connection with the foreign names for the field drum, since some of them are used for other, slightly different instruments.

The field drum is longer than the snare drum, and its tone is somewhat deeper and less brittle. It is usually equipped with gut snares. Although it is regularly used in bands, parts for it in orchestral literature are extremely rare. (One example occurs in Hindemith's *Symphonic Metamorphosis of Themes by C. M. von Weber.*)

THE TENOR DRUM

Italian: Tamburo Rullante   *French:* Caisse Roulante   *German:* Rührtrommel

Also longer and larger than the snare drum, but not nearly so large as the bass drum, the tenor drum is used much less frequently than either of these two. It has no snares, and its tone is more somber than that of the snare drum. It is normally played with wooden sticks.

THE TABOR

French: Tambour de Provence   *German:* Tambourin
         (or Tambourin)

This is a very long drum, equipped with a single snare in most cases. It is rarely seen in the United States. The part for it in Bizet's second *L'Arlésienne* Suite is labeled "tambourin," and even eminent conductors have been known to make the mistake of having it played on the tambourine. Examples of the use of the tabor in contemporary music can be found in Aaron Copland's *Appalachian Spring* and in his *El Salon Mexico.*

THE BASS DRUM

Italian: Gran Cassa   *French:* Grosse Caisse   *German:* Grosse Trommel
         (or simply "Cassa")

Because of its great size and its relatively slow response, the bass drum is obviously not suited to the involved rhythms possible on many of its smaller relatives; simple rhythmic patterns and isolated notes are more practical and effective. Repeated notes had better be no faster than eighths in moderate time (except in rolls). The instrument is normally played with a single soft beater, though two may be used to produce rolls. A rarely used special effect calls for the use of a wooden snare drum stick in place of the beater. (See Benjamin Britten's *Peter Grimes*, for example.)

Obviously the bass drum is well equipped to add volume or percussive accent. However, one must be a little careful about writing regularly recurring beats for it in serious symphonic music, lest the effect suggest parade music. Its effectiveness in soft passages is too often ignored; at lower dynamic levels it is "felt" rather than heard, and the lay listener may even be unaware that it is playing. Soft rolls, which give a faintly threatening sound not unlike distant thunder, are especially useful for color effects.

As with other percussion instruments of indefinite pitch, the bass drum part may be written on a single line or on a staff. It is often written on the same staff with the cymbals, and the two parts are sometimes played by the same person. This arrangement will be explained in the section on cymbals that follows.

THE CYMBALS

Italian: Piatti   *French:* Cymbales   *German:* Becken

The notation of the cymbals is the same as that of the bass drum. When the two instruments are written on the same staff or line, the part may look like any one of the three examples given here:

Ex. 2

There can be no objection to writing both instruments on the same staff, but it is highly unfortunate that both are sometimes played by the same person. One cymbal is attached to the top of the bass drum and the other is clashed against it, while the player uses his other hand to play the bass drum. Speaking about this arrangement, Berlioz says, "This economical procedure is intolerable; the cymbals lose their sonority and produce a noise similar to the sound of a falling bag full of old iron and broken glass."[2] Although this judgment may be a little extreme, there is no doubt that the

[2] Berlioz, *Treatise on Instrumentation.*

226

tone quality of both instruments suffers when they are played in this way. Incidentally, the combination of cymbals and bass drum, playing either simultaneously or in alternation, has figured in so many "war horses" that it has become dated and flat sounding, and it had better be used with caution if at all.

Among the various ways of producing sound on the cymbals, the crash or "two-plate stroke" is by far the most frequently used. The word "crash" must not be construed in this case as meaning only a loud sound, for this stroke can be performed at any dynamic level, from *ppp* to *fff*. One of the most ingenious and effective spots in orchestral literature occurs at the end of the *Fêtes* section in Debussy's *Nocturnes*, where the cymbals are merely rubbed together softly. Loud cymbal crashes are much more frequent and are apt to be used for moments of excitement or for climax points. Since there is considerable ring to a cymbal crash, it is wise to indicate in actual note values just how long the sound is to last before being damped. (Damping is achieved by touching the cymbals to the player's clothing.) If the sound is to be allowed to ring indefinitely, an easy indication is a small tie that

simply ends in the air: ├─○─┤ . Sometimes the French expression

laissez vibrer (let vibrate) is used. If, on the other hand, the note is to be

"choked" (made very short), it should be written like this: ├♪ ⁊ ⁊ ┤ .
                                                              sec

(*Sec,* or the Italian equivalent *secco,* means "dry.") "Choke" or "stop" may also be written in.

In the "two-plate roll" the cymbals are struck together repeatedly and rapidly. This is a difficult and infrequently used method which must be called for specifically when it is wanted. The French direction is *frottées.*

THE SUSPENDED CYMBAL

A single cymbal may be suspended from a stand and struck with a stick, or two sticks may be used to produce a roll. Single notes (which may be either damped or allowed to ring) are usable not only in a *forte* for purposes of percussive accent but also in a *piano* for a particular color effect. Rolls can produce anything from an almost imperceptible shimmer to a deafening volume of sound. They are especially useful for accenting a crescendo played by the rest of the orchestra. Normally, yarn-covered marimba mallets are used, but for special effects snare drum sticks, triangle beaters, wire brushes, darning needles, and so on, may be substituted. Soft timpani sticks, though frequently specified by composers, are relatively ineffective and are not recommended.

Cymbal parts are occasionally printed in diamond-shaped notes, while commercial arrangements commonly use an X in place of a real note. Although these systems make the cymbal part easy to spot in the score, they have certain disadvantages: the diamond-shaped notes are difficult to make in writing music by hand, and the X's do not show the actual value of each tone. Ordinary notes appear to be the best solution.

THE TRIANGLE

Italian: Triangolo   *French:* Triangle   *German:* Triangel
(Old name: Sistro)

Single notes, tremolos (rolls), and not-too-complicated rhythms are all effective on the triangle, and the *flam* and *drag* figures mentioned in connection with the snare drum are common. Normally, the instrument is suspended from one of the player's hands and struck with a single steel beater held in the other hand; more complex rhythms may be executed by suspending the triangle from a rack and using two beaters, one in each hand.

The silvery, ringing tone of the triangle is valuable for adding brilliance in either a *forte* or a *piano*, and a triangle roll at climax points can give an extra degree of excitement and intensity. The instrument should not be used too long at a time, however, for its distinctive tone tends to pall quickly.

Solos for the triangle are rare, though Liszt's E♭ major Piano Concerto includes a well-known one. Notation is either on a staff or on a single line.

Triangles are made in different sizes, and the tone quality varies accordingly.

THE TAMBOURINE

Italian: Tamburino   *French:* Tambour de   *German:* Schellentrommel
(or Tamburo Basco)   Basque   (or Tambourin)

The tambourine consists of a small wooden hoop with a calfskin head stretched across one side of it and pairs of small metal plates, called "jingles," attached in openings cut in the hoop. The instrument may be played in various ways:

1. It may be struck with the fist. This method is suitable for isolated notes and for fairly simple rhythms. It produces the percussive sound of the knuckles striking the head, along with the sound of the jingles. The word "fist" is sometimes written in. Some players prefer to strike the tambourine on their knee to produce the same effect, and in rapid passages alternate fist and knee strokes are sometimes used.

2. It may be shaken, in which case a roll on the jingles results. This is a brilliant sound, useful as an added touch of excitement and color, and especially good in dynamics of *forte* or louder. The notation is either $\vdash\!\!-\!\!\stackrel{\sharp}{\mathbf{\rho}}\!\!-\!\!\dashv$

or $\vdash\!\!\overset{tr\,\sim}{\underset{\rho}{\rule{0pt}{1em}}}\!\!\dashv$ (preferably the first).

3. The thumb may be rubbed over the head to produce a roll on the jingles. This effect is especially appropriate for softer dynamic levels, though it can also be played *forte*. Each note played as a thumb roll must be of short duration (no more than two or three seconds), since the player has only a small surface on which to move his thumb. Ravel uses $\vdash\!\!\overset{tr\,\sim}{\underset{\rho}{\rule{0pt}{1em}}}\!\!\dashv$ for this thumb method and $\vdash\!\!-\!\!\stackrel{\sharp}{\mathbf{\rho}}\!\!-\!\!\dashv$ when the tambourine is to be shaken, a simple and efficient way of distinguishing between the two effects.

4. The tambourine may be laid on a table or flat surface with the head facing upward (or downward for a slightly different effect) and may be played with sticks. The result is a combination of struck sound and jingle sound. When this method is to be used, some such direction as "Played with soft sticks" or "Played with snare drum sticks" must be included. For soft passages the tambourine may be placed head downward on a cloth and played with the fingers.

Of course no one method of playing need be used consistently. It is quite possible to have, for example, a "fist" note on the first beat of a measure and a roll on the succeeding beats. Obviously the fourth method takes a moment to set up and cannot be intermingled quickly with the others (except by using two tambourines). The tambourine is frequently used to back up vivid rhythms, or it may simply add color or accent at certain points. Characteristic parts for the instrument can be seen in Rimsky-Korsakoff's *Capriccio Espagnol* and Wagner's *Tannhäuser* Overture, among other works.

THE GONG OR TAM-TAM

Italian, French, and *German:* Tam-tam

This is a circular piece of hammered or spun metal which is struck with a soft-headed beater. Its tone is most effective when the instrument is allowed to vibrate a moment; therefore, when successive strokes are used, they should be spaced far enough apart to allow for ample vibration on each. However, rolls are possible. Although the gong is not ordinarily damped, *secco* (short) notes are occasionally used. In *The Rite of Spring* Stravinsky introduces a curious effect: the player describes an arc on the surface of the gong with the triangle beater.

The instrument need have neither oriental connotations (as it so often does in commercial music) nor the sinister and macabre character it assumes in the context of such works as Strauss's *Death and Transfiguration* or Tchaikovsky's Sixth Symphony. Sometimes it is used simply to add an unexpected and exotic touch of color, as in Example 4(h); or it may supply loud notes which have much the same function as cymbal crashes, as in Example 4(i).

Gongs are made in various sizes, and some composers specify "large gong" or "small gong" in their scores.

Incidentally, *tam-tam*, the European name for gong, must not be confused with *tom-tom*, the name for a snareless drum of a particular type.

THE CASTANETS

Italian: Castagnette   *French:* Castagnettes   *German:* Kastagnetten

The sound of castanets is familiar to everyone through Spanish music. But for the sake of those who have never seen them close at hand, they might be described as resembling oversized hickory nuts, chopped in half and partially hollowed out. The name itself means "chestnuts" and was presumably derived from the type of wood used. Today castanets are most often made of ebonite. They were designed originally to be clicked in the hand, but the current practice in orchestras is to use a mechanically mounted set that is played with the fingers.

Granted that castanets are most often heard in music with a Spanish flavor, they can sometimes be included effectively in non-Spanish music when a crisp rhythmic background is in order.

For more detailed information on characteristic castanet rhythms, the reader is referred to Forsyth's *Orchestration*.

THE WOOD BLOCK

Italian: Cassa di legno   *French:* Wood Bloc   *German:* Holztrommel

The wood block figures occasionally in modern scores, particularly in ballets and in music that is highly colored or strongly rhythmic, or both. It is, as its name implies, a small rectangular piece of wood (or of plastic), solid except for slits cut into it on two sides to give resonating space. Wooden drum sticks or xylophone mallets are used in playing it, and rhythms of all kinds are possible. The tone is dry and brittle—a little reminiscent of horses' hoofs, especially in certain rhythms. Single notes on the wood block have an impudent, unexpected quality that may verge on the comic.

CHINESE TEMPLE BLOCKS

Chinese temple blocks are a series of hollow wooden blocks, roughly circular in shape and painted in fantastic dragonhead patterns. Medium to hard rubber mallets are used in playing them. They may come in any number from two to five (five being the standard number) and are graduated in size, so that the pitch varies from one to the other. The tone is similar to that of the wood block, but a little "rounder" and hollower. Although temple blocks are tuned to a pentatonic scale, no attempt is made to notate their real pitches; a note is arbitrarily assigned to each block. Probably the best solution is to use the five lines of the staff to indicate the five blocks, respectively.

LATIN-AMERICAN PERCUSSION INSTRUMENTS

Some of the instruments frequently used in Latin-American music are the following:

The *claves*, two short sticks which are struck together. One is held in such a way that the cup of the hand resonates the sound.

The *maracas*, two hollow gourds with handles attached and dried seed or buckshot inside. They are shaken to produce the characteristic rhythms of the rumba, the beguine, and other dances. Claves and maracas are nearly always used together. Example 3 shows a characteristic passage for them.

Ex. 3

The *güiro*, a serrated gourd which is scraped with a stick.

Bongos, one-headed drums open at the bottom and played with the fingers.

Timbales, like the bongos but larger, and played with small sticks. For a special effect, the drum may be muffled with one hand and struck with a stick held in the other. It is also possible to play with one stick on the shell (side) of the drum and the other on the head.

OTHER PERCUSSION INSTRUMENTS

There are, in addition to the instruments already mentioned, others which are very rarely used. In this category might be listed the ratchet or rattle, the wind machine, and the thunder machine, all found in the Strauss tone poems; the slapstick or whip (see Copland, Third Symphony, and Mussorgsky-Ravel, *Pictures from an Exhibition: "Gnomus"*); cowbells, used by Milhaud in his *La Création du Monde;* sleighbells, which figure in the Mahler Fourth Symphony (see page 296) and in Respighi's *Roman Festivals*, for example; and the "anvil," which is a small steel bar made so as to sound like an anvil, and which appears in scores by Verdi, Berlioz, Mahler, Wagner, Copland, and others. The list could be extended still further by the addition of sandpaper blocks, switches, chains, the siren, and such realistic sounds as the clanking of steel plates in Mossoloff's *Iron Foundry* or the recorded song of a nightingale in Respighi's *Pines of Rome*. The foreign names for most of these instruments are included in Appendix. A.

THE PERCUSSION SECTION AS A WHOLE

Percussion parts fall into two broad categories:

1. Those that point up the actual thematic or structural aspects of the music (timpani parts, for example, are most often of this sort).

2. Those that are included chiefly for color purposes. But since the possibilities in both categories are almost infinite, an attempt to catalog them completely would be futile. Furthermore, each composition to be scored is an individual case with its own peculiar demands and possibilities. The best solution is to fix the sounds of the various percussion instruments in one's aural memory and draw on them as imagination and taste dictate.

It might be pointed out here that the dynamic range of the percussion section is greater (at both loud and soft extremes) than the dynamic range of the rest of the orchestra. This relationship can be illustrated on paper in the following manner:

Dynamic range of the percussion: ——————————————————————

Dynamic range of the rest of the orchestra: ——————————————

EXAMPLES

Ex. 4

(a) *Scheherazade*

Rimsky-Korsakoff

(b) *Bolero*

Ravel

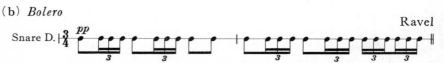

Permission for reprint granted by copyright owner, Durand et Cie, Paris, Fran-Vogel nce; ElkaCo., Inc., agents for the U.S.A.

(c) *American Festival* Overture

William Schuman

Copyright, 1941, by G. Schirmer, Inc.

(d) *Fire Bird* Suite

Stravinsky

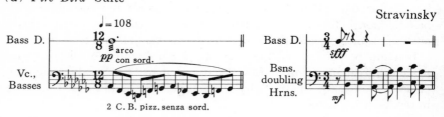

(e) *El Salon Mexico*

Copland

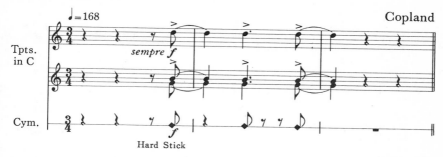

Tpts. in C

sempre f

Cym.

Hard Stick

Copyright, 1939, by Hawkes & Son (London) Ltd. By permission of the copyright owner, Boosey & Hawkes, Inc.

(f) *Capriccio Espagnol*

Rimsky-Korsakoff

Tamb-ourine

Vl. I

(g) *Carmen*

Bizet

Cast.

Carmen, dancing with Cast.

La ——— la — la ——— la ——— La ———

(h) *The White Peacock*

Griffes

Fl.

Harp

Tam-tam

Copyright renewal assigned, 1945, to G. Schirmer, Inc.

(i) *Bolero*

Ravel

(j) *Capriccio Espagnol*

Rimsky-Korsakoff

(k) *Symphonic Metamorphosis of Themes by C. M. von Weber*

Hindemith

(This passage is for percussion alone and continues for eight more measures.)

THE ARRANGEMENT OF PERCUSSION PARTS

In the score, timpani are generally listed first among the percussion instruments. Then follow the instruments of indefinite pitch, in any order, and finally the glockenspiel, xylophone, celesta, and piano (although few scores use all these instruments). Because the celesta and the piano are not usually played by members of the percussion section, they are discussed in another chapter along with the harp.

Most professional orchestras have at least three percussion players (including the timpanist). The usual plan is to hire extra percussionists for works that require them, although the orchestra's budget unfortunately enters in here, and percussion parts have been known to go unplayed for economic reasons. With a little judicious planning, it is usually possible to arrange the percussion parts so that one player can play several instruments (successively, of course).[3] For purposes of illustration, let us suppose that at a certain point the triangle must play a few notes; eight bars later there is a passage for snare drum, and sixteen bars after that the xylophone has a solo. There is no reason why the same player cannot handle all three instruments in turn. As for the player's part in that case, the three instruments can all be written on the same sheet, or the snare drum and triangle may be written on one part, the xylophone on another. In the latter case, there should be a cue in the snare drum–triangle part to show the player where the xylophone solo occurs. (Cues are discussed in greater detail in Chapter 20.) There is no hard and fast rule for the grouping of percussion instruments in either score or parts, because each score presents individual problems. Snare drum and triangle are often written on the same staff, usually with triangle notes

on the top space 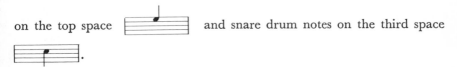 and snare drum notes on the third space

As has already been mentioned, bass drum and cymbals frequently share the same staff. It is normally impractical to write two percussion instruments of *definite* pitch on the same staff. Timpani parts are nearly always separate; that is, they have a staff to themselves in the score, and a separate player's part.

Probably the most practical plan, especially if a good many percussion instruments are involved, is to arrange the percussion parts with a specific

---

[3] However, it is possible for one percussionist to play certain *pairs* of instruments at the same time if need be. For example, a player can strike the triangle with one hand and shake the tambourine with the other, or play the bass drum with one hand and the gong with the other.

number of players in mind and to show each player's part on a separate staff (even in the score, in some cases). For example, in *The Rio Grande* Lambert calls for five percussion players (including the timpanist) whose parts are labeled 1 through 5. When all five are playing, the parts look like this:

Ex. 5

The Rio Grande

Lambert

(It happens that the timpani part has been put at the bottom here instead of in its usual place above the other percussion.) If only certain players are involved, the parts are designated by number (Ex. 6).

Ex. 6

The Rio Grande

Lambert

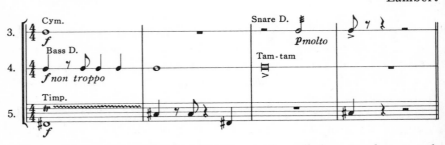

Under this system, each percussionist may be called on to play several different instruments in the course of his part (each new instrument being indicated at its entrance, of course). If the parts can be charted in advance in such a way that each player is responsible for certain specific instruments throughout the work, that is desirable. In any case, this arrangement has decided advantages. It solves in advance the problem of distributing the parts in a practical way among a given number of players, a problem which must otherwise be solved by the percussionists in rehearsal, often with a good deal of frenzied rushing from one instrument to another. It saves copying of several different percussion parts for the players if the following procedure is used: all the percussion parts (excluding the timpani in most cases) are written on the same sheet and copies of that sheet—as many as needed for the players—are then made by a commercial reproduction process. (See Chapter 19.) Furthermore, each percussionist has all the parts before him and can therefore relate his own part to those of the other percussionists.

Whatever arrangement of percussion parts is used, the number of players required should be indicated at the beginning of the score, along with the list of instruments. In a few rare instances, as many as six or seven percussion players are called for. An extreme example is Respighi's *Roman Festivals*, which lists fourteen percussion instruments, ten of which play at once at one point. But that sort of thing is obviously impractical as a general rule. It is, in fact, the kind of instrumentation that the aspiring composer had better not imitate if he expects to get his scores performed.

For a detailed discussion of percussion instruments and the notation of them, the reader is referred to *Scoring for Percussion and the Instruments of the Percussion Section* by H. Owen Reed and Joel T. Leach (Englewood Cliffs, N.J.: Prentice-Hall, Inc., 1969).

SUGGESTED ASSIGNMENTS

A. Be able to list the percussion instruments discussed here (except the Latin-American instruments and those included under "Other Percussion Instruments," page 231) and to translate the foreign names for them into English.

B. Know:

1. the strokes commonly used on the snare drum.
2. the various ways of playing cymbals and tambourine.
3. special abilities of each of the instruments.
4. proper notation in each case.

C. Select a march tune and write parts for snare drum, bass drum, cymbals, and any other percussion instruments desired.

SUGGESTED LISTENING

Percussion (Including Timpani)

Timpani Studies by Alfred Friese, with Edwin McArthur, pianist, and Dr. Philip James, narrator (recorded by Benjamin Sachs, Artist Recordings, 939 Eighth Avenue,

New York). The most valuable portion of this album is that which presents numerous solos and prominent passages for timpani from standard orchestral literature, with the orchestra parts reduced for piano.

Rimsky-Korsakoff, *Capriccio Espagnol; Scheherazade.*

Debussy, *Ibéria.*

Ravel, *Daphnis and Chloe* Suite No. 2; *La Valse; Rapsodie Espagnole.*

Kodály, *Háry János* Suite.

Respighi, *Pines of Rome; Fountains of Rome; Roman Festivals.*

Stravinsky, *Les Noces; L'Histoire du Soldat; The Rite of Spring.*

Bartók, *Music for String Instruments, Percussion, and Celesta;* Sonata for Two Pianos and Percussion; Concerto for Orchestra.

Hindemith, *Symphonic Metamorphosis of Themes by C. M. von Weber.*

Chavez, *Sinfonia India.*

Hanson, *Merrymount Suite.*

Lambert, *The Rio Grande.*

Copland, *El Salon Mexico; Appalachian Spring;* Third Symphony (especially 2nd and 4th movts.).

Shostakovitch, Fifth Symphony.

Piston, Suite from the ballet, *The Incredible Flutist.*

Varèse, *Ionisation* for eleven percussion instruments.

Music Educator's Series, *Percussion*, recorded by Capitol and Angel Records, Album No. HBR 21003. Record 1: *Bell, Drum and Cymbal.* All the percussion instruments of the symphony orchestra are described and played by Saul Goodman. As a finale he presents, through the technique of multiple recording, two arrangements for all the percussion instruments of *My Country 'Tis of Thee* and *Danse Macabre* by Saint-Saëns. Record 2: *The Percussion Instruments in Symphonic Form.* Includes Milhaud's Concerto for Percussion and Small Orchestra and Chavez' Toccata for Percussion (The Concert Arts Orchestra under Felix Slatkin) and Bartók's *Music for String Instruments, Percussion and Celesta* (Los Angeles Chamber Orchestra under Harold Byrns).

Chapter 15

THE HARP,
CELESTA, AND PIANO

The harp, celesta, and piano have been allotted a special chapter because they do not belong to any of the four orchestral groups already discussed. Although the harp and the piano have strings, they are not classed as stringed instruments because their tone is not produced by bowing. The celesta is listed with the percussion group in some orchestration books, but it is not normally played by a member of the percussion section; most orchestras have a separate player who performs either celesta or piano parts as required.

THE HARP

Italian: Arpa   *French:* Harpe   *German:* Harfe

Ex. 1

The harp differs from other instruments in being built on a nonchromatic basis; that is, instead of having twelve strings (one for each semitone) within each octave as one might expect, it has only seven. When the instru-

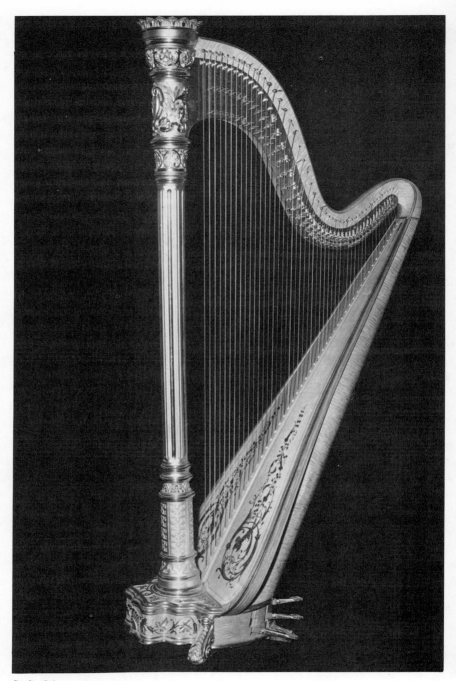

Studio Gilmore, Austin, Texas

Harp

ment is in its "home" key, these are tuned to the notes in the scale of C♭ major: C♭, D♭, E♭, F♭, G♭, A♭, and B♭. At the base of the harp are seven pedals, each one controlling all the strings of a particular letter-name on the instrument and capable of raising those strings either a half step or a whole step in pitch. For example, if the appropriate pedal is pressed halfway down (where it can be secured in a notch) all the strings that formerly sounded C♭ will now sound C♮; if we depress the same pedal still further to a bottom notch, the same strings will sound C♯. Using another pedal, the D♭'s in all octaves can be raised to D♮'s or to D♯'s; and so on, with all the strings. It is obviously impossible to tune the strings of one letter name differently in different octaves.[1] The reason for using the forbidding key of C♭ major as the basic key of the harp may now be apparent: it is the only one in which each pitch can be raised two semitones without the use of double sharps (or double flats to begin with); the three pitch possibilities of each string can be expressed by a flat, a natural, and a sharp.

The pedals are arranged in semicircular fashion around the base of the harp, three on the left, four on the right, in the following sequence:

D C B | E F G A

The three on the left are operated by the harpist's left foot; the other four, by the right foot. It takes only an instant to depress or release a pedal, and two pedals may be changed at the same time as long as they are on different sides of the instrument; for example, B and G, or D and A, or C and F. Harpists do occasionally take the E pedal with the left foot in cases when it is necessary to achieve a double change of pedals on the right side quickly. But the opposite arrangement (use of the right foot for pedals on the left side) is so awkward as to be impractical. Fortunately, these fine points need seldom be considered, since it is usually possible to make pedal changes one at a time rather than simultaneously.

The setting of the pedals at the beginning of a work should be indicated in the harp part. This may be done in any one of the three ways shown next:

D♭ C♯ B♭ E♮ F♭ G♯ A♭   ⌈E♮ F♭ G♯ A♭
                                                         ⌊B♭ C♯ D♭

The first method simply lists the letters in the same order as that of the pedals. The second, which is commonly used by harpists, consists of a diagram which is a "picture" of the pedals; a horizontal line corresponds with the middle notch on all pedals, and small marks above, through, or below this line show whether the pedals are in the top, middle or bottom notch,

---

[1] The only exceptions are the bottom C and D strings (and, on some harps, the top G string as well). These are not controlled by the pedal mechanism and must be tuned independently by hand.

242

respectively. The third way arranges the letters in a kind of radial fashion, with the order starting from the right on the bottom row and then moving from right to left on the top row.

Harp parts may be written either with or without a key signature. If the part is fairly diatonic, a key signature appears to be the most sensible solution. But if the harp has a part which would require constant cancellations of the signature, then it may as well be written without key signature, the accidentals being inserted. When there is a key signature and no pedal setting is shown, the harpist will normally assume that the pedals should be set according to the scale of the key involved.

Each pedal change needed in the course of the part should be shown beneath the bottom staff at the point where it occurs; the letter with the new accidental is sufficient. When two changes occur at the same time and when these involve pedals on different sides of the instrument (as will normally be the case), the change for the pedal on the right should be shown *above* the one for the pedal on the left; for example: $^{G\natural}_{D\natural}$. This standard placement (which conforms with the "radial" pattern given earlier) is an aid to the harpist in making pedal changes rapidly. There is often an advantage in indicating changes during rests that occur well in advance of the point where the new pitches will actually be needed, especially if a number of changes are involved. The pedal diagram is not used for showing pedal changes in the course of a work unless all or most of the pedals are to be changed.

To illustrate some points in connection with harp writing, let us suppose that the harp part in a given work starts in the thirteenth measure and involves the notes shown in Example 2.

Ex. 2

Although the key is E♭ major, the pedal setting at the beginning includes an A♮, since the first time an A of any kind occurs it is in the natural form. The three pedal changes necessary are shown beneath the music. Such changes as these, occurring from time to time in a tempo that allows them to be made comfortably, are entirely reasonable and are considered to be part of the harpist's normal assignment. But constant pedal changes become overtaxing, especially if they must be made quickly. Consequently, in highly chromatic music it is normally best either to omit the harp altogether or to give it a simplified part which eliminates some of the notes requiring changes. In the case of the example just given, for instance, the harp might play only on alternate beats (Ex. 3).

Ex. 3

Another solution in such cases (one used by Debussy, Strauss, and others) is to write for two harps, letting them take turns at playing. Each harp will then have rests during which pedal changes can be made. A further advantage of this arrangement is that greater volume is available from the two harps playing at once, in case that is wanted.

Two notes which sound the same but are spelled differently are spoken of as being "enharmonic." If we think back to the possible tunings of each harp string, we will discover that there are a good many possibilities for enharmonic notes where the strings overlap in pitch. For example, if we have the B pedal in the middle notch so that the string will sound B♮, and the C pedal in the top notch to produce C♭, the two strings will give the same pitch. The whole list of enharmonic possibilities follows:

C♭–B♮	E♭–D♯	G♭–F♯
C♮–B♯	E♮–F♭	G♯–A♭
C♯–D♭	E♯–F♮	A♯–B♭

The word "homophones" is sometimes used to describe these enharmonic tones on the harp. They are useful in various ways, but most frequently in connection with glissandos.

In performing a glissando, the player draws his hand quickly across the strings, touching each string included within the compass notated. Because it is not possible to skip over any of the strings, each one must be tuned in such a way as to fit into the musical scheme at that point. The glissando may consist of a scale or a chord. If a scale is used, there is no particular problem, since the strings can be adjusted to give any major or minor scale, each string sounding one note of the scale. But suppose that we want a chord,

say a dominant 9th sound on C , to be played as a glissando.

244

We could prepare C♮, E♮, G♮, B♭, and D♮ on the strings of those letter names. There is then the problem of what to do with the F and A strings. Can they be made to fit into the chord, and if so, how? By putting the F pedal in the top notch, the string can be made to sound F♭, equivalent to E♮ in pitch; by depressing the A pedal to the bottom, we can make that string sound A♯, or the same as B♭. Our complete pedal setting, then, would be: C♮, D♮, E♮, F♭, G♮, A♯, B♭. When the player's hand is drawn rapidly over the strings, the fact that certain pitches are sounded twice will not be apparent to the ear. The result will simply be a dominant 9th sound on C without any extraneous tones. To give another illustration,

suppose we want a diminished 7th chord on F♯  to be played

as a glissando. The pedal setting in that case would be: F♯–G♭, A♮, B♯–C♮, D♯–E♭. (The letters have been listed here in such a way as to show the enharmonic pairs.) Obviously, not all chords can be played as glissandos. In the case of a G major triad, for example, the A string cannot possibly be raised to the enharmonic equivalent of B nor lowered to the enharmonic equivalent of G; likewise, the E and F strings cannot be made to fit into the chord. The only solution, in such cases, and one that is commonly used, is to include extra notes. With the G major triad, the A string could be tuned to A♮, the E string to E♮, both extra; the C pedal would be tuned to C♭ (= B♮) and the F pedal to F♭ (= E♮). The notes played by the harp, then, would be: G♮, A♮, B♮, C♭, D♮, E♮, F♭. Although this is a more highly colored sound than the pure G major triad, the added notes would not sound as extraneous as might be expected. Of course another solution here would be simply to abandon the attempt at a chord glissando and use the notes of the G major scale as a glissando. Either way would give the requisite "splash."

Glissandos may be begun and ended anywhere on the harp, may be made in either direction, and may cover as much of the instrument as desired. They are usually at least two octaves or so in length, since it is difficult to work up much sound or sense of sweep within shorter distances; sometimes they cover nearly the entire range of the instrument. Various methods of notation have been used, but the clearest and most satisfactory one

(as applied to ) seems to be that shown in Example 4.

Ex. 4

Of course the proper pedal settings must have been indicated previously. It is possible to play up to six notes (three in each hand) in an ascending glissando and up to eight notes in a descending glissando. A triple glissando is included in the examples that follow.

Ex. 5

(a) *Daphnis and Chloe* Suite No. 2

Permission for reprint granted by copyright owner, Durand et Cie, Paris, France; Elkan-Vogel Co., Inc., agents for the U.S.A.

(b) *Fire Bird* Suite

Notice that in glissandos the actual notes (including any enharmonic sounds) need be written out for only one octave. If the strings are tuned to sound these pitches in one octave, they must sound them in all octaves. Consequently it would be superfluous, as well as a great nuisance, to write out every note in the glissando. The matter of time values is not of any great importance; orchestrators seem to use anything from sixteenths to sixty-fourth notes. Usually there are so many notes that the actual mathematical values would be hard to notate accurately in any case.

There is no denying the fact that the glissando is basically one of the most intriguing and effective sounds in the harp's repertory. But it has been so overused (particularly in commercial scoring) that it has lost some of its freshness and charm; it is best used sparingly nowadays.

Normally, the harp's tones are allowed to ring after being plucked, and they have considerable sustaining power. When that effect would cause a blur or be inappropriate to the music, the player may be directed to damp the sound with his hands. For a series of notes or chords, each one to be damped immediately after it is played, the French expression *sons étouffés* ("damped sounds") is commonly employed. Sometimes the single word *étouffez* is placed at the end of a passage or after a glissando, to show that the sound must not be allowed to ring.[2] The contrary direction is *laissez vibrer* (abbreviation, "1. v.") meaning "let vibrate."

As was intimated earlier, the harp is by nature more harmonic than melodic in feeling. As a rule, melodies played on it sound thin and ineffectual, though it occasionally doubles a slow melodic line for a special color effect. Arpeggios and chords are its most frequent assignments. Some typical and effective arpeggio figures are shown in Example 6.

Ex. 6

(a) *Prelude to The Afternoon of a Faun*

Permission for reprint granted by Jean Jobert, Paris, France; Elkan-Vogel Co., Inc., Philadelphia, Penna., copyright owners.

(b) *The White Peacock*

Copyright renewal assigned, 1945, to G. Schirmer, Inc.

(c) *Requiem*

---

[2] A convenient symbol for "damp" (or "muffle") is ⊕, which may be applied to individual notes, a specified group of notes, or an entire passage. For the notation in each case, and for information on special effects not covered here, the reader is referred to *Method for the Harp* by Lucile Lawrence and Carlos Salzedo (G. Schirmer, Inc., New York, 1929) and *Modern Study of the Harp* by Carlos Salzedo (G. Schirmer, Inc., New York, 1921).

Because of the angle at which their hands engage the strings, harpists do not use the little finger of either hand in playing. That means that chords involving more than four notes to a hand cannot be played, except by using a very pronounced roll or arpeggio effect. Incidentally, the stretch of a 10th on the harp is roughly equivalent in difficulty to the stretch of an octave on the piano and may be considered a safe practical limit.

It is traditional to roll all chords slightly in harp playing; a vertical wavy line in front of a chord should be used only when a much more decided roll is wanted. If a chord is to be played without any roll whatever (that is, with all the tones starting at exactly the same time), a bracket the length of the chord should precede it (Ex. 7).

Ex. 7

Double 3rds and 6ths are quite feasible, either harmonically or melodically performed (Ex. 8).

Ex. 8

Rapid repeated notes on the same string are not very practical: a sudden return to the string only damps out the vibrations of the previous note before they have had a chance to get well started. Here is another case in which the enharmonic possibilities of the harp prove useful. By tuning two strings to the same sound and playing them alternately, we get the effect of a repeated note, but each string has twice as long to vibrate as it would if used by itself (Ex. 9).

Ex. 9

Obviously, two strings will produce more sound than one. It is for that reason that we sometimes find a single sound written for two enharmonically tuned strings (Ex. 10).

Ex. 10

Daphnis and Chloe Suite No. 2

Ravel

2 Harps

Although the changing of pedals is part of the harpist's business, it is only humane and reasonable to avoid unnecessary pedal changes. This can often be done by using an enharmonic spelling for certain notes. For instance, Example 11, as written, requires constant changing of the B pedal and a double change of the D and B pedals. (The double change is especially bad since both pedals are on the left side of the instrument.)

Ex. 11

Allegro moderato

Harp

Db C♮ B♮ E♮ F♯ G♮ A♮   B♭ B♮ B♭   B♮ B♭ B♮ B♭
                              D♮   D♭   D♮

If the passage is written as in Example 12, different strings are involved, and no pedal changes are necessary.

Ex. 12

Allegro moderato

Harp

D♮ C♯ B♮ E♮ F♮ G♮ A♯

From the standpoint of harmonic spelling, the latter way is obviously incorrect. In fact, the whole system of false notation produces results that are often contrary to proper harmonic grammar. Nevertheless, its use is justified in harp writing by the fact that it makes for greater ease in performance.

The bottom notes of the harp are dark and sonorous in quality, the middle register rich and warm. Although the higher strings do not have much volume or sustaining power, their dry, slightly percussive quality enables them to come through more clearly than might be expected. It should be remembered, though, that whatever register the harp is playing in, it cannot compete with large masses of sound if it is to be heard prominently. Because harp strings are slightly more resonant in their "flat" position (in the top notch) flat keys should be chosen in preference to sharp keys where there is a choice. For example, if the rest of the orchestra were playing in B major, it would usually be best to write the harp part enharmonically in C♭ major.

Harmonics can be produced on the harp: (1) by touching the string lightly in the middle with the lower part of the left hand and plucking the string with the left thumb; or (2) by touching the string lightly in the middle with the knuckle of the index finger of the right hand, and plucking the string with the right thumb. The note that results in each case is the first overtone, an octave higher than the normal pitch of the string. (Although harmonics involving higher overtones are possible, they are almost never used.) Harmonics have an attractive crystalline, bell-like quality; but because they have little volume, there is no point in using them except in passages where the background is extremely light. They are useful for single notes or, rarely, for short melodic lines that move slowly enough to allow for the special technique involved in playing the notes as harmonics. It is possible to play two harmonics at once with the left hand—even three or four if they are within the range of a 5th—but only one with the right hand. The middle register of the harp is much the best one for harmonics. As regards the notation of them, there are, unfortunately, two different systems in current use: (1) the harmonic is written at its actual pitch; or (2) it is written an octave lower than the pitch desired. In both cases, a small circle above the note is the indication for a harmonic. The first way seems the simpler, but since the second has been used more often, any harmonics had better be accompanied by a note in the harp part telling which method is being used. In Example 13, the harmonics are intended to sound an octave higher than the written notes.

Ex. 13

(a) *Fire Bird* Suite

Stravinsky

(b) *Prelude to The Afternoon of a Faun*

Debussy

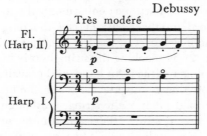

Permission for reprint granted by Jean Jobert, Paris, France; Elkan-Vogel Co., Inc., Philadelphia, Penna., copyright owners.

(c) *Daphnis and Chloe* Suite No. 2

Ravel

Permission for reprint granted by copyright owner, Durand et Cie, Paris, France; Elkan-Vogel Co., Inc., agents for the U.S.A.

There is not space here to describe all the other special effects possible on the harp. Many of them have been widely used in solo music for the instrument (particularly in pieces by the eminent harpist Carlos Salzedo) but have been little exploited in symphonic music. However, a few of the more important may be mentioned. There is, first, the brittle, somewhat metallic sound produced by playing with the fingernails. The usual symbol for this effect is a small crescent-shaped sign like a fingernail. The back of the nails may also be used in playing glissandos, to give what the Salzedo school calls a "falling hail" effect. Then there is the special tone quality that results from playing close to the sounding board. (*Sons près de la table* or simply *Près de la table* is the French direction.)

Among the devices more rarely used are the following: "timpanic sounds," produced by striking the most sonorous part of the sounding board with the third finger of the right hand, while the left hand plays normally; "fluidic sounds," which result from sliding the metal tuning key on the string; "metallic sounds," achieved by holding the appropriate pedal halfway between two notches; and "sliding of the pedals," which involves playing a note in the normal manner and then moving the pedal for that string one notch so that a pitch a half-step higher or lower results without being played by the hand (Ex. 14):

Ex. 14

THE CELESTA

Italian: Celesta   *French:* Célesta   *German:* Celesta

Ex. 15

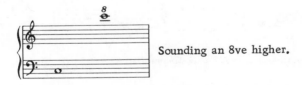

Sounding an 8ve higher.

In appearance the celesta is rather like a small piano. It has a keyboard like the piano's (though much shorter) and a damper pedal, which, when depressed, allows the tone to ring. But in place of strings, the instrument is equipped with small steel bars, each one with its own wooden resonator. These give out a delicate, bell-like tone. Gordon Jacob remarks, picturesquely, that the tone of the celesta always reminds him of the taste of a ripe plum.[3] In spite of its charm, however, it has little power and is drowned out by anything but the lightest of backgrounds.

[3] Gordon Jacob, *Orchestral Technique.*

The celesta is most often used to add a silvery edge to a melodic line. At other times it may merely provide "shimmer" via an arpeggio or some other figuration, as in Example 16(c). On rare occasions it may take a melody or a complete harmonic passage by itself, as in Example 16(a).

EXAMPLES

(Celesta sounding an octave higher)

Ex. 16

(a) *Nutcracker* Suite

(b) *Schelomo*

Copyright renewal assigned, 1945, to G. Schirmer, Inc.

(c) *Daphnis and Chloe* Suite No. 2

Permission for reprint granted by copyright owner, Durand et Cie, Paris, France; Elkan-Vogel Co., Inc., agents for the U.S.A.

Photograph courtesy of G. C. Jenkins Co., Decatur, Illinois
Celesta

THE PIANO

Italian: Pianoforte   *French:* Piano   *German:* Klavier

Ex. 17

The piano is not, strictly speaking, an orchestral instrument, but it is occasionally used in the orchestra for purposes of color or special effect. Its upper register can add sparkle or a bright clang, while the bottom notes are sometimes employed for their dark, faintly gong-like quality or to add percussive force and body to a bass line. The middle register, being more neutral in color, is less interesting in the orchestra. Furthermore, use of the piano for middle-register harmony parts is apt to be unpleasantly reminiscent of small studio and salon orchestras in which the piano must often take the place of missing horns, bassoons, and other instruments. Also to be avoided, as a rule, is the "fussy," rich-textured sort of writing that figures in piano concertos of the romantic period. Something simple and striking will be far more effective. In fact, parts for the piano as an orchestral instrument seem to be successful to the extent that they get away from overfamiliar solo-piano patterns.

It should be emphasized that the piano is called for relatively rarely in orchestral writing, even in contemporary works. When it is included, it is best used in small doses like other special orchestral colors. Excellent examples of its use in modern music can be found in Prokofieff's Fifth Symphony and in Copland's Third Symphony.

EXAMPLES

Ex. 18

(a) *Fire Bird* Suite

Stravinsky

(b) First Symphony

(c) *Pines of Rome*

By permission of G. Ricordi & Co., copyright owners.

SUGGESTED ASIGNMENTS

A. Know:

1. ranges of harp, celesta, and piano.
2. function of pedals on harp and order in which they are arranged.
3. enharmonic possibilities, false spelling.
4. proper notation of glissandos.
5. special effects on the harp.
6. transposition of celesta.
7. effective uses of celesta and piano in the orchestra.

B. (1) Give the pedal setting that would be used if each of the following harmonies were to be played as a glissando on the harp. If any of the chords are impossible as a glissando (without the addition of extra notes) indicate that opposite the appropriate number.

Ex. 19

(2) List the dominant 7th chords possible as glissandos on the harp and show the pedal setting for each.

SUGGESTED LISTENING

Harp

Berlioz, *Fantastic Symphony*, 2nd movt. (*Un bal*).

Wagner, *Love Death* from *Tristan und Isolde; Immolation Scene* from *Die Valkyrie*.

Franck, Symphony in D minor, 2nd movt.

Tchaikovsky, *Romeo and Juliet; Waltz of the Flowers* from the *Nutcracker* Suite.

Rimsky-Korsakoff, *Capriccio Espagnol*, near beginning of section IV (*Scena e Canto Gitano*).

Debussy, *Afternoon of a Faun; Nocturnes:* II. *Fêtes; Ibéria; La Mer.*

Ravel, *Introduction and Allegro; Daphnis and Chloe* Suite No. 2; *La Valse; Rapsodie Espagnole; Le Tombeau de Couperin; Pavane pour une Infante Défunte.*

Widor, *Chorale and Variations* for harp and orchestra.

Stravinsky, *Fire Bird* Suite; *Orpheus*, First Scene and Third Scene.

Bartók, Concerto for Orchestra, particularly Section III (*Elegia*) and latter part of Section II (*Giuoco delle Coppie*).

McDonald, Suite *"From Childhood"* for harp and orchestra.

Dello Joio, Concerto for Harp and Orchestra.

White, *Sea Chantey*, for harp and orchestra.

Mahler, Symphonies.

Copland, Third Symphony, 3rd movt., figure 72, figure 83 (both involving two harps and celesta); 4th movt., beginning; figure 120 (two harps, celesta, piano).

Celesta

Tchaikovsky, *Dance of the Sugar Plum Fairy* from the *Nutcracker* Suite.

Strauss, *Der Rosenkavalier*, number 303 (near the end) and following, also other passages.

Debussy, *Ibéria*, Section II (*Les Parfums de la nuit*).

Ravel, *Daphnis and Chloe* Suite No. 2; *Rapsodie Espagnole.*

Stravinsky, *Petrouchka* (celesta played 4-hands at figure 15).

Bloch, *Schelomo.*

Griffes, *The White Peacock.*

Bartók, *Music for String Instruments, Percussion, and Celesta.*

Shostakovitch, Fifth Symphony, end of 3rd movt.; Sixth Symphony, 1st movt., at number 28.

Schönberg, *Variations for Orchestra*, Op. 31, Var. I, Var VII; *Five Pieces for Orchestra*, Op. 16 (new version).

Webern, *Variations for Orchestra*, Op. 30; *Six Pieces*, Op. 6.

Copland, Third Symphony, 2nd movt., figure 40. See also the listings for the Copland Third Symphony under HARP, above.

Piano

Saint-Saëns, *The Carnival of Animals.*

Stravinsky, *Fire Bird* Suite; *Petrouchka; Symphony of Psalms;* Symphony in Three
    Movements; *Les Noces.*
Prokofieff, Fifth Symphony.
Respighi, *Pines of Rome; Roman Festivals.*
Shostakovitch, First Symphony.
Copland, *Rodeo: El Salon Mexico; Appalachian Spring;* Third Symphony.
Lambert, *The Rio Grande.*

Chapter 16

SCORING
FOR FULL ORCHESTRA

It should be clearly understood that the term "scoring for full orchestra" does not necessarily imply using all the instruments at once; an examination of a large number of scores would reveal that actual *tuttis* make up a relatively small portion of most of those scores. "Full orchestra" means only that all the instruments are on hand, to be selected as seems appropriate to the music being orchestrated. However, a good many of the examples in this chapter do involve most of the instruments, since they were chosen with the idea of illustrating techniques in scoring for large groups playing at once—a musical situation not encountered earlier in this book.

So far we have dealt principally with the scoring of chordal and homophonic music, reserving a full consideration of the scoring of purely polyphonic music until we had the entire orchestra to work with. In a sense, this last aspect of orchestration is one of the more difficult ones, for there are no harmonic masses which can be made to "sound" easily, and the relative weight of each line must be calculated with special care.

One of the main objectives in scoring linear music is to bring out the individual voices clearly. Here the orchestra has a certain advantage over the piano: whereas the piano has only one color to offer, the orchestra has many, and by allotting a different color to each voice we can give the lines a clarity and independence—a kind of third-dimensional feeling—that is impossible on the piano. For example, if three voices are involved, we might give one to oboe, one to clarinet, and one to bassoon. But it is not always necessary to use sharply contrasting colors. The three voices might be given, instead, to violins, violas, and cellos, respectively, in which case the differences of timbre, although less decided, would still afford a small color contrast between the parts. While it is possible to use instruments of different sections on the various parts, one must be careful to choose instruments that can be made to balance properly. It is also possible to contrast one composite color with another composite color or with a pure color.

Doublings of the top voice an octave (or even two octaves) higher and of the bottom voice an octave lower are useful and effective in arrangements of polyphonic music. But octave doublings of the inner voices are likely to be less successful, for they often involve a crossing of parts that may cause a muddled effect. When that happens, they had better be avoided.

Normally, an instrument or group of instruments that begins a particular voice should follow through on that voice to the end of the phrase or musical thought. In fugues, for example, it is usual to retain the same instrument on each voice at least up to the point where all the voices have announced the subject. After that, changes in scoring on the various parts are decidedly in order, at points where the structure of the music seems to warrant them. The re-entrance of a voice will be doubly effective if it can be scored in a timbre that has not been heard for several bars. To state the case another way, if an instrument is to make an important entrance, try to give it at least a few measures of rest beforehand.

With these brief remarks as a prelude, let us go on now to the fugue we are to use for our sample scoring. The first excerpt is the beginning or exposition of the fugue. Instead of including a separate example to show the actual orchestration, we have simply indicated here in the keyboard version the instruments that might be chosen. Since no dynamics or tempo indication are given in the original, we have had to supply our own. The third and fourth announcements of the subject have been marked a bit louder than the first two in order to make sure that they come through clearly against the upper voices.

Ex. 1

Fugue II (Book II of *The Well Tempered Clavier*)

Vc., *mf*; also Basses
(sounding an 8ve lower) if desired

Probably pure colors are best here at the beginning, mixed tone being reserved for later sections. By the same token, although it would be possible to give this opening section to brass instruments, it is much more effective to save them, or at least some of them, for the heavier, more emphatic announcements of the subject that usually occur later in the fugue.

The next excerpt is an ingenious *stretto* from about the middle of the fugue (in a *stretto* the subject overlaps itself). Here the subject appears in three different versions: (1) in the original form; (2) in augmentation (with note values doubled); and (3) in inversion (with the direction of the intervals reversed). If the musical content of this passage is to be made clear, each voice must stand out sharply on its own; that effect, in turn, can best be achieved by using a different color on each voice. Here again, we have merely suggested one of the many possible ways in which the excerpt could be transcribed (Ex. 2).

Ex. 2

The third excerpt consists of the last five and one half bars of the fugue, again an impressive *stretto*. (Each entrance of the subject or a portion of it is marked with an "S" here.)

Ex. 3

Ex. 4

Fugue II (Book II of *The Well Tempered Clavier*)

Bach
(Arr. by K.W.K.)

Although this fugue is usually played legato, a marcato effect seems appropriate, or at least possible, in this concluding section, and that interpretation has been used in the orchestral version in Example 4. The full orchestra, including brass, has been brought into play here. Since the voices seem to be about equally important and must therefore be balanced, it was necessary to distribute them among the brass instruments, strings and woodwinds being doubled with these parts either in unison or at the octave. However, instead of using the entire orchestra from the beginning of the passage, strings and woodwinds were added one or two at a time in order to accentuate each entrance of the subject and also to achieve a cumulative effect in leading to the *tutti* at the end. It would have been possible to reverse the orchestration by starting the final *stretto* with strings and woodwinds and adding brass at each entry of the subject.

It must not be concluded from these comments that the brass should be included only in *fortissimo*, heavily scored passages or that all the brass instruments must play if one plays. At lower dyanmic levels, balance can often be maintained between a single brass instrument and a single woodwind or a string group.

Example 5, from the Prelude to *Die Meistersinger*, combines three distinct musical ideas or elements. They are scored, respectively, as follows:

1. (consisting of three voices doubled at the octave): 2 flutes, 2 oboes, 1 clarinet, 3 horns (1 trumpet), violins II, violas;
2. 1 clarinet in unison with violins I; 1 horn in unison with cellos an octave lower;
3. 2 bassoons in unison with tuba; double basses an octave lower.

Although the greatest differentiation of the three elements could have been achieved by the use of sharply contrasting colors, Wagner chooses to present each element in a composite tone color produced by at least one woodwind, one brass instrument, and one string group. Yet in performance the three elements stand out sufficiently from each other, partly because of the differences between the *composite* colors and partly for purely musical reasons—differences in articulation, note values, and registers.

Despite the fact that we move into a totally different musical world in Example 6, the principles of scoring discussed in connection with Example 4 are still valid: because of the very high dynamic level, each of the lines involved must be included within the brass section if balance is to be achieved. Woodwinds and strings take unison or upper-octave doublings of them.

It is suggested that for each of the examples that follow the student make a listing (such as the one above for Example 5) of the instruments which take the various elements.

In this chapter and the next, the musical examples show the instruments listed as they are in the published scores (that is, in the abbreviated form of the foreign names) in order to accustom the student to identifying the instruments in scores using German, French, or Italian.

Ex. 5

Prelude to *Die Meistersinger*

Wagner

Ex. 6 Third Symphony

(a)

Copland

The reverse of the approach seen in Examples 5 and 6 is demonstrated in Example 7. Here, each one of the musical elements is given a separate color, and there is no mixing of timbres from different sections; in fact, except for some use of composite color *within* the woodwind section, the colors are pure, though produced in this case by more than one of each instrument. Even the two sections of violins differ from each other in quality, since the first violins are unmuted and in a high, intense register, while the second violins are muted and playing bowed tremolos in a much less brilliant register

Ex. 7

Six Pieces for Orchestra, Op. 6, No. 1

Instead of making exclusive use of either composite colors (as in Ex. 4–6) or pure colors (as, for the most part, in Example 7), the vast majority of contrapuntal scoring involves both. This is true of Example 8(a), though there is a preponderance of pure color there. In contemporary music that involves a complex linear fabric (as this passage does), considerable use of separate timbres is almost a necessity if the lines are to be kept distinct.

Example 8 illustrates certain tendencies in orchestration that are especially apparent in the works of serial composers:

1. There has been a reaction against the heavy, opaque, and often sumptuous scoring characteristic of late nineteenth-century orchestral music; composers today generally favor a leaner, more transparent sound. This does not necessarily mean, however, that a smaller orchestra is involved. A good many contemporary scores make use of a full orchestra but tend to employ the instruments consecutively more than simultaneously, so that much of the time relatively few of them are playing at once. Changes in the orchestration are likely to occur frequently, and instruments are often treated in soloistic fashion. In Example 8(a) all the instruments play at some point; yet because of the somewhat fragmentary individual parts and the fact that one group often drops out when another enters, the total effect is not particularly heavy.

2. Octave doublings, so heavily relied upon in eighteenth- and nineteenth-century orchestration, are often avoided. In the case of Schönberg and his followers, this avoidance probably stemmed chiefly from their desire not to give any note or notes a special importance that might lead to tonal implications, rather than from considerations of orchestration. But some nonserial composers also avoid octave doublings, simply to achieve the particular clarity and uncluttered sound which results.

3. There has been an increasing use of "C scores." In some of these, all the instruments are written at concert pitch, as in Example 8, but the majority still employ the octave transposition for the piccolo, double bass, and other instruments which otherwise are likely to need many ledger lines or an 8va sign. In any case, the players' parts for transposing instruments must of course be written in transposed form.

Examples 8(b) and (c), from Variation II of the same work, illustrate a pronounced use of the soloistic approach mentioned earlier. At the beginning of the variation (Ex. [b]), only pure colors are employed, and each voice is allotted to only one instrument, even in the case of the strings. In spite of the size of the orchestra, the effect at this point is actually that of a chamber group. Later in the variation (Example [c]) some unison doublings appear, but the texture and its orchestral garb remain essentially the same: a rather complex web of four to six highly independent lines scored in separate colors. (Interestingly, the short line for the trombone in the second measure of [c] is the much used B–A–C–H motive.)

Ex. 8

Variations for Orchestra, Op. 31   Schönberg

(b) II. Variation

Used by permission of Belmont Music Publishers, Los Angeles, California 90049. Copyright 1956 by Gertrud Schoenberg.

Note: In this work all instruments are written as they will actually sound.

Fragmentation, which stemmed chiefly from Webern's innovations[1] and which has been a major feature of much twentieth-century music, brought with it a parallel possibility in orchestration: melodic lines that formerly would have been taken by a single instrument are now sometimes divided among several. In serial music the row may even be fragmented to the point where each note is given to a separate instrument. In the Webern excerpt that follows (Ex. 9) the individual passages are so brief (some only one note) and there is so little use of instruments simultaneously that the total effect is extremely delicate and transparent. But it is worthy of note that nearly every instrument of the orchestra is used at some point on this page.

Octave displacement, a frequent device in serial music, obviously contributes to fragmented scoring when applied in the orchestra. Whereas extremely wide leaps are entirely feasible on the piano, for example, they often present problems of range for individual instruments of the orchestra, with the result that the allotting of a melodic idea to several instruments in turn may become a necessity.

The term "pointillistic," borrowed from a French school of painting that used small dots of unmixed color to achieve its effects, is sometimes applied to orchestration such as that in Example 9—as well as to highly fragmented lines themselves. While it is an appropriate and convenient term, it has the slight disadvantage of having been associated on occasion with a very different style of scoring—the impressionistic variety that makes use of small touches of color and subtle effects (as in certain Debussy works). Today, however, it generally has the first connotation.

The pointillistic technique of scoring may of course be applied to music of a nonserial character; Webern himself orchestrated a six-voice ricercar from Bach's *Musical Offering* in that fashion. Example 10 shows how the instruments are allotted during the first statement of the subject. Arrangements of this sort have met with reactions ranging from delight to outrage, and the esthetic validity of the approach has been widely debated. In the end, however, the answers to the questions raised remain a matter of individual taste and opinion.

Schönberg's concept of a "melody" made up solely of changing colors (*Klangfarbenmelodie*, meaning literally "tone color melody") should be mentioned here, since it anticipated and undoubtedly encouraged the pre-

---

[1] The fragmentation of lines is, in a sense, a return to the technique of "hocketing" employed in medieval polyphony.

Ex. 9

Variations for Orchestra, Op. 30

Webern

Note: All instruments are written as they will actually sound.

Ex. 10

Webern's Orchestration of Ricercar
from Bach's *Musical Offering*

occupation with individual timbres that is seen in the music of Webern and that of the many composers since his day who have adopted the pointillistic approach. It will be discussed briefly in the next chapter.

Example 11, from the Passacaglia section of Hindemith's *Nobilissima Visione*, affords a chance to study four orchestral settings involving the same theme as basis but with that theme orchestrated in a different way each time and with different counterpoints surrounding it. Example (a) includes all six measures of one variation (the seventh appearance of the theme) plus the first two measures of the next; (b) and (c) show, respectively, the first two measures of the two variations that follow. Here, again, the student will find it profitable to analyze the distribution of the instruments. He should, in the process, examine the weight of the passacaglia theme in relation to the other lines, and the weight of those lines in relation to each other. Stylistic differences between the scoring here and in preceding examples should be observed, and the ways in which principles discussed earlier apply here should be considered.

272

Ex. 11

Nobilissima Visione, 3. Passacaglia
(a)

Hindemith

274

As we turn now to the scoring of chordal and homophonic music for the complete orchestra, there is little new in the way of general principles that need be added. If the music is chordal, we can apply the material learned in Chapter 10, the only difference being that a succession of chords is involved instead of a single isolated chord. The important question of voice-leading between the chord tones enters in here too.

Suppose that we had set out to score the Brahms Rhapsody in E♭ major (Op. 119, No. 4), the beginning of which is a good example of chordal music. The first two measures are as follows:

Ex. 12

Rhapsody, Op.119, No. 4

Brahms

Allegro risoluto

Piano

Although, as we have seen, "scoring for orchestra" does not necessarily involve making constant use of all the instruments on hand, this particular example seems to suggest the full orchestral *tutti*. It also suggests a fairly brilliant coloring. We shall want to fill in the gap between the two hands, of course. It would probably be wise to sketch the orchestration (for at least the first chord or two) before writing out the actual score. Such a sketch, showing the layout of each section, might look like this:

Ex. 13

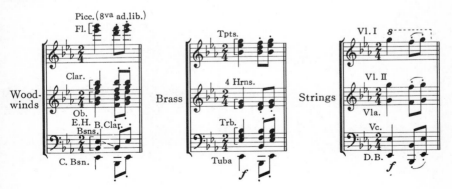

We would undoubtedly want to use timpani as well, either on the first beat of each measure

Ex. 14

(a)

or on the complete rhythmic pattern.

(b)

Having once set up this arrangement of instruments, our only problem during this opening portion is to let each note progress to the appropriate note in the next chord, so that good melodic lines will result for the individual instruments. Of course, there will be different arrangements of the instruments as the musical structure changes. An excellent exercise would be to write out the first ten measures (or more) of this piece in full score, using the sketch given here as the basis for the beginning.

The excerpt from Strauss' *Death and Transfiguration* in Example 15 is a good example of primarily chordal music scored for full orchestra. Incidentally, it illustrates the fact that full scoring need not be reserved for very loud passages; in this case the dynamic marking is *pianissimo*.

Another example of chordal texture is the Mussorgsky-Ravel excerpt (Ex. 16). There the original piano version is included at the bottom for purposes of comparison and is not meant to be played in the orchestral version.

Death and Transfiguration

Strauss

Ex. 16

Promenade (from *Pictures from an Exhibition*)

Mussorgsky - Ravel

The scoring of homophonic music was discussed in Chapter 12. There we used an orchestra consisting of woodwinds in pairs, horns, and strings. If a larger orchestra is involved, the problem is not altered as far as essential principles are concerned; the inclusion of additional woodwinds and of a full brass section merely gives us greater potential volume, increased range in the woodwind and brass sections, and new colors that may be used in a solo capacity. Some examples of homophonic music scored for full orchestra are shown next. (The first example makes use of the usual "full orchestra" of Beethoven's day, one which included no trombones.)

In Example 17 the melody is taken by first violins and first horn in octaves, with the second horn harmonizing in the same rhythm and bassoons joining in presently to double these two voices in a lower octave. The upper woodwinds have sustained harmony parts; second violins and violas take an idiomatic accompaniment figure, while trumpets, timpani, and lower strings reiterate the A pedal point.

In Example 18 the chief melodic line in octaves is given to a doubling of woodwinds, brass, and strings, with harmonic background and moving bass also distributed among the three sections.

Example 19 (a) demonstrates an arrangement that is uncommon in piano music but fairly frequent in the orchestra: the melody is in the bottom voice with harmonies above. Here, again, an octave doubling made up of brass, strings, and woodwinds is used for the melody. In this case the brass will predominate.

In Example 19 (b) the two melodic lines, played by trumpets and (in the last two bars) by trombones, are in middle voices, with harmonic parts above and below. Because of the power of the trumpet and trombone, two of each give enough sound to come through the rest of the orchestra.

In Example 20, the most important melody is given to the strings, a countermelody to the woodwinds, and a second countermelody to the upper brass. Except for an E pedal point which is shared by the lower brass and the double basses, this excerpt illustrates on a broad scale the principle we discussed in connection with polyphonic music, that of allotting a separate color to each voice to achieve the maximum distinctness and independence of line. Here we have not merely separate colors, but separate *sections* on the various parts. It might be argued that this example is actually polyphonic rather than homophonic in texture. The truth is probably that it lies somewhere between these two types; we are dealing in lines, to be sure, yet the countermelodies in woodwinds and brass seem to have the character more of ornamented harmony parts than of independent voices on a par with the melody in the strings.

This case brings up the point that music does not always fall exclusively into one of the three categories we have mentioned frequently in this book: chordal, homophonic, or polyphonic. We have used these categories in order to point out certain broad approaches to scoring, but hybrid types occur constantly. For example, we often have an important melodic line against a harmonic background (homophony) along with countermelodies that introduce a partially polyphonic effect. And some harmonic music consists of individual lines that move in an independent and musically interesting way, so that a polyphonic element is present.

When countermelodies are involved, one must be careful to weight the principal idea strongly enough, either by dynamics or sheer number of instruments, so that it will not be eclipsed by the secondary counterpoints. In Example 20, the countermelody in the trumpets and horns is marked one degree softer than the woodwinds and strings in order to insure that the greater power of the brass will not make that line too prominent.

In Example 21, the woodwinds and horns take the melody and its parallel harmonization, while the strings play a countermelody and the brass also has subordinate parts.

Example 22 illustrates impressionistic scoring for a fairly large orchestra. Features characteristic of the impressionistic approach include the following: a sensitive (and often sensuous) use of color, such as the frequent division of string groups into numerous parts, the velvety richness of the lower strings in the last two measures, the unusual doubling involving horn with piccolos two octaves higher, and the delicate touches in the xylophone, celesta, harp and tambourine; an avoidance of heavy masses of sound and of dynamic bombast; a constant concern for subtleties of dynamic nuance.

It is hoped that the distinction between the approach to color in this sort of scoring and in that of the Webern pointillistic school will be apparent from the examples given, and more will be said on this subject presently. In the first type, color has chiefly a decorative function, in the second, a constructional one.

Ex. 17

Seventh Symphony

Beethoven

Ex. 18

Symphony in D minor

Allegro non troppo   Franck

Ex. 19

Symphony in E minor *(New World)*

Dvorák

284

Ex. 20

Fifth Symphony

Tchaikovsky

Ex. 21

Les Préludes

Liszt

Ex. 22

Iberia. II. *Les parfums de la nuit*

Debussy

SUGGESTED ASSIGNMENTS

The following are suitable as exercises in scoring for full orchestra (although not all of them call for consistently heavy scoring). If it is possible to have a school or local orchestra try out student projects in orchestration, the instrumentation of that orchestra should be learned in advance and used for the pieces to be played.

1. Bach, any of the chorales.
2. Bach, Fugue XVI from *The Well Tempered Clavier*, Vol. I.
3. Bach, Fugue XXII from *The Well Tempered Clavier*, Vol. I.
4. Bach, Fugue in G minor from *Eight Little Preludes and* Fugues for the Organ.
5. Beethoven, *Sonata Pathétique*, Op. 13 (beginning in particular).
6. Beethoven, Sonata, Op. 10, No. 3, 1st movt.
7. Beethoven, Sonata, Op. 101, beginning; 2nd movt., meas. 1–11.
8. Beethoven, Sonata, Op. 106, beginning; 2nd movt., meas. 1–46.
9. Schubert, Sonata, Op. 143, 1st movt., exposition.
10. Schubert, Sonata in B♭ major, Op. Posth.
11. Chopin, Polonaise in A major, Op. 40, No. 1.
12. Schumann, Fantasia, Op. 17, 2nd movt., meas. 1–22.
13. Brahms, Rhapsody, Op. 79, No. 1.
14. Brahms, Rhapsody, Op. 79, No. 2.
15. Brahms, Rhapsody, Op. 119, No. 4.
16. Wolf, "Verborgenheit" (song).
17. Mussorgsky, "Ballet of the Chickens in their Shells" from *Pictures from an Exhibition*. (This offers a good chance for the use of special color effects: harp, celesta, percussion, etc.).
18. Mussorgsky, "The Great Gate of Kiev" from *Pictures from an Exhibition*.
19. Debussy, "The Engulfed Cathedral" from *Préludes*, Book I.
20. Rachmaninoff, Prelude in G minor.
21. Griffes, "The White Peacock" from *Roman Sketches*. (This lends itself well to impressionistic scoring.)
22. Griffes, Scherzo, Op. 6, No. 3.
23. Prokofieff, March, Op. 12, No. 1.
24. Prokofieff, Seventh Sonata for piano, Op. 83, 1st movt.
25. Tcherepnine, (Alexandre), Bagatelle I from *Ten Bagatelles*.
26. Bartók, No. 1 from *Fifteen Hungarian Peasant Songs*.
27. Rochberg, Bagatelle VIII from *Twelve Bagatelles*.
28. Mennin, "Aria" from *Five Piano Pieces*.
29. Kennan, Prelude III from *Three Preludes*.
30. Kabalevsky, Prelude 24 from *24 Preludes*, meas. 33–39.

OTHER EXERCISES

A word might be added here about certain exercises which have not been mentioned before. One consists in "de-orchestrating"; that is, reducing an orchestral score for piano, or for piano four hands, or for two pianos. Almost any orchestral music may be chosen for this purpose, though for the first attempt it would probably be wise to select a relatively uncomplicated score, say a Mozart or Haydn symphony. This is an excellent way to achieve an intimate acquaintance with a score and with the composer's characteristic use of instruments.

Piano reductions of many scores are available commercially. Another exercise consists in arranging such a reduction for the same orchestra that the composer originally used. The completed scoring can then be compared with the original orchestral version.

A somewhat similar exercise, mentioned earlier, is that of scoring a work which was written originally for piano (or another medium) and later issued in orchestral form. (A list of such works is given at the end of Chapter 11.) The student's version can then be compared with the published orchestral version.

Finally, there is score-reading at the piano—or at two pianos, with one player taking the woodwind and brass parts and the other taking the string parts. In any case, it is wise to begin with fairly simple material and progress to more complex.[2] Although this is a rather special technique which can be learned only by repeated practice over a period of time, a few advance hints may be of some help:

1. It will not always be possible to play all of the notes; sometimes octave doublings, secondary counterpoints, and the like will have to be omitted.

2. In widely spaced chords, string figurations, and other passages which are awkward pianistically, some rearrangement of the notes will be be necessary.

3. Try to keep going in spite of minor slips or omissions. It is more important to keep the music moving along at a steady pace (not necessarily up to tempo, however) and to aim at the general effect of the original than to worry too much about individual notes, although accuracy should be striven for, of course.

[2] In this connection, *Music for Score Reading,* by Robert A. Melcher and Willard F. Warch (Prentice-Hall, Inc., 1971) provides an excellent series of graded excerpts and is highly recommended.

Chapter 17

SPECIAL DEVICES

EMPHASIS ON INDIVIDUAL COLORS

In the remarks on pointillistic scoring made earlier, *Klangfarbenmelodie*, or "tone color melody," was mentioned. This concept forms the basis for the third of Schönberg's *Five Pieces for Orchestra*, Op. 16, entitled *Summer Morning by a Lake (Colors)*. A concert sketch of the first few measures is shown next in Example 1.

Ex. 1

Harmonic and melodic activity have been reduced to nearly zero here, the only "motion" being in the subtle shifting from one orchestral color to another. Although the *Klangfarbenmelodie* principle has not often been used in this particular fashion by other composers, it has been a major factor in music since Webern's day in the sense that there has been much emphasis on color as an actual compositional element rather than as a decorative feature. This approach has most often been applied to melodic lines, by assigning a different instrumental timbre to each note. While intriguing results can be produced in this way, there are certain inherent dangers. For one thing, there is a temptation to let color substitute for a strong and interesting melodic line; for another, a constantly changing orchestral palette can become just as monotonous as one that changes infrequently.[1]

THE CREATION OF PARTICULAR TONE QUALITIES THROUGH OVERTONE REINFORCEMENT

By having instruments play, softly, certain upper partials of a fundamental, it is possible to arrive at tone qualities not found in any one of the orchestral instruments. For example, in *Bolero* Ravel in effect creates a new instrument by having the horn play the theme *mf* while two piccolos softly play partials 3 and 5 and a celesta plays partials 2 and 4. The resulting sound is striking and exotically colored.

Ex. 2

Bolero　　　　　　　　　　　　　　　　　Ravel

Permission for reprint granted by Durand and Cie of Paris, France Copyright Owners; Elkan-Vogel Co., Inc., of Philadelphia, Pa., Sole Agents in the United States.

[1] For a perceptive commentary on this whole subject, the reader is referred to Reginald Smith Brindle's book, *Serial Composition* (Oxford University Press, London, 1966), Chapter 12: "Orchestration, Texture and Tone Colour."

This general technique is most often used in making orchestral transcriptions of organ music from the Baroque period. Organ registration of that day was characterized by the use of stops which strongly reinforced some or all of the upper partials—through the sixth, sounding two octaves and a 5th higher than the fundamental. In the orchestra the sound of that sort of registration can be simulated by placing high woodwinds (or occasionally strings playing harmonics) on the upper partials. However, not all these partials need be included; even doubling a line softly a 12th higher or two octaves and a 5th higher begins to suggest the "Baroque" effect, and either doubling combined with one two octaves above the basic pitch is moderately effective for that purpose.[2]

UNUSUAL SPACING

The suggestions concerning spacing given in the course of this book apply chiefly to pre-twentieth-century music. Many contemporary scores achieve highly interesting effects precisely by departing from traditional patterns. In Example 3, for instance, a triad is placed at the very bottom (where intervals would normally be wider) whereas in the middle register there are numerous gaps instead of the usual closer spacing.

[2] Readers who are interested in examining a score that makes considerable use of this whole approach are referred to *Toccata and Ritornelli* from Monteverdi's *Orfeo*, arranged and orchestrated by Maurice Peress (G. Schirmer, New York, 1967). There the intent is to "approximate and magnify" the sound of the orchestra that Monteverdi describes as having been used for a particular performance, an orchestra that included organs as well as a large number of early instruments.

292

Ex. 3

Agon, (Gailliarde)

With the special colors produced by harmonics in the flutes, harp and solo double basses and by the rarely used mandolin, the total effect is fresh and highly distinctive despite the fact that little more than a C major triad is involved, harmonically speaking. It need hardly be added that such exceptional spacing (and scoring) would be decidedly out of place in most music of earlier periods.

As a general principle, scoring that involves a wide gap in the middle register is likely to sound unsatisfactory and is normally avoided. Yet there are times when that very arrangement is employed for a particular effect. An instance is the following excerpt from Mahler's Ninth Symphony, where the two voices (one doubled at the lower octave) are separated by a vast distance. The passage is intensely affecting and dramatic to an extent it would not have been if it had been carefully "filled in" with octave doublings.

Ex. 4

Ninth Symphony

Mahler

Copyright by Universal Edition. Used by permission.

EMPHASIS ON TEXTURE

Texture, like color, has come to be considered by many composers an important element to be planned carefully and even utilized for its own sake on occasion. This idea is of course not an entirely new one. For example, in *The Rite of Spring* there are certain pages which suggest that Stravinsky's chief purpose was to build up a complex fabric of sound by superimposing many instruments playing different parts, as in Example 5. In such cases the listener tends to hear the overall texture rather than individual parts. Of course textural planning is often involved in music of a much thinner nature in which individual lines come through clearly and in which thematic content is more important.

Ex. 5

The Rite of Spring   Stravinsky

SPECIAL DYNAMIC ARRANGEMENTS

In addition to the more usual possibilities in dynamic effects, there are some special ones that appear from time to time in orchestral scoring. Among these are the following:

1. An instrument is introduced so softly that the listener is not aware of its entrance; it then raises its dynamic level to that of the other instruments playing. In commercial arranging this device is known as the "sneak-in." It can be used effectively in building an orchestral crescendo, the instruments entering one or two at a time until all are playing. The reverse process, though seen less often, is also useful when a decrescendo is wanted; individual instruments make a diminuendo and drop out successively.

2. "Contrapuntal dynamics" is a term sometimes applied to dynamic markings (including crescendos and diminuendos) that operate somewhat independently for the various parts. (This approach is the antithesis of the old "block dynamics" system that was the general rule during the Classical period.) Many composers of the Romantic era, including Wagner, Berlioz, Rimsky-Korsakoff and Strauss, made considerable use of differing dynamic levels in the same passage, but it was in the works of Mahler that the "contrapuntal" aspect was first carried to great lengths. For instance, in the third measure of Example 6 there are six different dynamic levels indicated, and at that point certain instruments are making a diminuendo while others are making a crescendo. The whole example demonstrates Mahler's intense concern with the most minute dynamic subtleties.

The simultaneous use of different dynamic levels in orchestral scoring stems in some cases from a desire to bring out a particular voice or tone color, in others from the need to compensate for inherent differences in weight between instruments. As examples of the latter situation, the brass section is sometimes marked one degree softer than the others in loud passages so that it will not overshadow them, and the harp, which tends to be easily covered, is often marked a degree louder.

3. The ultimate in independent dynamics occurs in certain serial music (especially the "totally organized" kind in which the dynamic pattern is one of the predetermined elements), where nearly every note has a separate indication. The levels indicated may vary widely and suddenly, so that abrupt changes between extremes of soft and loud are common. This approach is seen in Example 9.

296

Ex. 6

Fourth Symphony

Mahler

Published by International Music Co. Reprinted by permission.

4. In order to produce a distant effect, instruments are sometimes asked to play offstage. This device has probably been applied most often to a solo trumpet (Beethoven, *Leonore Overture No. 3;* Mahler, First Symphony) or a group of trumpets (Strauss, *Ein Heldenleben;* Verdi, *Requiem*). But it is also called for in woodwind parts on occasion. Two well-known instances (both involving the imitation of a shepherd's piping) are the passage for oboe, marked *lontano,* in Berlioz' *Fantastic Symphony* and the extended solo for English horn at the beginning of Act III of Wagner's *Tristan und Isolde.* The direction, in various languages, is as follows: Italian, *interna* or *dietra la scena* or *lontano;* French, *dans la coulisse* or *derrière la scène;* German, *auf der Bühne* or *in der Ferne* or *auf dem Theater.*

5. An instrument or a group of instruments which has been playing *forte* drops out, and as it does so another instrument or group enters *piano* on the last note. Stravinsky appears to be especially fond of this device; two examples from *Petrouchka* follow and numerous others could be quoted, including one from *Agon* in which three double basses playing harmonics take soft sustained tones as the other instruments drop out—a magical effect.

Ex. 7

Petrouchka

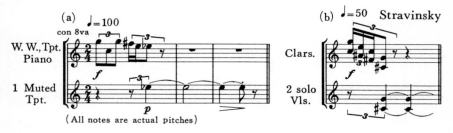

DIVISION OF A MUSICAL IDEA

A musical idea is sometimes divided between two instruments of the same kind. In certain instances this is done to ease a technical problem, such as fast passage work or awkward leaps or fast tonguing. This is the case in Examples 8(a) and 8(b). At other times the same approach is applied to wind parts that continue for some time without rests; by having two or more instruments of a kind play alternately, each has plenty of time to breath. This use is demonstrated in Example 8(c). (The passage continues in this fashion for another nine measures.)

Ex. 8

Schelomo

(a) Animato ($\quad$ = 108-112)   Bloch

Fl. I, II

(b)

Fl. I

Fl. II

(c) $\quad$ = 58

Bsn. I

Bsn. II

Reprinted by permission of G. Schirmer, Inc.

In the excerpt quoted in Example 2(c) in Chapter 5 Brahms makes use of a similar alternating and overlapping arrangement in the flute parts to insure that the melodic line will not be broken by even a brief retaking of breath.

THE USE OF SMALL INSTRUMENTAL GROUPS

Since the '50s or earlier, many composers have shown a fondness for small groups involving instruments of different sections of the orchestra, often with the addition of such extras as the harp, piano, and vibraphone. In terms of size, these groups clearly belong in the chamber category. But, especially when they include many of the regular orchestral instruments (normally no more than one of each), they sometimes suggest an orchestra in miniature. Such a work is Karlheinz Stockhausen's *Kontra-punkte Nr. 1* for nine instruments (Ex. 9).

Ex. 9

Kontra-punkte Nr. 1

Stockhausen

DIVISION OF THE ORCHESTRA INTO GROUPS

Ever since the earliest days of the orchestra, composers have occasionally used the device of dividing it into two or more parts; these may involve the same or different instrumentation. Such arrangements obviously suggest antiphonal effects and broad contrasts of weight or color. In contemporary usage they also lend themselves particularly to stimulating clashes between the groups, the clashes being either notated in the normal fashion or, in the case of aleatoric music, governed by chance.

Gabrieli's famous *Sonata pian' e forte,* which clearly reflects the divided-choir techniques of Venetian church music, is an example of an early venture into this genre. Mozart wrote a *Notturno* for four orchestras. Vaughan Williams' *Fantasia on a Theme of Tallis* and Bartók's *Music for String Instruments, Percussion and Celesta* both make use of a double string orchestra. In Stockhausen's *Gruppen* three orchestras participate. And Xenakis' *Strategy* involves two orchestras, each with its own conductor, which engage in a competition to see which one can produce the more interesting results under the same set of musical conditions, the winner being decided by judges.

THE USE OF EXTREME REGISTERS

Twentieth-century scores tend to make considerable use of the extreme registers of instruments, even extreme registers that were generally avoided in an earlier period because of difficulties in intonation, quality, or technique.[3] This tendency does not, however, rule out the validity of a normal *tessitura* for each instrument. Nor does the fact that such exceptional passages are written mean that they are always successful; frequently they merely confirm, in performance, the reasons why the registers involved were traditionally avoided for so long.

CUT-OUT SCORES

Example 10, an excerpt from a Boulez work, involves a small group of instruments (in this case with voice), but it has none of the "miniature orchestra" implications of Example 9. It is quoted here to illustrate the use of a "cut-out" score in which an instrument is given a staff only when it is playing, blank space being used in place of rests at other times. Proponents of this arrangement argue that it dispenses with needless clutter on the score page and allows the eye to concentrate on the points at which instruments are actually playing. Others feel that not enough is gained by this format to justify the extra effort involved in setting up the score.

NON-TRADITIONAL METHODS OF
PRODUCING SOUNDS ON INSTRUMENTS

Certain contemporary scores call for sounds produced by special and unorthodox means. In the case of woodwinds, the player may be asked to produce a clicking of the keys, either in the process of playing or as a separate effect. Or he may be directed to "crow" into the reed or, on the flute, to make a

---

[3] Listings of passages which make use of extreme or extended ranges are included in *Thesaurus of Orchestral Devices* by Gardner Read (Sir Isaac Pitman and Sons, Ltd., London, 1953).

Ex. 10

Improvisation sur Mallarmé

Boulez

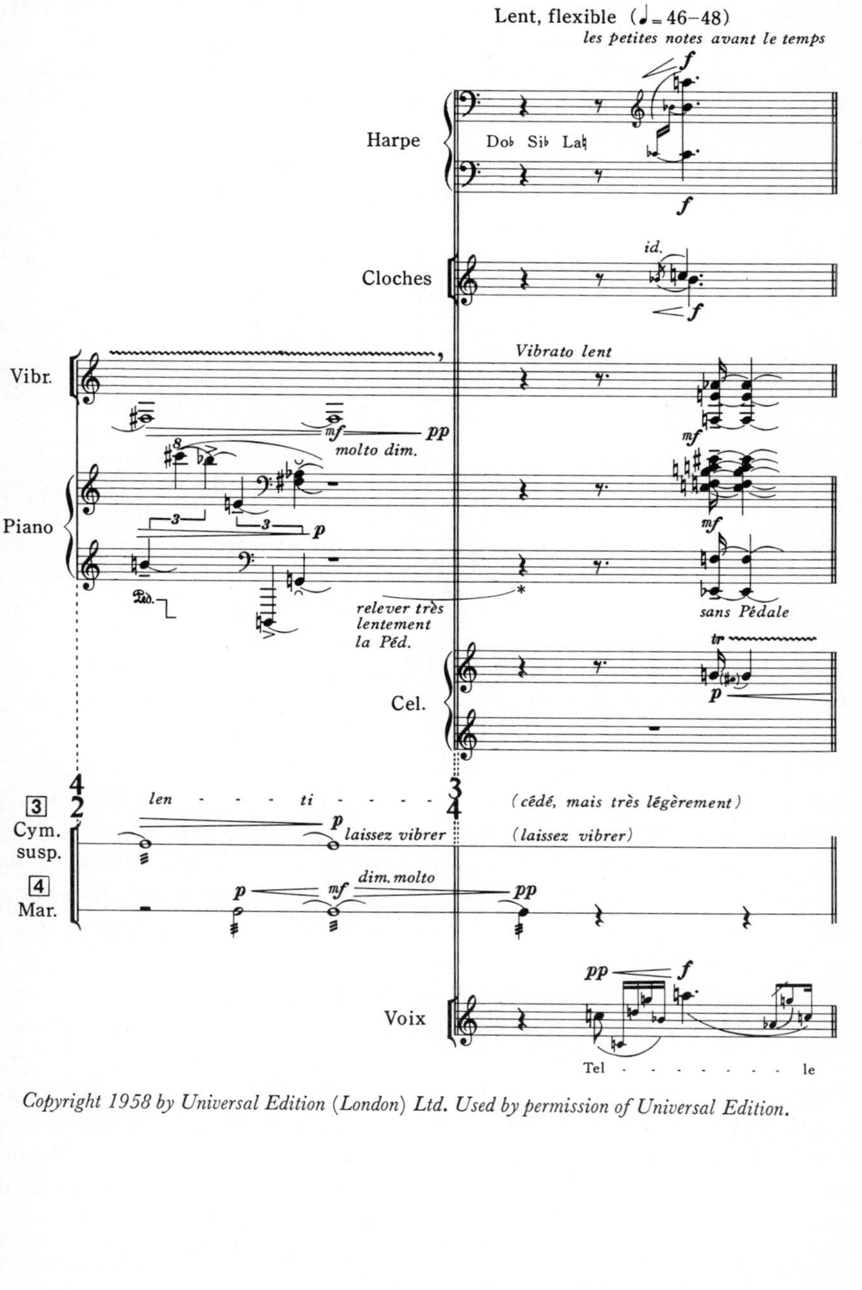

"kissing" sound at the mouthpiece. There has been considerable experimentation with chords on individual woodwinds, this effect being achieved through special fingerings that cause particular partials to sound as the upper notes. An intriguing discussion of these possibilities along with those in tonal and pitch variation is given in *New Sounds for Woodwind* by Bruno Bartolozzi, translated by Reginald Smith Brindle (London: Oxford University Press, 1967). A record demonstrating the sounds discussed in the book is included in an attached jacket.

On brass instruments, a clicking effect can be made with the valves. Other devices involve blowing air through the instrument, talking or shouting into it, striking the mouthpiece with the palm of the hand, or blowing into the mouthpiece alone. In the latter case the relative pitches of the notes are sometimes indicated by X's placed at various points on the staff. On the trumpet, "half-valving" produces a peculiar choked quality; arriving at exact pitches is difficult, however.

Among innovations involving the percussion are these: playing softly on the edge of an inverted cymbal that has been placed on the head of a timpano; playing a trumpet or trombone with the bell close to the head of a timpano, so that the drumhead sounds through sympathetic vibration; playing on the strings of the piano—most often the lower strings—with a gong mallet or marimba mallet (both soft) or occasionally with a harder stick.

Some composers now indicate particular percussion instruments in the body of a score by means of small symbols shaped like the instruments; an explanatory list of these symbols is provided at the beginning of the score. However, this system has not yet become standardized to the point where it has come into general usage.

A string device that is not new but that is seen more often today than formerly calls for the bow to be used behind the bridge. The sound is dry, thin, and somewhat eerie. Although the pitches (all higher than the corresponding open strings) vary from string to string, they are so uncertain that the usual notation consists simply of X's placed on the open pitches of the strings concerned; the values are indicated by means of stems, cross-beams, flags, and so on. For examples of this notation and two alternative methods, the reader is referred to *Music Notation* by Gardner Read (see Bibliography).

Although the tone cluster is, properly, a musical rather than an exclusively orchestral device, it might be mentioned here since it is a frequent feature of the string writing in the orchestral scores of certain contemporary composers (Penderecki, to mention only one). Generally the string groups—or some of them—divide, sometimes in many parts, to produce a block of sound in which the notes are bunched closely together, most often a minor 2nd apart. The result is not as dissonant as might be expected, especially when higher registers and softer dynamic levels are involved. Occasionally a score calls for the whole cluster to make a glissando.

Chapter 18

INFREQUENTLY
USED INSTRUMENTS

THE SAXOPHONES

Italian: Sassofono *French:* Saxophone *German:* Saxophon
       Sassofoni   Saxophones   Saxophone

Ex. 1

B♭ Soprano, sounding a major 2nd lower.
E♭ Alto,[1] sounding a major 6th lower.
B♭ Tenor, sounding a major 9th lower.
E♭ Baritone,[2] sounding an 8ve and a major 6th lower.
B♭ Bass, sounding 2 8ves and a major 2nd lower.

All the saxophones have the same *written* range and all are notated in the

treble clef, but each size transposes differently. The written note

would sound as follows on each of the saxophones:

---

[1] Many alto saxophonists are able to play the high F♯ or even G, although these notes are more difficult.

[2] Some older baritone saxophones do not have the top F. On the other hand, some of the newer models have the low (written) A.

Ex. 2

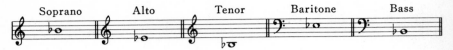

Therefore, in terms of actual sound we have five different ranges:

Ex. 3

Awkward as this system may seem, it has the advantage of enabling the player to use the same fingering on any one of the saxophones.

Let us suppose that we are scoring a piece for a combination that includes saxophones. We have decided that a particular melodic line lies comfortably within the range of the tenor saxophone and will sound well on that instrument. The part begins like this:

Ex. 4

In order to notate the passage correctly we must transpose up a major 9th (an octave plus a major 2nd). The written part will then begin with these notes:

Ex. 5

To write a part for the baritone saxophone we must think up an octave plus a major 6th from the actual sounds—and so on for the other saxophones.

A very small "sopranino" saxophone and a "contra-bass" saxophone are listed in some orchestration books, but these are not in current use. Likewise all but extinct is the "C-melody" saxophone which had a considerable vogue at one time. Even the bass and soprano instruments are little used today, although the latter has found favor with certain dance orchestras. (Incidentally, there are two types of soprano saxophone, one a miniature counterpart of the larger saxophones, the other, which is the one generally seen, straight like a clarinet.) But the alto, tenor, and baritone members of the family are in constant use in commercial arranging.

In the symphony orchestra, saxophones are employed only rarely. Examples that can be cited are the parts for them in Ravel's *Bolero,* the wonderfully effective solo for alto saxophone in the same composer's orchestration of Mussorgsky's *Pictures from an Exhibition* (in the section entitled *The Old Castle*), and the part for alto saxophone in Britten's *Sinfonia da Requiem.* School orchestras, however, sometimes use saxophones as substitutes for horns, bassoons, or other instruments that happen to be missing; some scores for school use include parts written for saxophones.

In general, the entire compass of the saxophone is usable, although the bottom two or three semitones on the soprano, alto and tenor instruments tend to be slightly inferior and are better avoided, while the top register of the tenor, baritone and bass saxophones is thinner and less characteristic. The instrument is remarkably agile technically. Almost every sort of figure is practical on it, but, being of the single-reed family like the clarinet, it is not well suited to playing rapid repeated notes. The bass saxophone, because of its greater size and ponderous operation, cannot be expected to perform quite as nimbly as the others, especially in the bottom 5th or so of its register.

It seems only fair to point out, in defense of the saxophone and its symphonic possibilities, that it need not have the blatant, wailing quality nor the wide, bleating vibrato that we hear so often in the dance band. That is merely one style of playing; the instrument can be made to produce a much more refined and sensitive tone, one that is more appropriate for serious music. Even so, it seems unlikely that the saxophone will ever become a regular member of the symphony orchestra.

The examples that follow show two different ways of arranging a chorale excerpt for groups of saxophones. The soprano and bass saxophones have not been included in these scorings since they almost never figure in symphonic orchestration. The original key of the chorale was E minor, but other keys have been chosen here with an eye to good key signatures and comfortable playing ranges for the saxophones.

Ex. 6

Jesu, meine Freude

Bach

THE FLUTE IN G

Ex. 7

Sounding a perfect 4th lower.

Strangely enough, the flute in G is known both as "alto flute" and as "bass flute." The first name appears to be the more logical of the two and is preferred.[3] Since the instrument has the same written range as the ordinary concert flute but sounds a 4th lower, its sounding range extends down to the G below middle C. Its tone is rich and velvety, although not quite so good in the top octave as in the middle and lower parts of its range. There is not much point in using the highest register anyway since the concert flute can ordinarily take these notes more successfully. All that was said in an earlier chapter about the technical possibilities of the flute applies here. The G flute appears conspicuously in Ravel's *Daphnis and Chloe* Suite No. 2 and in Stravinsky's *The Rite of Spring*, among other works.

THE OBOE D'AMORE

Italian: Oboe d'Amore   *French:*   Hautbois d'Amour

Ex. 8

Sounding a minor 3rd lower.

Used in Bach's day and revived by Strauss in his *Sinfonia Domestica*, the oboe d'amore is an extreme rarity today. Perhaps the most widely known part for it is the extended one in Ravel's *Bolero*. It is like the oboe as to fingering, but its tone is sweeter and less biting. Because it is midway in size between the oboe and the English horn, it is sometimes described as a mezzo-soprano oboe. In Bach's works, the part for it is written at actual pitch, but in modern scores the transposition given here is used.

THE HECKELPHONE

Ex. 9

Sounding an 8ve lower.

---

[3] At one time there was an actual bass flute, capable of going an octave lower than the concert flute, but it is no longer used, at least in this country.

This instrument, invented by Heckel in 1904, is an oboe pitched an octave lower than the normal oboe. It is longer than the English horn and has a larger distension at the bell. Its tone quality is extremely reedy and full, particularly in the lower register. Except for Strauss (in *Salome*) and Delius, few composers have written for the Heckelphone, but it is now finding some use in commercial orchestral arranging.

THE E♭ CLARINET

Ex. 10

Sounding a minor 3rd higher.

This is a small clarinet which has found great favor with military bands but little with orchestras. One reason for this state of affairs is that its tone lacks the mellow warmth of the B♭ clarinet and is, instead, rather hard and inelastic. On the other hand, this very quality has now and then been exploited with striking effect in orchestral writing, as in Berlioz's *Fantastic Symphony* (the section entitled *Dream of a Witches' Sabbath*), in Strauss's *Ein Heldenleben* (in the "critics" section) and in Ravel's *Daphnis and Chloe* Suite No. 2. Because its practical upward compass, in actual sounds, is slightly greater than that of the B♭ and A clarinets, it can take passages which would be too high for them. However, unless both instrument and player are first-rate, high passages for the E♭ clarinet are apt to be unpleasantly shrill or out of tune or both.

Strauss writes for a small clarinet in D, which has the same written range as the E♭ clarinet but sounds a major 2nd higher than written. The D clarinet is all but unknown in the United States, and the few parts for it (such as the important one in *Till Eulenspiegel*) are usually played on the E♭ instrument.

THE BASSET-HORN

Italian: Corno di Bassetto   *French:*   Cor de basset   *German:*   Bassethorn

Ex. 11

Sounding a perfect 5th lower.

The Basset-Horn is not a horn at all but derives the second part of its name from a man named Horn who introduced the instrument. Through an understandable confusion, "Horn" was translated literally as "Corno" by the Italians. The Basset-Horn was a forerunner of the Eb alto clarinet, an instrument that has been much used in bands. Examples of parts for Basset-Horn may be found in Beethoven's *Prometheus* and in Mozart's *Requiem* and several of his operas; Strauss later revived the instrument for use in *Elektra*. As a point of interest, it may be recalled that George Bernard Shaw used "Corno di Bassetto" as a pen name during his early days as a critic.

THE SARRUSOPHONE

Ex. 12

Sounding an 8ve lower.

An invention of a French bandmaster named Sarrus, the sarrusophone is a double-reed instrument very similar to the bassoon in construction but made of metal instead of wood. It came originally in six different sizes, pitched alternately in Bb and Eb. Of these, the only one used in the orchestra was the largest, which sometimes substituted for the contra bassoon. In order that the player might read from the contra-bassoon part without having to transpose, a contra-bass sarrusophone in C was introduced, and it is this instrument whose range and transposition are given here. The sarrusophone in Eb is still made today, however. Although the sarrusophone has had a considerable vogue in France, it appears only rarely in American orchestras. A part for it may be seen in Ravel's *Rapsodie Espagnole*.

THE CORNET

Italian: Cornetto   *French:* Cornet à pistons   *German:* Kornett
       (or Cornetta)   (or Piston)

Ex. 13

Sounding a major 2nd lower.

Some comments on the cornet were given earlier in the section on the trumpet in order to distinguish one instrument from the other. It was pointed out that the cornet, being predominantly conical in bore, produces a slightly mellower, less incisive sound than the trumpet. But the difference in tone quality is far less marked today than it was at one time. The cornet speaks a bit more easily than the trumpet and is technically facile.

Parts for cornets in symphonic music are seen principally in French scores of the late nineteenth century and early twentieth century. There are other instances, however such as the important cornet parts in Stravinsky's *Petrouchka*.

At one time, the cornet, like the Bb trumpet, had a slide by means of which the instrument could be pitched in A, but it is not included on cornets made today.

THE TRUMPET IN D OR Eb

Ex. 14

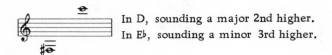

In D, sounding a major 2nd higher.
In Eb, sounding a minor 3rd higher.

The D trumpet can be converted to trumpet in Eb by means of a slide. This valve instrument is somewhat smaller than the Bb and C trumpets and only about half as large (in terms of tube length) as the natural trumpet in D used in the Baroque period. Its chief virtue is obviously its ability to play parts that would be uncomfortably high for the larger trumpets. Consequently, the lower register is likely to be little used. Parts for the D trumpet can be seen in Stravinsky's *The Rite of Spring* and Ravel's *Bolero*, among other works, and the instrument is often used to play the high trumpet parts in the music of Bach and his contemporaries.

Two other small trumpets sometimes utilized for the same purpose are those in F (sounding a perfect 4th higher than written) and high Bb (sounding a minor 7th higher than written).

Because all these trumpets are scarce, it is ordinarily impractical to score for them.

THE BASS TRUMPET

Ex. 15

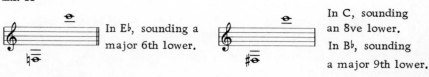

In Eb, sounding a major 6th lower.

In C, sounding an 8ve lower.
In Bb, sounding a major 9th lower.

The bass trumpet in E♭ is equipped with a fourth valve which allows it to go down to a written F♮, a half step lower than the trumpet's usual bottom written note (sounding the A♭ a major 6th below). Though the instrument is not often seen, parts for it such as that at figure 139 in Stravinsky's *The Rite of Spring* attest to its effectiveness, and Strauss also made notable use of it. Even when it does not go below the bottom limits possible on the B♭ and C trumpets, it has the great advantage of being able to take notes in the lower register with greater strength and security than those instruments.

Concerning the other bass trumpets listed here, Piston has this to say: "The bass trumpet, as written for by Wagner and Strauss, in the keys of 8-foot C and the B♭ below, is to all intents and purposes a valve trombone. It is played by trombonists, using the trombone mouthpiece."[4]

There are one or two instances of trumpet in F basso (sounding a 5th lower) in the works of Wagner and Rimsky-Korsakoff.

THE FLÜGELHORN

Italian: Flicorno   *French:* Bugle   *German:* Flügelhorn

Ex. 16

Sounding a major 2nd lower.

Once popular in bands but now seldom seen in this country, the Flügelhorn resembles the cornet in construction and size but has a wider bore. Its tone has been described by some as being similar to that of the horn though more open and less mellow, by others as being midway between those of the cornet and the baritone.

Two of the very rare instances of parts for the Flügelhorn in symphonic writing occur in Respighi's *Pines of Rome* (where *flicorni* are called for, obviously to suggest Roman horns) and in Stravinsky's *Threni*. In the latter work the instrument is listed at the beginning of the score as "Contralto Bugle in B♭ (Fluegelhorn)." Although the range of the Flügelhorn is theoretically the same as those of the cornet and the trumpet, the top 4th or so is not generally used.

---

[4] Walter Piston, *Orchestration* (New York: W. W. Norton & Company, Inc., 1955).

THE BARITONE AND THE EUPHONIUM (both in B♭)

Ex. 17

Sounding as written.

These two instruments are alike in general appearance and in range. They are built with either three or four valves, the current trend on the better instruments being toward four. They may have an upright bell or a "bell-front." The tone is smooth and mellow, and great technical agility is characteristic. The euphonium is often made with a slightly larger bore, which results in a broader and darker sound than that of the baritone. But even this distinction does not always apply, and it is, in fact, difficult to cite any consistent differences between the two instruments. Consequently, their names have become practically synonymous today.

The baritone and the euphonium are regular members of the band. They are mentioned here not because orchestral scores are likely to call for them by name but because they are often used to play orchestral parts labeled "tenor tuba" (as in Strauss's *Don Quixote* and Holst's *The Planets*) or the higher portions of parts labeled simply "tuba" (as in the passage from Stravinsky's *Petrouchka* quoted in Chapter 8).

Baritone players are frequently former cornet players, the fingering pattern on the two instruments being the same. For the benefit of those players who have not had occasion to become familiar enough with the bass clef to read parts written in it, publishers of band music generally print a treble-clef baritone part (in addition to the one in bass). Such parts are written a major 9th higher than the sounds; that is, when written in treble clef the baritone becomes a transposing instrument using the same transposition as that used by the bass clarinet in treble clef. In *scores*, the bass clef is more or less standard for the baritone, however.

THE WAGNER "TUBAS"

Ex. 18

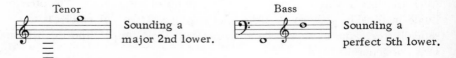

Tenor — Sounding a major 2nd lower.

Bass — Sounding a perfect 5th lower.

Wagner had these instruments constructed for use in his music dramas. It has frequently been pointed out that the name "tubas" is a misnomer, inasmuch as they are really modified horns. They have been little used by other composers, though parts for them are included in Bruckner's Seventh and Ninth Symphonies and in Strauss's *Elektra*.

THE GUITAR

Italian: Chitarra   *French:* Guitare   *German:* Guitarre

Ex. 19

 Range — Sounding an 8ve lower. Tuning of strings

The guitar is of ancient oriental origin and has appeared in various forms and under various names over the centuries. Unlike the lute, it has a flat back, and in its present form the sides curve inward. The neck is provided with frets (narrow strips of metal or wood attached to the fingerboard which mark the places where the strings are stopped by the left hand). The thumb and four fingers of the right hand are used in plucking the strings. In view of the unusual tuning of the instrument, a comment of Forsyth's may be of interest: "Its tuning, a series of perfect fourths broken between the 2nd and 3rd strings by a major third, perpetuates the old vicious tradition of the irregular lute system." Another inheritance from the days of the lute is the "tablature" type of notation still used for the guitar in popular music. Instead of showing actual notes, that system employs a small diagram of the fingerboard, with dots marking the points at which the player is to put his fingers. Standard notation is used in serious guitar music, however.

The extremely rare appearances of the guitar in the symphony or opera orchestra seem to fall into three categories: (1) those intended to provide a Spanish or Latin atmosphere; (2) those involving non-Spanish music in which the guitar contributes a folk-like feeling through a simple strummed or arpeggiated background (e.g., Percy Grainger's accompaniments for English folk tunes); (3) those that use the guitar simply for the sake of its distinctive plucked sound. In addition to opera scores which contain parts for the instrument (*The Barber of Seville, Oberon*), the following symphonic works could be cited: Mahler's Seventh Symphony, Gould's *Latin-American Symphonette*, Thomson's *Orchestra Suite from "The Plow that Broke the Plains,"* and Schönberg's Serenade, Op. 24.

It should be added that the electric guitar, on which the sound can be amplified, is having a great vogue in popular music today.

THE MANDOLIN

Italian: Mandolino   *French:* Mandoline   *German:* Mandoline

Ex. 20

Smaller than the guitar and roughly pear-shaped, the mandolin has eight strings tuned in pairs to the same pitches as the open strings of the violin. It is played with a *plectrum*, or pick. Not only are single short notes possible, but the double strings allow for a rapid alternation between two of the same pitch, so that a quasi-sustained effect with a kind of tremolo results. The fingerboard is fretted.

Like the guitar, the mandolin has occasionally been called for in the opera orchestra (Verdi's *Otello*, for example). The Mahler Seventh Symphony and the Schönberg Serenade, cited above as using the guitar, also contain parts for the mandolin, and the instrument is one of the many "extras" required for Respighi's *Roman Festivals*. A more recent instance of its use occurs in Stravinsky's *Agon*. (See page 292.)

THE PIPE ORGAN

Ex. 21

The organ is sometimes used in orchestral scores to supply added volume (generally at climactic points), liturgical atmosphere, or simply its own majestic tone quality. Occasionally the pedals alone, especially with 16-foot or 32-foot stops, are used to double the lower orchestral instruments for an extra-dark, ponderous effect.

Many timbres and textures are available through the stops. Eight-foot stops sound at the written pitch; four-foot stops sound an octave higher than the written pitch, 16-foot stops an octave lower, and so on. A system of couplers allows one manual to be linked with another or with the pedals. Music for the organ is written on three staves, the upper two for the manuals or keyboards, the bottom one for the pedals.

Although the organ was at one time a regular member of the instrumental group used to accompany oratorios and cantatas of the Baroque period (where it realized the *basso continuo* part), it later relinquished that role. Parts for it in symphonic music do not appear until the late nineteenth century. Scores that contain organ parts include Saint-Saëns' Third Symphony, Scriabin's *Poem of Ecstasy*, Mahler's Second and Eighth Symphonies, Strauss's *Thus Spake Zarathustra*, Respighi's *Pines of Rome* and *Roman Festivals*, and Holst's *The Planets*.

THE HARMONIUM

This is a small keyboard instrument sometimes described as a reed organ. However, the "reeds" in this case are thin tongues of metal set into vibration by an air stream that is provided by a pair of bellows operated by the player's feet. The principle involved, that of the "free single reed," is one that does not figure in the workings of any of the regular orchestral instruments. Some variety of timbre is obtainable by means of stops.

Scores that contain parts for the harmonium include Tchaikovsky's *Manfred* Symphony, Mahler's Eighth Symphony, Strauss's *Ariadne auf Naxos*, Hindemith's *Kammermusik No. 1*, and Shostakovich's ballet suite, *The Golden Age*.

THE HARPSICHORD

Italian: Clavicembalo (or Cembalo)   *French:* Clavecin   *German:* Cembalo (or Kielflügel)

Although the harpsichord was frequently used in combination with other instruments during the Baroque period (generally to supply the realized figured bass), its appearances in the modern orchestra have been few. One problem is the fact that its tone is so light as to be easily covered by other instruments and easily lost in a large hall. Even though many of the harpsichords built today are capable of producing more sound than their earlier counterparts, composers who use the harpsichord in an orchestral setting tend to make the orchestra a small one or to score relatively lightly for larger forces at points where the harpsichord sound must come through.

The instrument differs from the piano in that the string, instead of being struck by a hammer, is plucked by a plectrum made of crow quills or leather; this is attached to a jack which is set into motion by the depressing of a key. Doublings at the upper or lower octave, coupling of the two manuals, and some variation in tone quality are all available through pedals. There is no sustaining pedal as on the piano, and, quite apart from that, the sustaining powers of the harpsichord are somewhat less than those of the piano. In writing for the instrument, one must remember that it cannot make differences in volume by means of a lighter or heavier touch.

The meager list of orchestral works that employ the harpsichord includes Strauss's *Dance Suite after Couperin*, Falla's *El Retablo de Maese Pedro* and Concerto for Harpsichord and Five Instruments, Poulenc's *Concert Champêtre for Harpsichord and Orchestra*, and Martin's *Petite Symphonie Concertante*.

THE ONDES MARTENOT

Invented in 1928 by a Frenchman named Martenot, this instrument produces its tone through the amplification of air waves that result when two currents of slightly different frequencies are combined. The pitches may be controlled by a keyboard (with approximately the same range as that of the piano keyboard) or by a ribbon attached to a ring on the player's finger. In the latter case, all pitches between those on the keyboard are also playable, so that a "siren" effect is possible. The Ondes Martenot has been used chiefly by French composers, including Messiaen (*Turangalîla*), Honegger (*Jeanne d'Arc au Bûcher*), and Jolivet (Concerto for Ondes Martenot and Orchestra).

A somewhat similar instrument, developed in Germany and capable of imitating certain orchestral instruments (such as high trumpets) with surprising fidelity, is the Trautonium, named after its inventor, Trautwein.

THE TAPE RECORDER

Some readers may have difficulty in accepting the tape recorder as an "instrument." Nevertheless, it is the one natural purveyor of electronic music and *musique concrète*, and it has been used many times with orchestra, even to the point of being "soloist" in a concerto setting. Consequently, it seems to merit mention here. Since it is still in its infancy (relatively speaking), its potential has only begun to be realized.

THE VIOLA D'AMORE

Italian: Viola d'Amore   *French:* Viole d'Amour   *German:* Liebesgeige

Ex. 22

This curious instrument differs in several important respects from the ordinary viola. It is larger and heavier, and has seven strings tuned as shown. Beneath each of these is another string which vibrates sympathetically with the one above (but which is not touched by the bow). A serious limitation is the fact that the tuning of the strings centers so exclusively around the D major triad that passages which do not involve these notes are less resonant and effective. Also, the uneven spacing of the open pitches brings about some irregularities of fingering. Bach and Meyerbeer wrote for the viola d'amore; Charles Martin Loeffler included a part for it in *Le Mort de Tintagel,* and Hindemith even wrote a concerto for it (*Chamber Music No. 6 for Viola d'Amore and Chamber Orchestra*).

SUGGESTED ASSIGNMENTS

A. Know:

1. written range of all the saxophones.
2. transposition of the various sizes.
3. general abilities and limitations of saxophones.
4. transposition of Flute in G, E♭ Clarinet, Trumpet in D or E♭.

B. Score the first 6 bars of *America* for:

1. two alto and two tenor saxophones.
2. two alto, one tenor, and one baritone saxophone.
   Use other keys if you feel that the original key (F) is unsatisfactory.

Chapter 19

SCORING FOR
HIGH SCHOOL ORCHESTRA

From time to time in the course of this book there have been brief comments on the subject of arranging for school orchestra. It may be helpful to gather together some of these remarks and to expand on the problem as a whole. However, this chapter should be considered more a collection of pointers than a full-fledged treatise on the subject.

There have been notable improvements in the state of high school orchestras during the last twenty years or so: instrumentation has become much more nearly standardized, at least in the case of senior high schools; the average performance ability of players has increased; the music used is of generally higher quality. Of course there are still differences in instrumentation, ability, and musical sophistication between the larger schools with highly active music programs and those schools less fortunate in terms of musical and material resources. But these differences are far less extreme than they once were.

Most published arrangements for senior high school orchestras make use of an instrumentation essentially the same as that listed for the "medium-sized orchestra" in Chapter 1:

2 flutes

2 oboes

2 Bb clarinets

2 bassoons

4 F horns

2 or 3 Bb trumpets

2 or 3 trombones
(1 tuba)
timpani (2 or 3)
other percussion
strings

Some scores also include parts for saxophones, usually two altos and a tenor. These are generally marked *ad libitum*—to be included or not at the discretion of the conductor. They are often duplications of the horn parts and can be used to replace or bolster the horns. The tenor saxophone can be helpful in doubling the bassoon and/or the cellos. Other instruments for which a part is occasionally included are the piccolo, English horn, bass clarinet, harp and celesta.

Many high school orchestras do not have players for all the instruments listed under the normal instrumentation. Second oboe, second bassoon, and third and fourth horns are the instruments most likely to be missing. And even when players are available, they are likely to be inexperienced, so that it is normally unwise to give them a part which they must carry entirely on their own. Consequently, parts for these instruments are generally made "non-essential"; that is, the same notes are assigned to other instruments as well. This is largely true of viola parts also, since some schools do not have enough violists to make up a section that can provide adequate strength and balance.

Partly because of the popularity of bands today, we find that most schools have plenty of performers on flute, clarinet, saxophone, trumpet, trombone, and percussion. But oboists and bassoonists present more of a problem. It is not merely a matter of training the players; the high cost of the instruments is also a stumbling block, particularly in the case of the bassoon.

As a result of these considerations, important passages and even solos can be given to flute, clarinet, trumpet, or trombone with a reasonable assurance that players for these parts will be on hand. But solos for oboe, bassoon, or horn are often "cued" in another part so that the passage can be played by another instrument if necessary. Oboe solos may be cued for trumpet (usually muted) or for clarinet, flute, or violins, depending on which is convenient. Sometimes they are cued for two or more of these, in which case the conductor will decide which instrument is to do the substituting. Bassoon parts may be cued for trombone or cellos, while horn passages may be taken over by trombone, trumpet, or strings—or saxophones, if used.

However, solos are somewhat less frequent in scoring of this type than in actual symphonic orchestration. And there is likely to be more doubling between strings and winds, although today there seems to be a laudable tendency to break away from constant doubling of that sort and to introduce more use of pure colors and of individual sections.

What has been said so far applies chiefly to arrangements for the senior high school orchestra. Some junior high school orchestras are sufficiently well-staffed and proficient to use the same arrangements. Others, with fewer and less-experienced players available, use publications scored for the following more modest instrumentation:

> 1 or 2 flutes
> 1 oboe
> 2 B♭ clarinets
> 1 bassoon
>
> 2 F horns
> 2 B♭ trumpets
> 1 trombone
>
> timpani (2)
> other percussion
>
> (piano)
>
> strings

The piano part that is sometimes included may be placed either above the strings or at the bottom of the score page. It is usually a condensation of the score (or salient elements of it) and may be played or not, depending on whether it is needed to replace missing instruments, to reinforce weak instruments, or to reinforce the orchestra as a whole.

Some directors of junior high school orchestras use the following plan in making arrangements for their groups: each instrument has a part written for it throughout the piece, instruments being allotted according to a kind of "type-casting" system such as this:

Melody	Upper Register Harmony Parts	Middle Register Harmony Parts	Bass
Flute	(1st Clarinet?)	Horns	Bassoon
Oboe	2nd Clarinet	2nd Violins	Trombone
1st Clarinet	(and/or 2nd Violins)	(and/or 2nd Clarinet)	Cellos
1st Trumpet	2nd Trumpet	Violas	Basses
1st Violins			

When the time comes to play the arrangement and the conductor is sure what instrumentation he will have, he can cut out certain instruments wherever he feels that to be advisable, in order to get away from a constantly heavy scoring and to introduce a lighter texture and pure colors. Although this system may seem at first to be roundabout, and although it is certainly an unimaginative one, it has certain points in its favor: (1) It insures that there will at least be enough volume, where volume is needed, and that, barring hopelessly deficient instrumentation, each voice will actually be played. (2) It eliminates the need for writing cues as such (the cues being "built in," so to speak), and it allows for the maximum number of possibilities in substitution. In the case of orchestras which vary radically in make-up from year to year, this type of arrangement may be more useful than one with only limited cross-cueing. (3) Arrangements made according to this plan can often be used for smaller instrumental ensembles, such as wood-wind quartet or quintet, brass quartet, or small string group. That is, it is possible to plan the scoring so that certain groups of instruments playing by themselves will sound complete and satisfactory. (4) In working with an orchestra, it is easier to delete parts than to add them. For example, the conductor can, if he wishes, simply tell a player not to play a particular passage; but if he should decide, in rehearsal, that he wanted to add that instrument, he could not do it without writing out a new part—assuming that the instrument was not cued at that point.

On the other hand, there are some serious disadvantages to this system. For one thing, it tends to involve much heavy doubling, which, in turn, brings about a constantly mixed tone that becomes monotonous. Also, because the arrangement must be contrived in such a way as to sound well whether it is played by a large or a small group, instruments are often not used in the most interesting or effective way. This whole method is one born of practical necessity rather than artistic choice; obviously there is no point in adopting it in the case of orchestras that have a more or less complete and constant instrumentation.

Of course there is nothing hard and fast about the allotment of instruments to various voices in the chart shown on page 320. In the first place, it applies, as given here, chiefly to homophonic music, and even within that category it would have to be altered from piece to piece to fit the individual structure of each. If a countermelody were present, that might involve changes in the distribution of the voices, and if the music were entirely contrapuntal, a different approach to the labeling of the musical elements would be needed.

Some technical points to keep in mind in scoring for school orchestra are given next, arranged by section.

WOODWINDS

In arranging for senior high school woodwind players, a good axiom is to stay within the "practical" woodwind ranges given earlier (but in the case of the bassoon the top note had better be G or at most A, rather than B♭). With junior high school groups, it is safest to work within upper wood-wind ranges that are about a 3rd lower than the usual practical ranges.

Be sure to give the flute and oboe sufficient rests (though not necessarily extended ones). This is a good principle to follow even in writing for seasoned players, and it is doubly important in the case of young performers, whose breathing powers are not as fully developed. Remember that the flute is by nature weak in its bottom octave and must be written higher if it is to add anything in a *tutti* or to come through any but the lightest background in a solo.

First clarinet parts may be of considerable technical difficulty, but second clarinet parts are best kept simpler to accommodate the less skilled players who will probably be assigned to them. Keep in mind the fact that particularly in the hands of an inexperienced player the clarinet becomes shrill above about (written) ◻ .

Some directors have found it helpful to include a bass clarinet and/or a contra-bass clarinet borrowed from the band to reinforce the bass. Although scores do not normally include a part for either of these instruments, it would seem sensible to include one for the bass clarinet at least, in the interests of compensating for missing or weak bassoons if necessary.

Whereas in symphonic scores bassoon parts that go relatively high are customarily written in the tenor clef, parts in school scores seldom depart from the bass clef. This is a debatable practice, inasmuch as players who go on to more advanced work are unprepared to read the passages in tenor clef which they are certain to encounter. The same question comes up in connection with tenor trombone and cello parts.

BRASS

Horn parts should be kept within a written range of about ◻ .

Notes above the F are risky, while passages that go below A or G are more difficult for young players and ungrateful to play. Besides, as intimated earlier, not all school orchestras include an actual fourth horn player. Even when four players are available, it sometimes happens that one or more of these are too inexperienced to manage separate parts, and in such cases a frequent solution is to use only two horn parts (I and II as a rule) with two players to each part. Probably the safest approach to horn writing for school use is to score for four horns but to plan their parts in such a way that the music will sound satisfactory if only the parts for Horns I and II are played.

High school trumpet players, on the other hand, are apt to be quite proficient, and the same is true to a slightly lesser degree of the trombonists. In fact, there are few limitations that apply to writing for these players— apart from the natural limitations of the instruments themselves, which have already been discussed. Remember especially that entrances on high notes should be avoided. (See page 153.) Trombone parts, like bassoon parts, use the bass clef as a rule.

PERCUSSION

Most schools now own at least two pedal timpani, and the more affluent schools may have three or even four. Remember that even with pedal timpani available, it is unreasonable to demand extremely fast changes or a great number of changes in quick succession from an inexperienced student player, though a tuning gauge will allow for more accurate and rapid tuning than would be possible otherwise.

Thanks to the band, there is rarely any dearth of players for the snare drum, bass drum, cymbals, and the other percussion instruments. Many school orchestras include a set of chimes, a glockenspiel, and a xylophone (or a marimba). Vibraphones are considerably scarcer, however.

HARP, CELESTA, AND PIANO

Some scores (more than formerly) now contain parts for the harp, and there has been an increase, in recent years, in the number of high schools that own harps and have student harpists available.

Although parts for the celesta appear occasionally, they are most often played on the piano, since few schools own a celesta.

The role of the piano in arrangements for junior high school orchestras has already been mentioned. It is chiefly a utilitarian role, rather than a coloristic one as in symphonic scoring.

STRINGS

At one time many scores for school use subdivided the violins into three parts labeled A, B and C or I, II and III. The third part was generally a simple one designed for beginning players, and it often involved the same notes as the viola part, to the extent that the difference in ranges permitted. Although some publishers still provide a player's part labeled "Violin III

(Viola 𝄞)", such parts are not often shown in the score; today the strings

are normally listed in the usual symphonic format: Violin I, Violin II, Violas, Cellos, Double Basses.

All the string groups may be written as high as the third position with safety, and the use of fifth position is by no means uncommon in the case of the first violins and the cellos (especially in advanced-level arrangements). The following notes may be considered safe upward limits for high school players of average ability:

Ex. 1

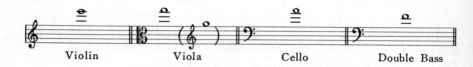

If higher notes are required in the first violin part and there are doubts as to whether all the players in that group can manage them, the part can be written in octaves, *divisi*, so that the less experienced players can take the lower octave.

The tenor clef is rarely used for the cellos in school music.

Only the easier multiple stops should be called for, preferably those making considerable use of open strings, especially in the case of triple and quadruple stops.

Harmonics are seldom seen in school scoring, although the natural harmonics on the E string of the violin may occasionally prove useful for color effects or for very high notes that would be too difficult if played in the ordinary way.

Because the string groups are likely to be small, the players inexperienced, and the instruments of generally inferior quality, *divisi* passages should be used sparingly (and not at all for the violas). Division into more than two parts had better be ruled out altogether, unless the string section is well above average in size.

As to the size of string sections, a word should be added about the number of string parts included in published arrangements. Some publishers make a practice of including only one of each string part, any additional parts being ordered separately. Other firms classify their arrangements in three sets of different sizes, according to the number of string parts contained in each. The proportions used by one leading publisher are as follows:

	Set A	Set B	Set C
1st Violins	2	5	8
2nd Violins	2	5	8
Violas	1	3	5
Cellos	1	3	5
Basses	1	3	5

It must be remembered that these figures represent parts and that since two string players normally read off the same stand, the number of string players will be roughly twice as large as the number of string parts.

GENERAL

Sets A, B and C also include one of each woodwind, brass and percussion part, a full score, and a "piano-conductor" score. The latter is a condensed version of the music on two or three staves, with general indications as to what instruments are taking the respective musical ideas. While such scores can be used to conduct from, they have the disadvantage of not showing the exact part for each instrument as specifically as the full score does. They are not actually played at the piano except, perhaps, in the case of junior high school orchestras with deficient instrumentation, which occasionally use them (in the absence of an actual piano part) to supply missing parts.

Arrangements for high school orchestra should be made with an eye to providing individual parts that will be grateful and enjoyable for the players, parts that will be challenging enough to be interesting yet not so difficult as to be impractical. In general it is wise to choose the easier keys, preferably those involving no more than three sharps or four flats. Remember that a concert key of three sharps will put the B♭ instruments in five sharps, while a concert key of four sharps means six sharps (or six flats) for them.

CONCERNING THE EXAMPLES THAT FOLLOW

Examples 2–5 are excerpts from works written or arranged by American composers for high school orchestras. Some employ the instrumentation given on page 318, others the smaller one shown on page 320.

Example 2 (from *Vignettes*, by Kirk) gives a good idea of normal cross-cueing for the instruments that are often missing; the third and fourth horn parts are cued for the trumpets in the first measure, while the oboe and bassoon parts are cued for the clarinets and trombones, respectively, in the last two measures.

Example 3 (from *Poem*, by Grundman) shows a more extensive—and perhaps less typical—use of cues. Even the violins are cued (for the first trumpet), presumably not with any idea that there would ever be a total absence of violins and that the trumpet would play in place of them but rather so that it may play along with them for added body and support if that seems desirable. This example also illustrates the inclusion of optional saxophone parts. They involve cues which may be played if the conductor so directs. The melody in the strings has obviously been written with easy (first-position) fingering in mind.

Example 4 shows the part in *The Orchestra Song*, by Schuman, at which a number of traditional Australian melodies, which have been presented earlier, are all combined. Probably because of the polyphonic nature of the piece, only a single-line part is written for each of the woodwinds, but a note at the beginning of the score explains that more than one of each woodwind may be used on each part, at the discretion of the conductor, and that the number of horns, trumpets and trombones may be reduced.

Example 5 ("Rustic Dance" from *Three Miniatures* by David Ward-Steinman) shows an excerpt from a piano piece and an arrangement of the music made especially for school orchestras. All the voices have been doubled at the octave in the orchestral version for greater fullness and brilliance. Bowing indications have been carefully marked. Although many multiple stops are too difficult to be used safely in arrangements for school orchestras, those assigned to the violas and cellos here involve open strings and are therefore ultrasimple to perform. They also have the virtue of providing great resonance.

Ex. 2

Vignettes, I

Theron Kirk

Ex. 3

Two Sketches for Orchestra, I. *Poem*

Clare Grundman

Ex. 4

The Orchestra Song

William Schuman

330

Ex. 5

*Three Miniatures for School
Orchestras, I. Rustic Dance*

David
Ward-Steinman

SUGGESTED ASSIGNMENTS

A. Know:

1. ranges practical for (a) senior high school orchestras; (b) junior high school orchestras.
2. the instrumentation generally used in published arrangements for (a) senior high school orchestras; (b) junior high school orchestras.
3. which instruments are most likely to be missing or weak in high school orchestras.
4. how to write cues, including those involving a transposition; for example, an oboe part cued for muted trumpet or a horn part cued for clarinet (the latter involving a double transposition).
5. the written range of the saxophones and the transposition used by the alto and tenor saxophones (if not learned earlier).

B. Make an arrangement for high school orchestra of one of the following, keeping in mind the points discussed in this chapter and including cross-cues wherever advisable.

1. A short piano piece.
2. A short piece written originally for a small instrumental group.
3. A song from a school song book.
4. A work written originally for symphony orchestra which lends itself to an arrangement playable by high school orchestras.

Chapter 20

WRITING
SCORE AND PARTS

Unfortunately, most students (like many composers) cannot afford to hire a professional copyist and must write out their own scores and parts. This aspect of orchestration may appear to be mere hack work requiring no special knowledge; actually, it involves some problems that students have seldom had occasion to learn before. Therefore this list of pointers on the subject is included here.

CONCERNING THE SCORE

If a single copy of the score is needed, ordinary music paper (from 12-line to 30-line, depending on the size of the orchestra) may be used. Naturally, an ink score is much preferable to one in pencil and would be expected by the conductor of any professional orchestra.

If, however, more than one copy of the score is required—as, for example, in the case of a composer who wishes to make his music available to several conductors at the same time—the procedure generally used is this: the music is written with engrossing ink or special pencil on translucent master sheets which can be reproduced by the Blackline Diazo process. These thin master sheets, which are available in a variety of sizes and formats designed for various combinations of instruments, can be bought from several firms, three of which are listed here:

Independent Music Publishers
205 East 42nd St.
New York, N. Y. 10017

Circle Blue Print Co.
225 West 57th St.
New York, N. Y. 10019

Cameo Music Reproduction
1527½ North Vine St.
Hollywood, Cal. 90028

These same firms can make copies of the sheets and can also supply cardboard covers and spiral binding, or "saddle-stitch" binding for scores of only a few pages. Many blueprint companies in other parts of the country are equipped to make reproductions by the Blackline Diazo process, but few sell the blank master sheets or handle covers and bindings. Specially prepared music pens are available through the last firm listed above.

As explained earlier, dynamics must be shown beneath each part, but it is usually sufficient to show tempo indications in only two places on the page, at the top and just above the violins. Sometimes they are also shown at the bottom of the page.

Meter signatures may be written in each part, or two or three meter signatures written in large elongated figures may be used instead. The latter system is preferable in certain modern music where the meter changes frequently, for the larger figures are more easily visible to the conductor. In cases where there is a change on the first measure of a new page, the new meter signature is generally shown in advance at the end of the preceding page as well.

In order to save time in student scoring, it is possible to omit whole rests, and to leave the measures blank instead. But rests of a fraction of a measure must always be shown. Of course whole rests are included in printed scores and in manuscript scores intended for professional use.

When a single melodic line appears on a staff that is shared by two woodwind or brass instruments, be sure to indicate whether the passage is to be played by both instruments or by the first or by the second ("a 2" or "1." or "2.").

When only a portion of the orchestra is playing, either one of two systems may be used: (1) All the instruments are listed on each page, with rests (or blanks) for those that are not actually playing. (2) Some or all of the instruments that are resting are omitted from the listing on the page. Since fewer staves are required this second way, it is sometimes possible to put on one page what would have taken up two full pages under the other system; that is, the page is divided into an upper score and a lower score with "slash marks" (short diagonal bars) between the two at the left-hand side to call attention to the division (as in Ex. 8 in Chapter 12). While this method saves paper, it has the disadvantage of not keeping the instruments in the same relative places on the page and therefore makes score-reading a bit more difficult. In any case, the first page of a score should show all the instruments to be used.

The sections of the orchestra can be more clearly distinguished from each other if there is a gap in the bar lines between them. The horns may have a separate bar line or be grouped with the brass.

"Rehearsal letters" (or numbers) must be included in both score and parts so that the conductor can tell the orchestra where to start when particular passages are to be rehearsed. Sometimes these letters or numbers are placed at likely starting points throughout the score. Another method is simply to write in the number of the measure above the staff every 10 or 20 bars (or as often as desired). In either case, the letter or number should be enclosed in a square or circle so that it can be found easily. (This applies to both score and parts.)

CONCERNING THE PLAYERS' PARTS

Use 12-line or 10-line manuscript paper.

Copy in black ink. Manuscript written in pencil is difficult to read and soon gets smudged. Be sure to make the notes large enough, especially in the parts for such instruments as double bass and tuba, whose players must read from some distance. Also, allow enough room so that the notes are not crowded. Ledger lines should be the same distance apart as the lines in the staff.

Ordinarily the part for each wind instrument is written on a separate sheet. However, it is possible to write each pair of woodwinds or brass on one sheet, usually with a separate staff for each part. In rare cases where the two instruments play "a 2" much of the time or have very similar parts, it may be practical to write the parts for both on the same staff. In the past, horn parts have usually been written with horns I and II on one sheet, III and IV on another; today it is more usual to write a separate part for each horn.

For directions on writing percussion parts, see the final portion of the chapter on percussion.

In planning string parts, be sure to remember that you will need only half as many parts as there are players, because two players read from each part. Instead of copying out each individual string part, most composers and arrangers have copies made via the Blackline Diazo process or some other method of reproduction. This entails making only the original master part for each string group. Of course the same procedure may be used for wind and percussion parts in case more than one set of parts is needed. Whereas orchestral scores are generally too large to fit into most Xerox copying machines, players' parts written on ordinary music paper may be reproduced in that way.

Each part must include indications for tempo, dynamics, expression, phrasing, slurring, bowing, and muting—in short, every direction that is necessary in telling the player exactly how the part should sound.

Rehearsal letters or numbers, described in the section on the score, must be shown in each part.

Rests of more than one or two measures are indicated in the manner shown in Example 1.

Ex. 1

Notice that when a rehearsal letter occurs in the middle of a rest, the rest must be divided to show the number of measures before and after the rehearsal letter. Rests of only one or two measures are often shown by simply putting a whole rest in each measure.

The expression *tacet* (literally translated, "is silent") in a part indicates that the instrument in question does not play for a specified length of time. For example, if the tuba had nothing to play in the second movement of a particular symphony, we might write, "2nd Movement, tacet" in the part. Or if it played at the beginning of the movement but had nothing to play for the last 200 bars, we could write, "Tacet to end of movement (200 bars)" rather than bothering to ennumerate the separate rests and rehearsal letters.

Example 1 illustrates the use of cues in parts, in this case the fragment of the trombone part included in the trumpet part. Cues are a great help to the player and one which he has the right to expect. They are most often included just before an entrance after a rest of some length, but they are also useful as "landmarks" in the middle of very long rests. One or two bars are usually sufficient for a cue, though longer cues are common. Be sure to select an important voice that can be easily heard and not a minor part that is apt to be covered up by other instruments. Cues should be written in small notes with stems in the "wrong" direction to allow for the rests that are included. A question that arises here is this: in writing a cue for a transposing instrument, should the cue also be transposed or should it be written as it actually is in the score? Both systems have been used, and each has its advantages, but as a general rule the first seems preferable. It should certainly be used in any case where a cued passage may have to be played (for example in school orchestra music, where important passages for one instrument are often cued for one or more other instruments, any one of which may substitute if necessary).

Label each part carefully, giving the name of the composition in the middle of the page at the top, the names of the composer and the arranger in the upper right-hand corner, and the name of the instrument that is to play the part (for example, "Clarinet II in B♭") in the upper left-hand corner.

If page turning is involved, copy the part in such a way that at the bottom of the page there will be a rest of sufficient length to allow for the turn. This is more important in wind parts than in string parts, since one of each pair of string players can turn the page while the other continues to play, if necessary. However, that arrangement is better avoided.

Appendix A

LIST OF FOREIGN
NAMES FOR INSTRUMENTS,
ORCHESTRAL TERMS

Unless one has taken the trouble to learn the Italian, French, and German names for instruments and the abbreviations for those names, score-reading is likely to degenerate into a kind of guessing game. Of course it is easy enough to guess, correctly, that *Klarinette* means clarinet in German or even that *timbales* is the French name for timpani. But it is also easy to guess, *incorrectly*, that *cors* means cornets (instead of horns) or that *trbe.* stands for trombone (instead of for trumpets—in the Italian plural form). And how is one to decipher such names as *Posaunen* (trombones in German) or *piatti* (cymbals in Italian)?

Presumably the student who has covered the material in this book has already learned a good many of the foreign names as he went along. The complete list (given on the following pages) is for purposes of reference or study. Also given are the foreign equivalents of some important terms commonly found in orchestral scores. The blanks in the latter list are caused by the fact that some of the terms are seldom or never used in certain of the languages. Also, there are cases in which the Italian term is used even in French and German scores. For example, one finds *sul ponticello* and *con sordino* in German scores, while such terms as *arco* and *pizzicato* are universal.

NAMES OF INSTRUMENTS

English	Italian	French	German
WOODWINDS	LEGNI (OR FIATI)	BOIS	HOLZBLÄSER
Piccolo	Flauto Piccolo (or Ottavino)	Petite Flûte	Kleine Flöte
Flute	Flauto	Flûte	Flöte
Oboe	Oboe	Hautbois	Oboe (or Hoboe)
English Horn	Corno Inglese	Cor Anglais	Englisch Horn
Clarinet	Clarinetto	Clarinette	Klarinette
Bass Clarinet	Clarinetto Basso	Clarinette Basse	Bassklarinette
Bassoon	Fagotto	Basson	Fagott
Contra Bassoon	Contrafagotto	Contre-basson	Kontrafagott
BRASS(ES)	OTTONI	CUIVRES	BLECHINSTRUMENTE
Horn	Corno	Cor	Horn
Trumpet	Tromba	Trompette	Trompete
Trombone	Trombone	Trombone	Posaune
Tuba	Tuba	Tuba	Tuba (or Basstuba)
PERCUSSION	PERCUSSIONE (OR BATTERIA)	BATTERIE	SCHLAGZEUG
Timpani (or Kettle Drums)	Timpani	Timbales	Pauken
Xylophone	Silofono (or Xilofono)	Xylophone	Xylophon
Marimba	Marimba	Marimba	Marimba
Glockenspiel	Campanelli	Jeu de Timbres (or Carillon)	Glockenspiel
Vibraphone	Vibrafono	Vibraphone	Vibraphon
Bells or Chimes	Campane	Cloches	Glocken
Antique Cymbals	Crotali	Cymbales Antiques (or Crotales)	Antiken Zimbeln
Flexatone	Flexatone	Flexatone	Flexaton
Snare Drum (or Side Drum)	Tamburo (Militare)	Tambour (Militaire) (or Caisse Claire)	Kleine Trommel
Field Drum	Tamburo (Militare)	Tambour	Rührtrommel
Tenor Drum	Tamburo Rullante	Caisse Roulante	Rührtrommel
Tabor	Tamburo	Tambour de Provence (or Tambourin)	Tambourin
Bass Drum	(Gran) Cassa	Grosse Caisse	Grosse Trommel
Cymbals	Piatti	Cymbales	Becken
Suspended Cymbal	Piatto Sospeso	Cymbale Suspendue	Hängendes Becken (or Becken frei)
Triangle	Triangolo	Triangle	Triangel

English	Italian	French	German
Tambourine	Tamburino (or Tamburo Basco)	Tambour (de) Basque	Schellentrommel (or Tambourin)
Gong or Tam-tam	Tam-tam	Tam-tam	Tam-tam
Castanets	Castagnette	Castagnettes	Kastagnetten
Rattle (or Ratchet)	Raganella	Crécelle	Ratsche
Wood Block	Cassa (or Cassetta) di Legno	Wood Bloc (or Bloc de Bois)	Holzkaste
Cowbells	Campanelli di Vacca	Grelots	Heerdenglocken
Sleighbells	Sonagli	Grelots	Schellen
Slapstick (or Whip)	Frusta	Fouet	Peitsche
Celesta	Celesta	Célesta	Celesta
Harp	Arpa	Harpe	Harfe
STRINGS	ARCHI	CORDES	STREICHINSTRU-MENTE
Violin	Violino	Violon	Violine
Viola	Viola	Alto	Bratsche
Violoncello	Violoncello	Violoncelle	Violoncell
Double Bass	Contrabasso	Contre Basse	Kontrabass

ORCHESTRAL TERMS

English	Italian	French	German
muted	{con sordino[1] {con sordini	sourdine(s)	mit Dämpfer (or gedämpft, in horns)
take off mutes	via sordini	enlevez les sourdines	Dämpfer(n) weg
without mute	senza sordino	sans sourdine	ohne Dämpfer
divided	divisi (div.)	divisé(e)s (div.)	geteilt (get.)
divided in 3 parts	div. a 3	div. à 3	dreifach
divided in 4 parts	div. a 4	div. à 4	vierfach
in unison	unisono (unis.)	unis	zusammen (or einfach)
a 2	a 2	à 2	zu 2
at (near) the bridge	sul ponticello	sur le chevalet	sul ponticello (or am Steg)
over the fingerboard	sul tasto (or sulla tastiera)	sur la touche	am Griffbrett
with the wood of the bow	col legno	avec le bois	col legno (or mit Holz)

Note: Nouns are always capitalized in German.

[1] May also be spelled *sordina,* in which case the plural is *sordine.*

English	Italian	French	German
at the point of the bow	punta d'arco	(de la) pointe	Spitze
at the frog	al tallone	du talon	am Frosch
bells in the air	campane in aria	pavillons en l'air	Schalltrichter auf
half (a string group)	la metà	la moitié	die Hälfte
stopped (horns)	chiuso (chiusi)	bouché(s)	gestopft
brassy		cuivré	schmetternd
open	aperto (aperti)	ouvert(s)	offen
with soft stick	bacchetta di spugna	baguette d'éponge (baguette molle)	mit Schwamm-schlägel
with hard sticks	bacchette di legno	baguettes en bois	mit Holzschlägeln
change G to F♯	sol muta in fa♯	changez sol en fa♯	G nach Fis umstimmen
near the sounding board (harp)		près de la table	
desk or stand	leggio	pupitre	Pult
in the ordinary way (after sul pont., etc.)	modo ordinario	mode ordinaire	gewöhnlich
string	corda	corde	Saite

Appendix B

RANGES OF INSTRUMENTS

In each case the limits of the extreme possible range are shown in open notes, the limits of the practical or commonly used range in black notes. These are written ranges.

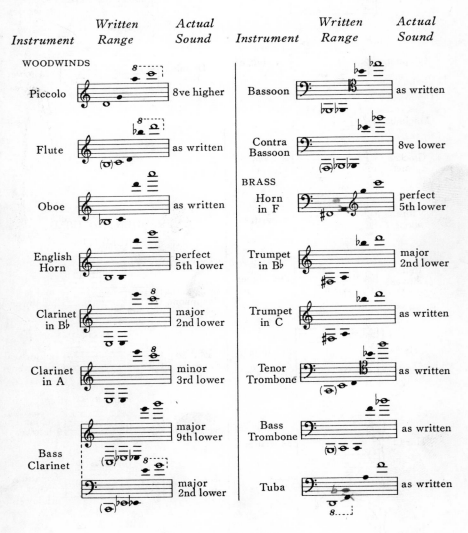

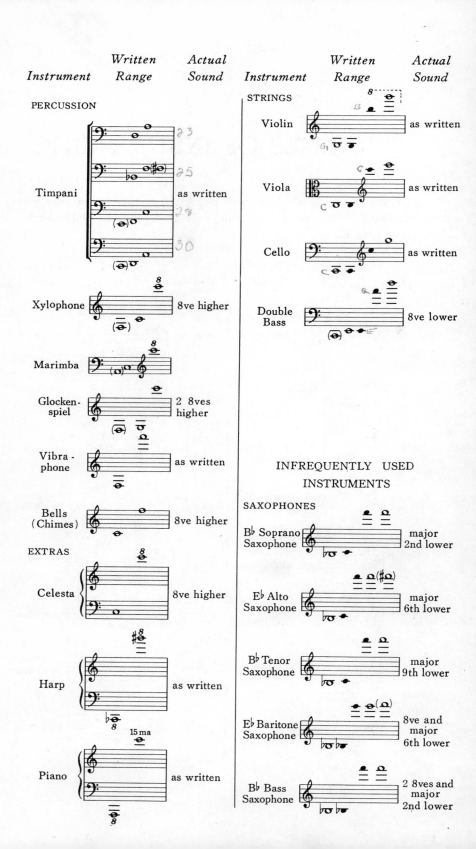

Instrument	*Written Range*	*Actual Sound*	Instrument	*Written Range*	*Actual Sound*
WOODWINDS			**BRASS, cont.**		
Alto Flute (in G)		perfect 4th lower	Flügel-horn (in B♭)		major 2nd lower
Oboe d'Amore		minor 3rd lower	Baritone or Euphonium		as written
Heckel-phone		8ve lower			major 9th lower
E♭ Clarinet		minor 3rd higher	Tenor		major 2nd lower
Clarinet in D		major 2nd higher	Wagner "Tubas"		
Basset-Horn (in F)		perfect 5th lower	Bass		perfect 5th lower
Sarruso-phone		8ve lower	**EXTRAS** Guitar		8ve lower
BRASS Cornet (in B♭)		major 2nd lower	Mandolin		as written
Trumpet in D or E♭		D: major 2nd higher E♭: minor 3rd higher	Manuals Organ Pedals		depends on registration
Bass Trumpet in E♭		major 6th lower	Harmo-nium		as written
Bass Trumpet in C		8ve lower	Harpsi-chord		as written
Bass Trumpet in B♭		major 9th lower	**STRINGS** Viola d'Amore		as written

BIBLIOGRAPHY

BOOKS ON ORCHESTRATION

1. Relatively recent books designed primarily as texts:

Isaac, Merle. *Practical Orchestration: A Method of Arranging for School Orchestras.* New York: Robbins Music Corp., 1963.

Jacob, Gordon. *The Elements of Orchestration.* London: Herbert Jenkins Ltd., 1962. (Reissued by October House, New York, 1966.)

———. *Orchestral Technique.* London: Oxford University Press, Inc., 1931, 1965.

McKay, George Frederick. *Creative Orchestration.* Boston: Allyn & Bacon, Inc., 1963. (There is a workbook to accompany the text.)

Piston, Walter. *Orchestration.* New York: W. W. Norton & Company, Inc., 1955.

Rauscher, Donald J. *Orchestration: Scores and Scoring.* New York: The Free Press, 1963.

Rogers, Bernard. *The Art of Orchestration.* New York: Appleton-Century-Crofts, 1951.

Wagner, Joseph. *Orchestration: A Practical Handbook.* New York: McGraw-Hill Book Company, 1959. (There is a workbook to accompany the text.)

2. Other recent books and articles of value to the student of orchestration:

Bartolozzi, Bruno. *New Sounds for Woodwind,* trans. Reginald Smith Brindle. London: Oxford University Press, 1967. A compendium of new monophonic and multiphonic possibilities for individual woodwind instruments, with fingerings and other directions for producing the sounds. A recording is included.

Galamian, Ivan. *Principles of Violin Playing and Teaching.* Englewood Cliffs, N. J.: Prentice-Hall, Inc., 1963. A book aimed chiefly at the teacher and solo performer; cited here because of its detailed discussion of bowing types and string techniques.

Green, Elizabeth A. H. *Orchestral Bowings and Routines* (2nd ed.). Ann Arbor, Michigan: Ann Arbor Publishers, 1957. A manual in which the emphasis is on basic principles of orchestral bowing as related to specific musical situations.

Leibowitz, René, and Jan Maguire. *Thinking for Orchestra*. New York: G. Schirmer, Inc., 1960. A book consisting of two parts: (1) reductions of excerpts from orchestral scores, which the student is to orchestrate; (2) the excerpts in their original scored form, to be studied by the student and compared with his version. There are accompanying comments on various styles of orchestration.

Read, Gardner. *Music Notation: A Manual of Modern Practice*. Boston: Allyn & Bacon, Inc., 1964. A highly comprehensive book containing much valuable information on the notation of orchestral instruments, singly and in combination.

———. *Thesaurus of Orchestral Devices*. New York: Pitman Publishing Corp., 1953. An encyclopedic compendium of possibilities in the use of orchestral instruments, with listings of the places in orchestral literature where each device may be found. Foreign terms are included.

Reed, H. Owen, and Joel T. Leach. *Scoring for Percussion and the Instruments of the Percussion Section*. Englewood Cliffs, N.J.: Prentice-Hall, Inc., 1969. A detailed treatment of percussion instruments, both singly and in combination, and the notation for them.

3. Standard reference books:

Forsyth, Cecil. *Orchestration* (2nd ed.). New York: The Macmillan Company, 1935. (First edition, 1914).

Rimsky-Korsakoff, Nicolas. *Principles of Orchestration*. Berlin and New York: Edition Russe de Musique, 1922, 1964. Later reissued by Dover Publications, Inc., New York, 1964, and by Peter Smith, Publisher, Gloucester, Mass. (n.d.).

4. Books which, though outmoded in some respects, contain much material that is still valid and have historical interest as important earlier treatises on orchestration:

Berlioz-Strauss. *Treatise on Instrumentation* (English translation). New York: E. F. Kalmus, 1948. (First issued in German in 1904.)

Gevaert, François Auguste. *Nouveau Traité d'Instrumentation*. Paris: Lemoine & Cie, 1885.

———. *Cours Méthodique d'Orchestration*. Paris: Lemoine & Cie, 1890.

Prout, Ebenezer. *The Orchestra* (in two volumes). London: Augener, Ltd., 1897.

Widor, C. M. *The Modern Orchestra*. London: J. Williams, 1906.

BOOKS ON THE HISTORY OF INSTRUMENTS OR OF THE ORCHESTRA

Baines, Anthony, ed. *Musical Instruments Through the Ages*. Baltimore: Penguin Books, Inc., 1961.

Bekker, Paul. *The Story of the Orchestra*. New York: W. W. Norton & Company, Inc., 1936.

Bessaraboff, Nicholas. *Ancient European Musical Instruments*. Cambridge, Mass.: Harvard University Press, 1941.

Carse, Adam. *History of Orchestration*. New York: E. P. Dutton & Co., Inc., 1925. (Reissued by Dover Publications, Inc., New York, 1964.)

———. *Musical Wind Instruments*. New York: Da Capo Press, 1966.

———. *The Orchestra from Beethoven to Berlioz.* Cambridge, England: W. Heffer & Sons Ltd., 1948.

———. *The Orchestra in the XVIIIth Century.* Cambridge, England: W. Heffer & Sons Ltd., 1940.

Coerne, Louis Adolphe. *The Evolution of Modern Orchestration.* New York: The Macmillan Company, 1908.

Daubeny, Ulric. *Orchestral Wind Instruments.* London: William Reeves, 1920.

Galpin, Francis W. *A Textbook of European Musical Instruments.* London: Williams and Norgate Ltd., 1937.

Geiringer, Karl. *Musical Instruments.* New York: Oxford University Press, Inc., 1945.

Hayes, Gerald R. *Old Instrumental Music* (Book I of series entitled *Musical Instruments and Their Music, 1500–1750*). London: Oxford University Press, 1928.

———. *The Viols and Other Bowed Instruments* (Book II of series listed above). London: Oxford University Press, 1930.

Rensch, Rosalyn. *The Harp.* New York: Philosophical Library, Inc., 1950.

Sachs, Curt. *The History of Musical Instruments.* New York: W. W. Norton & Company, Inc., 1940.

Schlesinger, Kathleen. *Instruments of the Modern Orchestra and Early Records of Precursors of the Violin Family* (in two volumes). London: William Reeves, 1910.

Schwartz, H. W. *The Story of Musical Instruments.* New York: Doubleday & Company, Inc., 1939.

Terry, Charles Stanford. *Bach's Orchestra.* London: Oxford University Press, 1932.

BOOKS ON BAND SCORING

Johnson, Clair W. *Practical Scoring for the Concert Band.* Dubuque, Iowa: William C. Brown Co., 1961. (There is a workbook to accompany the text.)

Lang, Philip J. *Scoring for the Band.* New York: Mills Music, Inc., 1950.

Wagner, Joseph. *Band Scoring.* New York: McGraw-Hill Book Company, 1960. (There is a workbook to accompany the text.)

BOOKS ON COMMERCIAL ARRANGING

Delamont, Gordon. *Modern Arranging Technique.* Delevan, New York: Kendor Music, Inc., 1965.

Mancini, Henry. *Sounds and Scores: A Practical Guide to Professional Orchestration.* Northridge Music, Inc., 1962.

Skinner, Frank. *Underscore.* Hollywood: Skinner Music Co., Inc., 1950. On scoring for motion pictures.

BOOKS ON CHORAL ARRANGING

Davison, Archibald T. *The Technique of Choral Composition.* Cambridge, Mass.: Harvard University Press, 1945.

Wilson, Harry Robert. *Choral Arranging for Schools, Glee Clubs, and Publication.* New York: Robbins Music Corp., 1949.

INDEX

347

360